5/07

FENG SHUI
FOR THE REST OF US

*What You Can Do Right Now
to Change Your Life*

GABRIELLE ALIZAY

THE WRITERS' COLLECTIVE
Independent Books for Independent Readers

Book Cover Design: Robert Aulicino
Book Interior Design: Barbara Hodge
Illustrations: Kelly Barber

ISBN-13: 978-1-59411-132-7
ISBN-10: 1-59411-132-4

LCCN: 2005903266

Printed in the United States of America

10 9 8 7 6 5 4 3 2 1

Published by The Writers' Collective ♦ Cranston, Rhode Island

I dedicate this book to each one of you. May you take this information, apply it, and then watch as your life transforms into a work of art.

Making sure there are plenty of individual life masterpieces on the planet shall heal the earth, her people, and future generations. It is then that we become activists, and with a bit of luck, in step with the power of amplification. It is then that all things become possible; world peace, one dwelling at a time.

WHEN I AM WORKING ON A PROBLEM I NEVER THINK ABOUT BEAUTY. I ONLY THINK ABOUT HOW TO SOLVE THE PROBLEM. BUT WHEN I HAVE FINISHED, IF THE SOLUTION IS NOT BEAUTIFUL, I KNOW IT IS WRONG.

— Buckminster Fuller

TABLE OF CONTENTS

ACKNOWLEDGMENTS

Foremost I recognize that all that I am and everything that I do are bestowed by my Higher Power. Without this connection, I am nothing.

My heartfelt thanks to: my publisher for believing in me in the first place; to Kristin Robison, Dawn Griffin, Cindy Wathen, and Bonnie Hearn Hill, my wonderful editors; to Kelly Barber for her illustrations; to Bob Aulicino for the book cover; Barbara Hodge for the interior design; Galen Schroeder for the index; and Natalie Calder for her photo artistry. I am also indebted to Jaya Leandra Aaron, Audrey Sirota, Liz Boyens, and especially Jean Feingold for proofreading the galley. Lastly, I am grateful to my publicist, Javier Perez.

I appear tall only because I stand on the shoulders of many Helpful People. A shower of chi falls on all who have assisted me in any way, and a sincere thank you to:

Dr. Jeff and Mary Smith; Bryana Garcia; Katherine Ideker; Sharon Julien; Jeanne Bessette; Carol Johnson; Catherine Young; Ron Septimus; Mariposa; Nancy MacAllister; Kendra Rose Hunter; Kelly Edwards; Mary Conn; Lisa and Henry Carter; Sharyn Adams; Tom Murray and his wife, Vivian; Susanne Breubeck; Erika Cianciulli; Ruby; Steve Palmisano; the staff at the Teahouse Spa; Mudra of VMudra Studios; Rachel McMullin; Limor Inbar; Ian and Pamela Chambers; Ellen-Mother; and Charles E. Koch.

Finally, a special thank you to D.F., who brings me laughter and miracles daily. My appreciation for this gift of love continues to grow—as large as there are stars in the night sky.

THE ESSENCE OF
FENG SHUI

AN INTRODUCTION

Feng shui is an enchanting art form. You may have even imagined bringing this ancient Chinese tradition into your home and office. After all, who couldn't do with more—as they vow in Feng Shui articles—harmony? So you study countless volumes on the subject. You sign up for a five week adult education class on Feng Shui. You even look in the paper to see if one of those fancy Feng Shui consultants is local. Who knows what you will tell your mate if you actually take the financial risk and become a client to this outlandish person who claims she can transform your home, your castle?

You are attracted and at the same time, repulsed by the Feng Shui ideals. Clearly, Feng Shui is for movie stars, heads of state, and New Age cronies or for those people who already have big, rambling homes found in *Architectural Digest*. But here is a mind-boggling fact: Feng Shui is for everyone. Even you. You don't have to change your religion, your style, or your ideals to get access to this incredible art.

News Flash: Everyone has problems and issues, even if some people have shinier chrome on their bathroom sink. No one is immune from the challenges of life on earth, whether you start your day in a yoga pose, or you make pancakes for the kids with Extract of Cow Butter. This book is written for you and me and the rest of us. Finding harmony and peace is great. Only it is difficult to be harmonious when the electric bill is through the roof and your right foot hurts every time you put weight on it. Plus, you know you have a mate. Yet between kids, work, and dinner, you have lost some of the passion you once had. Take heart, this book will help you work out all of those issues since Feng Shui is an exquisite problem-solving tool, sometimes even miraculous. So whether you're someone who needs to hide from the *Society Press* reporters or always dashing around town on errands, this guidebook will show you another reality, one which revolutionizes the experiences of your life in radically positive ways.

"Ho Hum," you say in your head. "Yet another Feng Shui book. Still another guarantee to change my life. Why is this book (yawn) any different?"

Look at it this way: your home and office hold the keys to satisfaction with your life in general. Make intentional changes in your dwelling and you will alter your life in positive, wide-ranging ways. You can keep your values and beliefs. You don't need dogma to solve your problems, get empowered, stay strong, or to feel marvelous things happen on a regular basis— like having more than enough money to pay that electric bill or having your foot heal by moving the symbols in your home and office. Plus, the grand prize: the return of a lot more passion into your life.

Of course, no one can change your life but you. But this book contains a lot of information about an amazing life-altering tool, and it will show you how to integrate it into your harried existence, gently, and with tremendous effectiveness. There are recommendations in each section of this book to help make your adventure into the world of Feng Shui both positive and successful. It's best you read the entire book before you actually implement the Feng Shui suggestions, unless you are inspired to take action immediately.

You won't be bored. In fact, you'll become an active participant in the Alpha Principle which states that when a person is giggling (out loud or silently), they relax, which naturally stimulates the brain into creating alpha waves—the super-learning state. In other words, chuckle your way through learning this lovely art of Feng Shui. Become skilled at the many ideals of Feng Shui, then apply them to your dwelling. While so doing, may you roll with laughter, deep and long, as your life is transformed in glorious and fantastical ways.

PART I

THE BASIC STEPS

THE ABCS OF FENG SHUI

Pronunciation of these two simple words ranges from something which sounds like the scientific name for bacteria—fing swui—to a tasty dish which could be served at the local Chinese restaurant, fong shooey. Regardless of how you pronounce it, Feng Shui will work wonderfully when properly applied to your space. Here is an easy phonics technique to employ. Say the word "fun" and add a "g" to it. *Fung*. First word covered. Then stand and swish your hips from side to side. *Sway*. Second word covered. Now put the words together: Fung Sway.

There are many emotional reactions when the term Feng Shui is verbalized. They occur regardless of whether the person truly understands this science or not. The effects are always breathtaking:

(a) *Staggering, mind-blowing fear.* You are doomed. You do nothing Feng Shui correct. You might as well get a cart, fill it up with your prized possessions, and live on the street. Everything in your house or office, you are certain, is bad Feng Shui and horrible Feng Shui nightmares invade your fitful sleep. You are paranoid because you assume there is nothing you can do to remedy anything.

Welcome to *Fear Shui.* It is a common but unnecessary inclination. Frequently, it exists because a person is erroneously convinced that to employ Feng Shui in their home and office, major stylistic and religious changes must first be made. Relax, this is not true! The marvels of Feng Shui can be integrated into your life easily and effortlessly. It is not needed, nor even recommended, to alter any values in your life. Proper education about the science of Feng Shui is usually the cure for *Fear Shui.*

(b) *Astonished, all-out rejection.* You are disgusted. You have never been told such incredible hogwash. You would rather clean the grout between the tiles of your shower than listen to such unbelievable babble. Everything in your home and office is the way it is because that's how you like it. Besides, you have a gift for design. You have "Inner Feng Shui."

This phenomenon is called the "Feng Shui is an airy-fairy crock" belief. Ironically, the Feng Shui Life Value represented by the bathroom in your home, which might stand for career, love, or health for instance, will improve as you clean the tile in your shower. That's how powerful it is. It works in spite of you. It's true Feng Shui promotes many unusual principles and ideals, and your normal comfort zones are certain to get pushed. Approach the Feng Shui theories with the manner of a scientist. Conduct experiments with the concepts, especially those rumored to problem-solve an area of your life which needs help. Feng Shui is a concrete discipline grounded in the third-dimensional world of objects and things, and is extremely successful in transitioning your home, office, and your life in general into a work of art.

(c) *Enormous, far-fetched love.* You are smitten. Feng Shui is the answer to all of your problems. There is nothing you would not do for a Feng Shui treated environment. If you are obliged to get a divorce, you will. If the kids have to go live with your mother, they must. You have a new lover. Your latest devotion is harmonious, sleek, and free of excess baggage. Everything in your home and office is a study in the science of Feng Shui. You own every book ever published about the art to prove it. They are neatly shelved in the Feng Shui research area (the kids didn't need a playroom anyway. Too much clutter!).

I label this response to the science: *The Feng Shui Geek.* However, you can be over-the-top with Feng Shui and still keep the mate and the children. Sometimes, *The Feng Shui Geek* adores this art so much they inadvertently embrace the ills of *Fear Shui* because of an extreme desire to apply its principles in their home and office properly. But you do not need to walk on Feng Shui eggshells to assimilate this fantastic wisdom into your life

FENG SHUI IS A SIMPLE, POTENT, ARTFUL SCIENCE

It is an ancient belief system born in China thousands of years ago. It speaks the language of symbols. It is a discipline of home and office arrangement which follows the Laws of Nature and the universe. It promises to create maximum joy, love, health and abundance in return. It heals the breath of your building. It creates a feeling of peace, well-being, and service in your surroundings. Feng Shui is also an amazing problem-solving tool, which when applied to your dwelling, causes this intentional change of symbols which positively affect your life in general.

There are Many Misconceptions about Feng Shui:

(a) Feng Shui is interior design: False. It goes much deeper than the simple arrangement of furniture. It means more than what shade the curtains should be. A Feng Shui treated space does have the feeling of an environment which has been attentively put together. Yet, it makes no difference whether you are color blind or adore that ratty couch in the corner. Feng Shui is an artful science. Get an interior designer if your primary concern is art.

(b) Feng Shui is only for the New Age crowd: False. To be good at reading the symbols your home and office give you, you must be solid and stable. If you spend all your time with your thumb stuck in your belly button and your head in the heavens, how can you see that the faucet is leaking in your Love Union/Marriage kitchen or how fixing it can have a profound affect on your date Friday night? Feng Shui is just as effective with Ross Reality as it is with Princess Leabria from the Stellar Federation of the Starship, Karta. Scary, but true. Reading the third-dimension messages a home or office reveals is a valuable lesson. They reflect the tangible, albeit hidden, convictions of the subconscious mind. The symbols do not lie. There is nowhere to hide, regardless of whether you just dusted and the books on the shelves are set just so. Feng Shui is a captivating study of the self. Whatever the problem or issue, your life has symbolic reflections found by diagnosing the area of your home and office which corresponds to that Life Value on the Bagua. Armed with this knowledge, you can intentionally change the symbols to improve your life. To have true talent with this skill requires that you are grounded.

(c) You have to spend lots of money to apply the principles of Feng Shui in your dwelling: False. It is true the Feng Shui paraphernalia aspect can be confusing. Lots of stores these days have everything from Feng Shui candles to Feng Shui bath salts guaranteed to bring you abundance, health, or love, depending on the color of the capsule you melt in the water. Sure, it will. In truth, it doesn't take a special kind of Chinese symbol thingy to hang from your Fame/Reputation ceiling to secure an acting part in the local play. It *does* take disciplined intentional application of the Fame/Reputation Life Value ideologies. This book will teach them. Applying the values of Feng Shui to your home and office is not free of charge, but it doesn't have to put a huge dent in your bank account. The real price tag comes as you spend time proactively changing your environment around to heal emotional, mental, and spiritual patterns. It also requires the courage to evolve into an empowered being. Although Feng Shui is not free, application of its ideals will create a surrounding which supports ultimate liberation. Such a promise is priceless.

Applied Feng Shui remedies transform the home and office into a sanctuary. Your environment begins to assist you. You uncover solutions to your day-to-day issues; life improves. Your space starts to heal you. Because you are nurtured, you have the energy to support others. You become a walking endorphin. The pebble thrown in the pond effect is obvious with Feng Shui. Circles create bigger rings, create larger spheres. The world is in synch.

Here is a Chinese proverb: "When there is harmony in the home, there is order in the nation. When there is order in the nation, there is peace in the world."

I am making my contribution to world peace, one dwelling at a time, but I require the help of like-minded others. So read on.

THE BAGUA

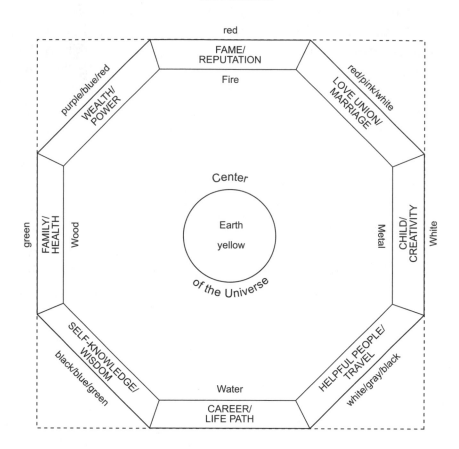

BAGUA BASICS

Imagine this scenario: You turn the knob to your home's door, enter, and smile. The day has been long and rough, but you instantly dump all that yuck as soon as you step inside your sanctuary. Why? Because your surroundings serve you. They soothe all the way to the core. Applying the ideals of Feng Shui to your environment has been a slow, revealing but rewarding process. Amazingly, the physical adjustments have been minimal, except for clutter-clearing. Instead, it has been the symbolic gestures which have been conscientiously applied which have transformed your space, your life, and your universe into something remarkable. Now, an invisible, powerful, and healing force moves in your world. This difference can be attributed to the language of symbols, Feng Shui. It has changed your life definitively. Here's a secret: The next section of this book contains one of the essential components of this practice, understanding the Bagua. Learn about this and you will go far.

The Bagua is the diagnostic tool used in Black Hat Tibetan Feng Shui. This eight-sided figure greatly resembles the outline of an American stop sign. The Bagua is an age-old symbolic shape in Chinese history representing power and protection. Feng Shui philosophies believe the Bagua mirror has significant influence preventing negative energy from entering any space that it has been placed, with intention, to guard.

Like the western stop sign, the Feng Shui Bagua asks: pause before proceeding forward. Stop, look, and listen to what the symbols say. In the science of Feng Shui, the Bagua shape is also superimposed onto a bird's-eye view of the house or office plan of a building. Incredible emblematic truths reveal themselves. For instance, when you learn where the Love Union/Marriage section is in your surroundings, you also discover what you have in that area. Black Hat Tibetan Feng Shui assigns a Life Value to each of the eight sides of the Bagua, with the interior representative of the Center of the Universe. Included in these values are Career/Life Path; Self-Knowledge/Wisdom; Family/Health; Wealth/Power; Fame/Reputation; Love Union/Marriage; Child/Creativity; Helpful People/Travel; and Center of the Universe.

To comprehend the different areas fully, each Life Value will be investigated in detail in Part II of the book. Colors associated with each Life Value, as well as symbolic representations of the Elements, will also be examined. In this section of the book, you will learn how the Bagua is superimposed on top of a bird's-eye view floor plan of your space. This will, in turn, teach you how correlations exist between the Life Value areas of the Bagua and the corresponding areas in your life.

The essential aspects of each of the Life Value areas are described next. First you will see the colors which are the traditional tints suggested for each Life Value section. These color choices are hardly strong, fast rules; each can only benefit you if the suggested hue influences you positively. In other words, if you hate all shades of purple, which falls symbolically in the Wealth/Power section, please don't assume your economic strife is over now that you have painted your study a bold shade of eggplant. Learn the dogmatic, traditional approaches with all Feng Shui values and cures, but then balance this information with what genuinely makes you feel upbeat. Being positive when you see any color or cure in a certain Life Value is how you'll start to see real miracles occur in the corresponding part of your life. Following the color is the symbolic natural element which contributes to the enhancement of chi, or life force, in a certain Life Value of the Bagua. Honor and attempt to understand these traditional ideas. On the other hand, know with every Feng Shui principle, you can grasp the conventional rule, and then alter it into your own lifestyle. Please remember: No *Fear Shui*—Fun Sway instead!

Finally, the areas of one's life represented in each Life Value are addressed. This knowledge reveals the places where your various issues symbolically exist in your home. Armed with this awareness, you can implement solutions to positively affect your life in general. Keep in mind this Feng Shui premise: the microcosm environment, your home or office, reflects the actuality of the macrocosm environment, your life in general.

Career/Life Path Color: Black Element: Water	Family/Health Color: Green Element: Wood
Areas investigated, enhanced, and/or problem-solved: • Job (full or part-time). • Parenthood. • Life path (easy or difficult). • Decisions related to choosing a life path.	Areas investigated, enhanced, and/or problem-solved: • Ancestors, dead or alive, who are part of your lineage. • Health on every level; physical, emotional, mental, and spiritual. • Foundation money: to pay the mortgage or rent, put food on the table, and take care of the bills. This Life Value teaches until the holes in the symbolic foundation of money are plugged up, you cannot hope to gain the true wealth of having "more than enough."
Self-Knowledge/Wisdom **Color: Black, Green, Blue** **Element: None**	
Areas investigated, enhanced and/or problem-solved: • Self in general. • Self-esteem. • Self-worth. • Self-image. • Education, learning, and study. • Issues of addiction and grief. • Personal growth and spiritual practices, such as yoga and meditation.	

Wealth/Power Color: Purple, Blue, Red Element: None	Fame/Reputation Color: Red Element: Fire
Areas investigated, enhanced, and/or problem-solved: • Prosperity lives here. Not just abundance of money, but the plenty of all things—love, health, time, creativity, friends, and so on. This is the feeling of having more than enough of whatever. • This is also the *power* area. There is a knowledge acquired when you understand where the power lives in your space. • Do not have pets, children, housemates, or guests inhabit this area. Unless you desire authority disputes, boundary issues, and power struggles as a part of your world. • The owners, parents, or lessee named on the lease should occupy this part of the house or office, whether it is a bedroom, office, kitchen, or say, a meditation room.	Areas investigated, enhanced, and/or problem-solved: • All types of fame and distinction. • Marketing. • Goal setting. • The things you are remembered for in life. • The symbolic time travel into past and future desires is possible here. Transform the emotional charge of a past issue or assist the manifestation of an unrealized goal.
	Love Union/Marriage **Color: Red, Pink, White** **Elements: None**
	Areas investigated, enhanced, and/or problem-solved: • Sacred union. • Sex, passion, and mate communication. • Business partnerships.

Child/Creativity
Color: White
Element: Metal

Areas investigated, enhanced, and/or problem-solved:

- Children.

- Inner child.

- Pets.

- Conception desires.

- Creativity, whether this is the artistry of paint on a canvas or the inventiveness of marketing your business.

Helpful People/Travel
Color: White, Grey, Black
Element: None

Areas investigated, enhanced, and/or problem-solved:

- Invisible and Visible Helpful People are represented here. Gurus would be on the visible side. Other illustrations of earth dimension helpers are friends and/or handy workers who know how to listen to your heart or fix a leaky sink in the bathroom. Some examples of hidden aides would be guides, angels, Jesus, and other such beings.

- Helpful People are also benefactors, patrons, bosses, and protectors. Paying customers as well as clientele, with their word-of-mouth advertisement, are included here.

- This area represents any and all real estate, whether buying, selling, or renting.

- All legal issues are solved here, regardless whether it is a helpful attorney, judge, jury, or ruling which is needed.

- Finally, the balance of travel happens here. Some people travel frequently with their work. Other people would just love a trip to the Bahamas. Attention to the Helpful People/Travel area of your home can bring an equilibrium of travel so symmetry is restored in your life.

**Center of the Universe
Color: Yellow
Element: Earth**

Areas investigated, enhanced, and/or problem-solved:

- This area allows for the simplification of any Life Value, especially if there are many issues present in a particular Life Value. Any one of the aspects which exists in a particular Life Value can be placed in the Center, so you can divide the qualities represented into smaller areas of focus.

- Also, this Life Value is a location to honor anything central in your life, be it for a day or for a lifetime. You can address an issue in the Life Value where it naturally falls, as well as place it in the Center area. This action doubles your concentration toward the creation of that particular goal.

- Multiple concerns can be concurrently addressed by the Center of the Universe Sacred Space. A more detailed explanation will follow in Part II of this book. Breathe.

OPPOSITE-ATTRACT LAW[1]

This is another tool to employ to get the results in Feng Shui which will astound you. The Opposite-Attract Law states: If you have performed the suggested Feng Shui cures for an area and are not content with the results, proceed to the Bagua Life Value directly opposite of it. Make sure everything is in order in this opposed section because its condition can affect the quality of your original concern.

Here's how this theory works: Fame/Reputation affects Career/Life Path and vice versa; Wealth/Power affects Helpful People/Travel and vice versa; Child/Creativity affects Family/Health and vice versa; Self-Knowledge/Wisdom affects Love Union/Marriage and vice versa. Remember this law. It is an important step to having Feng Shui work for you. Keep in mind, laws do not lie.

THE COST OF CLUTTER

Clutter is directly opposite to the values of Feng Shui. If you want Feng Shui to be effective in your life, to problem solve your issues, and to make your living and working environment feel like a shrine, it is necessary to follow the "no clutter laws" of Feng Shui. Interestingly, a place full of clutter is hardly just a room with chaos. It also signifies the need to clear up issues on the emotional, mental, and spiritual levels of your being. An environment is meant to serve you, not limit you. It should heal, inspire, relax, and protect you. Applying Feng Shui principles to your space, which includes clutter-clearing, will help transform the material into the sacred. When the house is used as a storage unit, self-esteem is negatively affected. Furthermore, it challenges the extraordinary art of Feng Shui to problem solve, say a health issue in the Family/Health area, if you use that part of your house to store your collection of classic record albums even though you no longer have a record player.

---

1. The Opposite-Attract Law is not a new concept in regard to the workings of the Feng Shui Bagua, but I love how Karen Rauch Carter named it in her book *Move Your Stuff, Change Your Life*. It's clear, concise, and simple. I wouldn't change a thing, so I didn't.

Surprisingly, the true Feng Shui definition of clutter might fascinate you:[2]

1. If an object, picture, memorabilia, and such lowers your energy, it is clutter. It is strongly recommended, in such case, that it leave your premises.

2. If it raises your energy, or said in another way, makes you pop (think effervescent), then it enhances your environment and your life. That "thing" has permission to stay.

3. The Higher Power, or whatever your spiritual source is, gifts on the physical, emotional, mental, and spiritual plane when space is made.

Here's an example of a true clutter-clear. If a room has nothing in it but a table, but the table lowers your energy (because every time you look at it you are reminded of an ex-lover, either consciously or subconsciously), then the room is cluttered according to Feng Shui terms. And suppose that particular room represents the Child/Creativity area of the house and one of the issues in your life is that you want to paint landscapes again but lack the inspiration to get started. So get rid of the table, which is clutter, and then expect gifts, in the Highest Good, to flow into the Child/Creativity area of your life.

For instance, you purge your life of the table, which is the unconscious symbol of failure—a former love relationship. Suddenly you can imagine the room takes the shape of a painting studio. You find your easel in the attic, come across old tubes of paint, a few brushes and then spend the rest of the weekend drawing a mountain scene. Such gifts happen when clutter is removed from the environment.

Whenever you have an issue, pick the corresponding area of the Bagua. Figure out where that section is in your space, then do a clutter-clear there. For example, let's assume you have a Love

2. The rightful definition of clutter is taken from the brilliant conceptual work on clutter by Karen Kingston, *Clear Your Clutter With Feng Shui*. If her ideas were truly followed by the majority of people, the world would be a better place to live. Promise.

Union/Marriage issue. You want a mate. Go to the Love Union/ Marriage area and the Self-Knowledge/Wisdom area and clutter-clear both sections. Always remember the power of the Opposite-Attract Law to assist the manifestation of positive results.

Excuse 1: I don't know what to do with all the stuff I no longer want.

Have a garage sale. Make money to buy things which raise your energy. Or, put on a "give away." This assures a great party-like atmosphere. Arrange your clutter in a room and then invite your family and friends over to pick and choose what they fancy. Remember, your clutter is someone else's treasure. The "give away" is also a great karma activity. It's a fabulous way to show the Higher Power, or whatever your spiritual source, that you are abundant. Naturally like attracts like, and in such cases, more wealth and prosperity of whatever Life Value shall come your way. If the first two options are not a possibility, then take your stuff to a thrift store. Often these businesses will come and pick up larger items like couches, appliances, and mattresses.

Please keep in mind, clutter is clutter even if it is organized. I had a client who, after our appointment, immediately gathered up a box of things which brought her energy down. She placed the box by the front door. Two months later, when I returned for the follow-up, the box of clutter was still there and, thus, still negatively affecting her life. Even if you systematize the clutter, it can nonetheless affect you. Do not let clutter have control over you. If you cannot remove your clutter from your premises in a reasonable amount of time, create a storage area with mirrors— the details on how will be given in the mirror section of this book. Move all your clutter into this self-created storage unit until you take action to release it from your life. Then it won't be a distress to the flow of chi in your environment.

Excuse 2: I could not possibly get rid of that because:

1. *it was given to me by my favorite niece, and if she came over and did not see it, she would be crushed;*
2. *it was given to me by an old flame; or*
3. *it was very expensive and would be impossible to replace.*

Let me remind you, clutter is clutter, no matter what. If something lowers your energy, it will negatively influence you and most likely the area it corresponds to in your environment. Clutter-clearing is not a time to caretake others. Of course you love your favorite niece, and she, you. Given that, she would not want you to be harmed by less than favorable conditions in your environment. So please unshackle yourself of whatever lowers your energy. Your psyche will be much happier. This will reflect positively on your future relation with all family members.

What if an old flame gave it to you? The flame is called "old" for a reason. This object is a reminder that you are living in the past. Clutter-clearing asks you to get current in your life. If you look at things from the perspective of what "was" rather than what "is," *and* if they lower your energy, do yourself a favor. Eliminate.

What if the object cost big bucks but it lowers your energy? Is your well-being worth a few hundred dollars? Try an ad in the "miscellaneous for sale" column of the paper. People pay more for items listed there than at garage sales. Regardless, if it lowers your energy, the price is too high to cling to it. If all else fails, Hippie Cure it. Cover it with a piece of fabric. See if your reaction to it changes positively. You'll learn how in the Bathroom section.

Excuse 3: I could possibly need it someday, so I might as well keep it.

When somebody's place is full of stuff which clearly does not raise their energy, that inhabitant has serious "poverty-consciousness." Ironically, the very people who are worried the most about survival issues have the largest amount of earthly possessions. It takes great trust to simplify through clutter-clearing. But it also allows the space symbolically for offerings to come into those people's lives. It can do the same for you. Many of my clients, chronic savers, tell me they had a parent who survived the Great Depression. They have been taught to accumulate. Yet here is another principle to realize:

THE LAW OF UNIVERSAL ABUNDANCE—FLOW OUT INCREASES FLOW IN.

Give and you shall receive: not hoard and you shall receive. Clutter-clear to expect gifts—physical, emotional, mental, and spiritual—to enter your life. Want to cure poverty-consciousness? Give away. The healing will come. Promise.

In deference to the true Feng Shui definition of clutter, I have a friend who loves used things, old car parts, pipes, even rusty pieces of machinery, which he can use in his many construction projects. Anytime I catch a glance into his trunk, my stomach curdles. I think to myself, *useless old stuff!* Yet for him, that same car trunk absolutely raises his energy. What he sees is *possibility*. No one can choose for you what clutter truly is. It is different for everyone. Apologies are unnecessary. If it makes you pop, it makes you pop. That said, please realize when going through your house to clutter-clear, this is not an intellectual activity. In fact, the mind does not enter into the process, only your intuitive being does. For you heady types, ask for assistance until you learn the drill of turning off your mind. For instance, a whole room, regardless of size, can be perused and clutter-cleared in less than an hour if you don't let the mind decide things for you. All objects are decided on instantly, in five seconds or less. Any longer, and the mind tells you a story, or tries to convince you of something.

Futhermore, beware of the comfort zones. They are the patterns in your life which you are used to—positive or negative. This very strong inclination towards familiarity loves to stop you from evolving into the potential of who you could be. Avoid getting overwhelmed into non-action. Comfort zones have this effect on the psyche. Clutter-clear a drawer, a closet, or a bookshelf a day. Soon your environment will be free of clutter and serving you well.

Finally, the Navajo have a belief system: Never have more than you can carry. Not a realistic goal for most of us, but a wise perspective to hold when you decide whether or not the lamp with the multicolored balloons really raises or lowers your energy. True wealth is invisible to the eye. Learn to see the beauty of simplicity. Form is function in Feng Shui. Let the things which surround you assist your life. Anything else is poverty in its truest form.

IMPLEMENT INTENT

From the Black Hat Tibetan Feng Shui perspective, it is imperative that every action you take is done with purpose. When I, as the Feng Shui consultant, recommend a particular action or cure, and you do it because you heard it from me, the effect will be a mere 10%. In fact, little or no outcome is guaranteed. However, if you take my advice as the information giver and apply your will, your intention, and your desires to all your changes and actions, the deed performed will be 120% effective.[3] Thus, the situation will not only be balanced but improved as well. Not bad numbers considering it simply takes intention to change the Feng Shui results radically. As you progress, you see how central this step is because intentional cures also create solutions in that general part of your life.

3. Master Lin Yun has always insisted, "Do things with intention!" His successor, Sarah Rossbach shares this same sentiment in her book, *Interior Design with Feng Shui,* and gives the specific numbers: no intention, little or no effectiveness (10%); full intention, big changes for the better (120% effectiveness).

Even though what follows is a ritual, and treated with reverence, Feng Shui should not be confused with a religion. It does produce benefits similar to a spiritual practice, like prayer or chanting, yet it is most clearly a problem-solving tool. This ancient Chinese art is most effective when you instill your own values, belief systems, and Higher Power into the formula. In short, any devout approach is powerful when you apply intention, so just do it. What ensues is a simplier, westernized version of the intention ritual which is used by the Black Hat Tibetan Feng Shui School. The traditional name of this ceremony is called the Three Secrets Reinforcement Ritual. You may call it anything you like. Just make use of it.

THREE SECRETS REINFORCEMENT RITUAL:[4]

With every action taken (for instance, hanging a chi catcher, installing a mirror, placing a Feng Shui anchor, or even energetically clearing your space), perform these steps:

1. *Placement of Object*

   Place the new object in the recommended location and/or take the suggested action, such as to install a mirror over the stove or remove clutter from a certain Life Value room.

2. *Visualize/Imagine the Action Already Occurring*

   Be sure to "see" the action or "cure" object in present tense, as if improvement has already happened. Relax about the visualization part. This also means "to imagine."

3. *Speak Your Intention Out Loud*

   Verbalize from your heart, and remember always to add "...This or something better for the Highest Good now occurs" to the end of each statement. Such a disclaimer ensures that "my will" is balanced with "Thy Will" and is a fail-safe method to avoid manipulation of any kind.

---

4. Prototype of westernized version of Three Secrets Reinforcement Ritual of Intention. Ideas on affirmation laws in the book, *Creative Visualization*, by Shakti Gawain.

Here is an example. You have been given the recommendation, through reading Feng Shui material or by getting a personal Feng Shui consultation, that you should hold chi or life force in a particular room which represents a certain value of the Bagua. You want to work on your health, and the Family/Health section of the Bagua lines up with your living room. To increase the attention and energy of that area, it is suggested that chi be held in the room. Similar to when you go to an acupuncturist, regardless of the malady, the practitioner puts needles into various vital points to bring chi, or life force, to the struggling area. It is the chi which heals the complaint. In Feng Shui, when you hold chi symbolically in each Life Value, especially ones which have corresponding problems in general life, it is likewise effective in promoting positive change. You hold chi inside your dwelling very easily. More details will be explained in the bathroom section. But here is the general idea:

Step 1 of the ritual is to hang the object used to catch chi. Suspend a crystal, which is traditional, or whatever item is within your personal style, from the ceiling with a hook or tack. Then execute step 2, which is to envision the action—the holding of chi in the area—as if it had already occurred. Visualize or imagine light energy, like a form of glitter, floating in the room. The chi catcher's function is to keep the energy from escaping out of the windows or skylights in the room. In this example, its function would be to hold energy in the Family/Health area of one's life. Complete the ritual with step 3. In this example, you would say out loud, "The chi of Family/Health stays in this room, and in my life. This or something better for the Highest Good now occurs." If you are still confused about this ritual, don't worry. It is explained in every application part of this book.

Important to note, the term "Highest Good" is rather deceptive. From the sound of it, you like whatever happens in your life. After all, the Highest Good is the gift of the Higher Power, or whatever your spiritual source, so it must be wonderful. Yes and no. The outcome might look like what you imagined or it might not. Regardless, whatever happens in your life, it is always the Highest Good but it often takes hindsight to give you this particular slant. Learn to accept whatever happens as the Highest Good, and if something occurs which is hard to figure out, ask yourself, "What is the Highest Good in this situation?"

I have many clients who love Feng Shui and its concepts. They move around furniture, or transfer a certain picture to a different wall because its symbolic reference is better. The clients hang chi catchers, install mirrors, get new mattresses, turn work desks around, and put away their kitchen knives. They proudly report back to me after making the changes. I ask, "Have you done those things with intention?"

Silence.

Quietly I add, "What you have done is great. Now if you just add intention to your actions, the results will be incredible."

Intention is the bonding agent which makes Feng Shui magic adhere to your life. Don't be afraid to ask for what you want. If you don't know what to request, but know you want energy placed into a particular area, just surrender it to the Higher Power and declare something like, "The Highest Good Career Path now comes to me!" You can make general statements like this for any of the areas of concern. If you do have an idea of what you want, you can be more specific and say something like, "I want Jim to adore me. This or something better for the Highest Good, now occurs!"

The more you do the ritual, the easier it becomes. Someday, it will be second nature to place your object, visualize the outcome as if it's already occurred, then speak your intention. In the beginning, bring a copy of the ritual around with you so that when you have intention rituals to perform throughout your house, the confusion is minimal. Having intent is as basic to life as the amoeba. Somehow, we have forgotten this fact. Remember it again. Use Feng Shui to refresh your memory.

Important Note: The next two sections—The Element Plunge and Sacred Spaces—are included in this section of the book to give a brief understanding of their importance to the effectiveness of the Feng Shui treatment of your space. However, their in-depth exploration will occur in Part II.

THE ELEMENT PLUNGE

There is often a fear that learning the Elements is complicated and boring. Feng Shui Element theory, however, can be presented in such a manner that you stay awake, feel tranquil, and even understand the concepts. Feng Shui embraces the five different Elements which exist on earth. Their placement with the different Life Values follow:

The first Element is Water. It is listed with the Career/Life Path region in the Bagua of Feng Shui. This value is about your work and passageway on the planet. If you want your Career/Life Path to flow, think "river of life." In Part II of the book, you'll find numerous examples to represent the Element of Water.

The next Element is Wood. It is placed in the Family/Health section. This Bagua Value deals with ancestors, health on all levels, and also includes paying the mortgage, rent, buying food, as well as the basic bills. One signifier of Wood is the image of a tree. Trees have roots, the origination associated with family ancestors. Trees are stronger when they have deep roots, a foundation for deep pockets to pay the bills. It can also be viewed as a healthy, rooted being, an ideal description of a hearty person. Examples of the Wood Element are listed in Part II.

The next Element is Fire. It is located in the Fame/Reputation Life Value of the Bagua. Fame is like a movie star. Reputation is what you are remembered for, like being a good parent, a great worker, a caring friend, or not. If you want your celebrity status to spread like wildfire and your flame to burn bright so you are thought of well, then honor the Fire Element in this Life Value. Examples of Fire Element come later.

The Metal Element lives in the Child/Creativity Life Value of the Bagua. This area deals with children, the inner child, procreation, and pets. It also focuses on creativity in all things: artistic, marketing techniques, and other. Imagine the coin treasures in fairy tales—gold, silver, and copper. These are riches just like our children and pets. To discover our talents and gifts is also like finding treasure. Examples of the Element Metal are forthcoming.

Finally, the Earth Element represents the Center of the Universe Bagua section. This quality touches every other Life Value in the Bagua because of its central placement. Thus it is grounded. Perfect for Earth. Examples of Earth Element are in Part II.

The four remaining Bagua Life Values do not have Elemental representation: Self-Knowledge/Wisdom; Wealth/Power; Love Union/Marriage; and Helpful People/Travel. These areas are neither more nor less significant. In every Life Value area of your home and office that does have a symbolic Elemental representation, the results of Feng Shui applications can be much more profound when the specific Element is respected and the various cycles for growth or hindrance are understood. Enter the Creative and Destructive Element Cycle. It is really quite simple. Relax and breathe.

The Creative Element Cycle enhances a specific Element and encourages it to grow larger. Once you understand this cycle, it is wonderful to apply it to a Bagua Life Value that has an

Element representation. In this way, you can increase the symbolic influence of that particular Element.

Breathe!

The Destructive Element Cycle is equally important. Avoid placing negating Elements in Life Value areas which are represented by one of the Elements. For example, don't put a fish tank in your Fame/Reputation area, which symbolizes the Fire Element. Doing so could destroy or make smaller your intended action.

Breathe!

Here is the Creative Element Cycle: Metal creates Water: Think metal bowl with condensation generated on the outside of it. Water feeds Wood: Just like how watering a tree makes it grow. Wood feeds Fire: To build a bigger campfire, feed it wood. Earth creates Metal: Consider a dig in the earth to mine for gold. Fire creates Earth: Reflect on the ash created from the blaze. See Creative Element Cycle diagram.

CREATIVE ELEMENT CYCLE

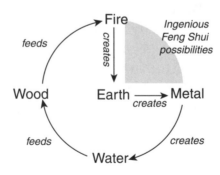

DESTRUCTIVE ELEMENT CYCLE

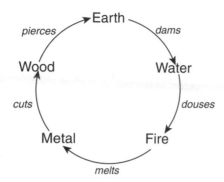

The Destructive Element Cycle is also quite straightforward. Earth dams Water: To stop the flow of water, dam with Earth. Metal cuts Wood: Imagine the power of the ax. Water douses Fire: If you want the campfire out, add Water. Fire melts Metal: Hold a flame under a metal bowl and eventually it turns to liquid. Wood pierces Earth: Consider trees maturing from Earth, absorbing its nutrients. See Destructive Element Cycle diagram.

Here is an example of how to apply these Cycles. You want a new job. You completed many of the recommended Feng Shui treatments for the Career/Life Path area. You also know that the symbolic Element here is Water. You definitely want flow in your work life. So, besides Water and water images, regard the Creative Element Cycle and see what increases the flow of Water—Metal. Metal chairs, metal tables, and metal sculptures are ideas. Another example would be a picture of coinage in a treasure chest. You could add any of these things to enhance the Career/Life Path so the Highest Good could flood into this area. Next, be sure you know what decreases the symbolic torrential flow. The Destructive Element Cycle tells you—avoid Earth.

Rocks, crystals, bushy plants, or pictures of Native American landscapes would not be so superior here.

Your next step is to memorize these relationships:

	Good Element	*Not So Good Element*
WATER	Metal	Earth
WOOD	Water	Metal
FIRE	Wood	Water
METAL	Earth	Fire
EARTH	Fire	Wood

Surprisingly, the Element relationships do have some tricks which make them interesting and like putting together a puzzle. Suppose you have lush, flowery plants in your Career/Life Path dining room and happen to love them there. Looking over the chart, you discover that Earth dams Water. You need a new job, but the plants add so much to this room. You hate Feng Shui. It is stupid and severe.

But here is the fun part. Realize effective ways to use the Creative and the Destructive Element Cycle to meet all of your wants. For this sample, it is critical to know short, bushy plants are representative of Earth; and tall, woodsy plants that remind you of trees, represent the Wood Element. So if you keep the short, bushy plant in your Career/Life Path dining room, the flow of the Water which gets that new job will be dammed by the Earth of the plant. You have the following choices:

1. Remove the plants to another place where Earth is either represented (Center of the Universe) or enhances the Element which exists already in that area (Child/Creativity).

2. Leave the plants in the dining room. You jump for joy at this idea. Figure out how to weaken the Element Earth so it won't inhibit your flow of Water (Career/Life Path). Study the chart above and see what Element is not good for Earth. That's right—Wood. One piece is all it takes. Driftwood, a branch from your tree outside, or other such Wood examples are all satisfactory. Make sure it raises your energy, however. Next comes the Three Secrets Reinforcement Ritual again. Place the piece of Wood in the dirt of a potted plant located in the Career/Life Path area. Visualize or imagine that the Wood weakens all the Earth in the dining room. Say out loud, "The Wood pierces the Earth so my Career/Life Path Water can flow. This or something better for the Highest Good now occurs."

The implications here are huge. Whenever you have an Element which does not support the Element of a Life Value, either move the offending Element, or keep it where it is, but weaken it. If these concepts confuse you, reread the last few paragraphs until this Element stuff is pleasant to you after all. Even still, you may nonetheless struggle with the concepts. Here is The Make My Day, Everything's Okay Cure. With this treatment, you alleviate confusion, insecurity about proper Element use, and mind fog. This cure balances the Elements so you don't worry if an area perplexes you.

MAKE MY DAY, EVERYTHING'S OKAY CURE:

When each of the five different Elements—Water, Wood, Fire, Metal, and Earth—are equally represented in a spot, the Destructive Element Cycle no longer exists. This is to be used when you can't move a certain obstructing Element out of its placement. Or it can be used whenever you feel baffled about the Element relationships in any Bagua Life Value. The effectiveness of this cure is to place all five Elements in equal amounts in any Life Value area which has an Element representation but also a Destructive Element which cannot be altered. Here is an example. You have a fireplace situated in your Child/Creativity section where the Element representation is Metal. Fire melts Metal. This symbolic Fire melting Metal could affect your relationships with your children, pets, creativity, or even your chances of becoming pregnant. Clearly, you can't move the fireplace to a better Bagua location, and relocating to a new home is unrealistic. The Make My Day, Everything's Okay Cure comes in. Regard the example, but be sure to perform this cure in your own style.

Fire is already represented in the fire pit of the fireplace, regardless of whether you ever have a fire in it or not. Use the fireplace and its surroundings to hold the rest of the Elements. For instance, add a large mirror over the mantle, which can represent, with intention, the Element Water; some cedar logs (Wood); a copper container for the wood (Metal); and a few nice-sized rocks for the mantle (Earth). Now all five Elements are present in the area. Fire will no longer melt the Metal, symbolically. At this point, babies and artistic projects flourish.

With such a cure in existence, why deal with learning the Elemental relationships? Simply put, the Elements have the power to revitalize the mind, body, and soul. Anyone spending a relaxing day out in nature knows this to be true. The same healing forces of the Elements are available inside your home and office. You only need to learn how to respect and honor these components of Life. They, in turn, renovate your dwelling into a refuge. Embrace the Elements. Don't panic about them. They are basic. The more you work with them, the more they let you into their simple little psyches. When the world of Elements opens for you, you will see not only the simplicity of each of the five Elemental forms, but the building blocks of the entire universe as well.

SACRED SPACES

Feng Shui can do many things for your life. When you apply its values, the magic begins. Not only does it bring harmony, peace, and order to a space, it also solves problems when its principles are faithfully practiced. For instance, when you turn your desk around so you can see the door as you sit behind it, employees will treat you differently, the patterns of procrastination diminish, and even job promotions and financial raises can occur.

To capitalize on Feng Shui as a problem-solving tool, develop the use of Sacred Spaces. A Sacred Space is a special spot someplace in your room(s) where life issues are consciously addressed. Use Feng Shui as a problem-solving tool to help resolve general issues, such as the desire to get a promotion at work or attract the perfect mate. A Sacred Space is an area of focus which assists you to unravel more specific issues.

Things to know about Sacred Spaces

1. *A Sacred Space is a place to solve both general and specific problems within a particular Life Value topic.*

   Examples of statements which can be addressed in a Sacred Space: "The Acme Widget Company has promoted me to General Manager. This or something better for the Highest Good now occurs." Or, "Phil has asked me out on a date for this Friday night. This or something better for the Highest Good now occurs." Or even, "The Highest Good Career Path is now here."

2. *A Sacred Space is designated by the person doing the Feng Shui.*

   You choose the place where the Sacred Space goes, either in its Life Value room or somewhere else in your dwelling.

3. *A Sacred Space can be horizontal, like an altar table, or it can be vertical, like a picture.*

One is not more influential than the other. Whatever you choose for your Sacred Space should raise your energy. No clutter is allowed.

4. *Designate a Sacred Space in an area and choose power objects (for the table) or power images (in the picture) to place your intention on for a specific issue. This particular Sacred Space then assists to solve that concern.*

For instance, let's say the Sacred Space is for Family/Health and you have a health issue. There are many basic Feng Shui shifts which need to occur in this area of your home and office (and also in The Opposite-Attract Child/Creativity area). After those steps have been made, you can specify your future health desires. For example, choose a stone you really like and place it on the Family/Health Sacred Space to hold the intention. Remember to visualize the outcome you desire, and then make the appropriate statement out loud. If you have an ailing back, you might say, "I now have a healthy and strong back. This or something better for the Highest Good now occurs." The same can be done with your Sacred Space picture. Point to an image within the picture, visualize the desired result, then speak your intentions.

5. *Do not mix the secular and the sacred.*

This premise applies to all Feng Shui cures and every Sacred Space you create. If you select a place in your Love Union/Marriage kitchen for a Sacred Space, last night's dirty dishes are forbidden to be stacked on it. This space is to solve specific issues, not accumulate whatever you have not had time to deal with yet.

6. *Always add, "This or something better for the Highest Good now occurs" to your specific requests.*

This takes the manipulation out of the appeal and puts "Thy Will" aligned with "my will." As explained before, the Highest

Good might be better than you could have imagined, or the situation might seem to move your life into a negative place. In time, however, you will always find the "why" something happened and understand the Highest Good result.

7. *Do not choose to put Sacred Spaces in bathrooms, garages, roommates', or children's rooms.*

The bathroom is the symbolic place for drainage of abundance (yes, Feng Shui can cure that). Suppose you have a bathroom in your Child/Creativity area of the Bagua and your teenager thinks you are pond scum. Perform the bathroom cures explained later. But don't work on this specific teenager angst inside there. Choose a table or picture outside of the bathroom to become the Sacred Space, which helps to solve all individual Child/Creativity issues, including this problem.

If a garage is attached to the house, you always include it in your Bagua. Thus, it is a representation of some Life Value of the Bagua. Suppose your garage is Helpful People/Travel and you want a vacation to The Florida Keys. Perform the necessary cures recommended for any garage. But do not find a Sacred Space between the car oil and the bicycle. Bring the Sacred Space inside your house, and, if you want, put it somewhere near the garage. Interestingly enough, as long as you know the place of a particular Life Value Sacred Space, it can go anywhere allowed.

Clearly, because roommates and children have their own lives, they should not be held responsible if their rooms fall in your Fame/Reputation area of the Bagua, for instance. It is unrealistic, therefore, for you to solve status problems from work in your child's or roommate's space. Perform the suggested cures for children's and roommates' rooms as explained later. Then choose a location outside of their rooms to create a Sacred Space for that Life Value. Everyone will be happier.

It is wonderful to have the Sacred Space which represents a certain Bagua Life Value in the actual room that it signifies. For example, the Career/Life Path Sacred Space can live in your Career/Life Path part of the house. But this is not necessary, nor is it always possible. We don't always live alone. It doesn't always feel safe to have a Sacred Space in the TV room where everyone is. Many clients have every Sacred Space in their bedroom. It really doesn't matter, as long as there is a Sacred Space representation for every Life Value of the Bagua somewhere in your home and office.

8. *Sacred Spaces solve life problems by using the wisdom of the Highest Good.*

Consent to whatever is brought your way. Some things are not meant for you to understand or evaluate right now. Practice acceptance. You will be more satisfied with existence then.

9. *Always use the Three Secrets Reinforcement Ritual to place requests upon the power objects (or images) of your Sacred Space.*

The effectiveness of desires and the promise of manifestation are contingent upon the intention added. The nine separate Sacred Spaces are tremendous problem-solving tools for your home and office. This does not mean, however, they stop tribulations from ever happening. Welcome to Earth and the human condition. They do offer you a three-dimensional passage to pull yourself out of the victim role and into the proactive behavior of problem solving.

Troubles on Earth always change. When one is solved, another is born. Feng Shui ideals, inclusive of Sacred Spaces, give you the chance to operate with dignity by grounding your issues into solutions. Think about the challenge of digging a hole without a shovel. Now think about life without Feng Shui.

THE SPONGE IS FULL

You think you already have a huge amount of information? True. Have I recommended caffeine yet? In addition, be gentle with yourself. Reread the last pages again if necessary. Work consciously not only to understand the information shared in these pages, but to sense the ideas as well. Believe it or not, a building structure responds to positive energy and care, not unlike a human, a car, or even a project you perfect at work. When your home and office has the Feng Shui beliefs applied to them, differences are noticed not only by the occupants, but by everyone who steps through the door. Along with sensing the improved arrangement of the place, people also report "feeling" the peace, balance, and healing which occurs when Feng Shui unleashes its enchantment in a space.

Why does Feng Shui work? It follows the Laws of Nature and Universal Principles. The philosophies of Feng Shui are as certain as the sunrise every day and the leaf dropping off a deciduous tree in the fall. However, Feng Shui will only work in your home and office if you actually employ its ideals. Many clients have profusely thanked me for the consultation, shaken my hand, and then kindheartedly invited me to leave their home. The door slams shut. So do their minds. Not a solitary change is made to their homes, their lives. And guess what? Not a thing happens.

I have also experienced the direct opposite of this non-action. Here are some examples. A client had boxes, each filled to the rim with stuff, strewn all over his house. He offered apologetically, "Sorry about all the boxes. I have not really moved in. I hate this place! I'm not going to stay!"

I nodded. "How long have you lived here?"

"Five years."

I smiled. "Take your things out. Show the Higher Power, or whatever your spiritual source, that you can make a home out of any place. Then when that is done, the Highest Good home will come to you."

He diligently followed the various Feng Shui suggestions, added his intentions, and within a month moved into a different house. And this time with a mate.

Another client called with excitement. "I have lost weight in this past week. It just falls off me."

"What are you doing differently?" I asked.

"I am clutter-clearing every drawer, every closet, and every shelf in my house."

A favorite story was the client who had a dead refrigerator leaning up against her outside bedroom window. She moved it to a junkyard since her bedroom represented the Wealth/ Power Life Value. Hours after the release of that symbol from her world, she received a call which promised money was to be hers. Coincidence? New Age mumbo jumbo? Try proven Natural Laws manifest. Feng Shui works. Undeniably. You have a chance to add your voice to the chorus of success stories. Just do one Feng Shui application a day, nothing overwhelming. See what happens. A home or office does not need a completed Feng Shui space before the marvels start to occur.

Know, however, Feng Shui is a process. It takes time, patience, plus a willingness to move beyond your comfort zones. The effort you make will give you outcomes which far exceed the input. When Feng Shui values have been completely employed in your space, you see amazing transformations. Not only is your living and working space now sacred, healing, and helping you to resolve problems, it blesses all who enter. Good luck and congratulations!

THE TRUTH

To put into operation the science of Feng Shui is a bit like peeling an onion. You diligently remove one layer, only to be met by yet another layer. Your eyes tear up and you hold your breath, but hard as you try not to, the crying begins. Then the stinging. You can't even open your teary eyes anymore, not to mention the paper cut on your index finger burns. It feels as if a lit match is being held to your skin. Surprise, it is only onion juice. You endure all of this suffering just to add a bit of zing to the soup.

In the Feng Shui model, the pain of growth adds spice to your life. To peel and prep an onion, what does this have to do with Feng Shui? Expect multiple layers. Expect resistance. Expect joy. Expect miracles to happen and at times expect nothing. Yes, tears. Yes, the burn of change. In barter, I guarantee incredible results; spice, bliss, peace, and more will eventually supersede the pain of the preparation.

Fast forward: Your guests have arrived. Everyone sits down for the soup dinner. As the cook, you take the first tentative bite. The crowd joins you and goes wild. The soup is delectable. Everyone praises you and ask for seconds and thirds. Where are the tears or even the memory of the sting now?

The following information is some of the multiple layers of the Feng Shui onion. Regardless from whom you receive your Feng Shui facts—the Feng Shui book, the Feng Shui consultant, the baker at the corner store who knows his Feng Shui—please remember that they are all just information givers. It is the power of intention which will take all this information and turn it into magic. Look again carefully at the informational section about the Three Secrets Reinforcement Ritual. Even though the ritual is simple, learn how to direct it in your dwelling. This will change your life.

THE BEGINNING FENG SHUI DO AND DON'T LIST

DO:

Draw a Bird's-Eye View Plot Diagram of Your Home and/or Office.

This first step stops many people from ever beginning a Feng Shui diagnostic of their space. It is not necessary to have an architectural quality line drawing or draw your building to scale. Do have a semi-accurate rendering of your space. This is much more helpful to you when you diagnose with Feng Shui. So if the bathroom takes up only a small portion of the upper left corner of the plot, avoid having it take up half the building space when drawn. Though flawlessness has its good qualities, when someone is stopped by this first step, I usually ask, "So, are you a perfectionist?" Nod.

Perfectionists never start the process, because whatever they do in the form of a house plot will not be good enough. So why begin? Feng Shui is a language of symbols. If you won't undertake that house plot, what other projects in your life are waiting for the green light? Thus, self-named procrastinators oftentimes are really perfectionists not wanting their output to be anything less than flawless. For the truly floor plan challenged, ask a mate, your teenager, or a friend to draw it for you. It really doesn't matter who does it, just get it done. The glory of Feng Shui awaits this initial step.

What you are looking for in your floor plan is the overall shape of your home and/or office. Garages which are attached to the building are included. In fact, any out building which is connected to your house counts. Covered porches, screened rooms, and other attached buildings with a roof are a part of the necessary diagram. Multi-level houses are drawn one floor plan level at a time. Be sure to indicate where the stairs are on each level since the stair landing represents that floor's front door. You will find plenty of house plan diagram examples throughout the book.

Learn the Proper Placement of the Bagua Superimposed Over the House or Office Diagram.

This part can be the most challenging, but without a doubt, one of the more enjoyable aspects. This section will help you to understand the whys and the ah-has about your life. Feng Shui uses not English or French, but the language of symbols to express itself. Thus the building you analyze has many stories to tell. Learn to read these symbol stories. Feng Shui converts then from an ancient Chinese treatise to something which has fascinating relevance in your life.

Remember there are nine sections, called Life Values, located in the Bagua. When the Bagua is superimposed over your building plot, these nine sections fall somewhere in the various rooms and locale of your space. Every building has a Wealth/Power locale. Every structure has a Love Union/Marriage site and so on. For example, the Family/Health location could fall in your guest bathroom and, as you will later learn, that could very well contribute to your health issue, of say, low energy in the afternoon. Perhaps you store all your potential garage sale clutter in that small, multi-task bedroom which falls into your Child/Creativity section. Because this is the art of symbology, having lots of stuff in the room which also represents Child/Creativity could mean there is similarly lots of stuff, or issues, between you and your love (cough) child, preteen Billy.

So how do you figure out which Life Value falls where in your space?

On a flat surface, place the plan of your building with the line which represents the wall where the front door opens, facing your body. The front door is the front door that the architect intended. It doesn't matter if you never use it. You, your children, your friends, and even your mother-in-law use another door, the one from the garage to the kitchen. That's still not the entrance we're looking for. The front door is where strangers and sales people come. This is the door where the newspaper hits.

Suppose you live in a multifamily dwelling on the second floor and stairs enter into your space, not a door. You use the stair landing as the front door. At times, the landing for the stairs runs straight into a wall, or the stairs open into the center of an upstairs space. Alignments of the Bagua on upper and lower levels of a dwelling are not always as straightforward as they are on the ground floor of the building. It becomes necessary to use your intuition then. Often, at the top of the stairs, as I stand on the landing, I move my body exactly 90° and place the Bagua from this angle. At first this can seem confusing, but the more comfortable you become being your own self-expert of your life, the more confident, skilled, and intuitive you get about proper placement of the Bagua. Remember, the same rules do apply as on the ground floor, the upper level just might have some fancy moves added.

If you live in an apartment, it is interesting to know what Life Value your apartment represents from the perspective of the front door of the building. However, use the door to your private space as the front door for your overall analysis. Here's another scenario: You, or even the architect, has added a covered screen room as your front porch. Even though you count covered porches in the back and on either side of the home and office in the Bagua diagnostic, you do not count the front covered porch in this instance. Still use the door which is the main entrance into the house for your front door, not the first screen door you come to. Regardless of your particular set of circumstances, the front door on the building plot faces you.

Next, put the eight-sided Bagua, complete with all nine Life Values, on top of the plot of your building—with the Self Knowledge/ Wisdom, Career/Life Path, and Helpful People/Travel part of the Bagua—towards your body.

The Bagua is very flexible. It can get taller, wider, smaller, and shorter. It stretches or shrinks to serve you. You do not have to draw your plan the same size as the Bagua. What you are looking for is whether or not your home and office is a holistic shape—a square, a rectangle, or a circle. If it is, then all the different Life Values are represented in your building plot. See diagrams A-1, A-1a, and A-1b to see how a Bagua fits into various types of spaces.

HOW THE BAGUA FITS INTO A BUILDING (A-1)

Wealth/ Power	Fame/ Reputation	Love Union/ Marriage
Family/ Health	Center of the Universe	Child/ Creativity
Self-Knowledge/ Wisdom	Career/ Life Path	Helpful People/ Travel

ANOTHER VIEW OF THE TRADITIONAL BAGUA SUPERIMPOSED INTO A BUILDING (A-1A)

THE BAGUA SUPERIMPOSED ON EACH
LEVEL OF A 2-STORY HOME (A-1B)

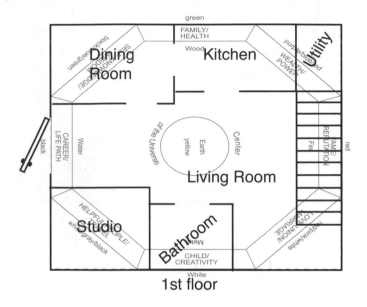

1st floor

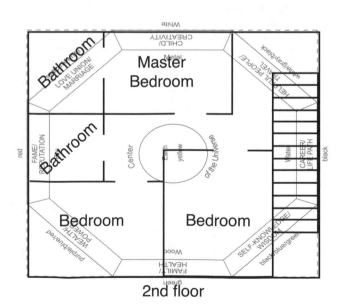

2nd floor

If your building is an irregularly shaped structure, instructions on how to balance this issue will be addressed shortly. If the front door, as the architect intended, is located on the left side of the building front, then the front door is a Self-Knowledge/ Wisdom front door. If it is located in the center of the building front, then it is a Career/Life Path front door. On the right side of the building front it is a Helpful People/Travel front door. The true front door can only be one of these three Life Values or a mixture of two if the door falls somewhere in the middle of two Life Values. See diagram A-2 for clarity.

**THE THREE POSSIBLE LIFE VALUES THAT THE
MOUTH OF CHI CAN BE IN EVERY DWELLING (A-2)**

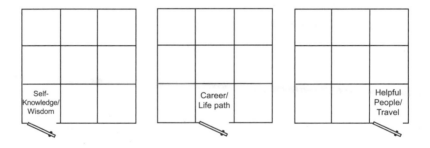

The quality of the front door is also important, as it is also called the "Mouth of the Chi." Chi is the Chinese version of life energy. The Hindus call it prana. The Hawaiians call it mana. You can call it anything you like as long as you recognize the importance of it. Think "open gate." For chi to bless the rest of your house, and most importantly the quality of life, it must feel welcomed into the front door. Interestingly, the front door is symbolically your entrance to the self. Notice yours.

Figure out Which Part of Your Space is Represented by Which Part of the Bagua Life Values.

True, it is exciting to determine whether your front door represents Self-Knowledge, Career, or Helpful People. More thrilling still is to learn where all of the other Life Values live in your space, and if they symbolically reflect what's happening in your life. Go over the Life Value section again in the informational section to master the different themes represented by each and every Life Value.

Let's say you have a Love Union/Marriage concern. Your mate has not turned out to be what you expected when you married. First, determine where in your home or office the Love Union/Marriage area resides. Go into the room(s) and look with Feng Shui detective eyes. Find out what exists in this area which symbolically represents the disillusionment in your relationship. What if you found a box on top of a dresser in which you stored all of your old creative writing stories that were never published? You knew they had great potential, yet they were never respected by the outside world. Every time you see this box it brings up feelings of disappointment, whether consciously or subconsciously, and the box has come to represent symbolically disenchantment in your life. Fascinating, as well, is that you keep this box of disappointment in the Love Union/Marriage area of your house. Are any ah-has going off in your head? Though Feng Shui can be miraculous, please don't assume by just moving the box, suddenly your mate will bring you flowers, stop reading the paper when you talk, and cook a great, romantic meal for the two of you. This *might* happen. To remove the symbol of letdown from your Love Union/Marriage area alerts the subconscious mind that the symbols have changed, you are aware of the patterns, refuse to be a victim to them anymore, and are open for the Highest Good to occur. The Highest Good might be a snuggle date in front of the fire as you watch a girlie flick, couple counseling twice a month, or both.

Here is another scenario, this time more complicated: Suppose you do not get enough recognition from your boss at work. You were in line for that promotion and instead, Joe, the pimply faced, just out of college nerd who needs a life, got the impressive desk in an office with the bay window. How would you deal with such a situation so it doesn't get repeated? Since boss relationships are dealt with in Helpful People/Travel, start there. However, this is also a Career/Life Path and Fame/Reputation issue. You are not acknowledged at your job.

Locate these values in your home and/or office with your newfound knowledge of how to align the Bagua onto the diagram of your space. Let's say the Helpful People/Travel area includes your kitchen, and sadly, your stove is broken. You have not bothered to get it fixed. The Fame/Reputation area is the hall bathroom. Enough said. Explanation to follow soon. Your Career area is actually where your front door opens. It's a long, dark hallway and the front door sticks. The symbolic reading: Doors of opportunity can't easily open in your Career/Life Path. You drain away any abundance of having a good reputation. The stove, which is the symbolic representation of prosperity, is busted. A broken stove means your relationships with Helpful People who show you generosity are also broken.

Once you diagnose a problem in your home or office—which translates to your life—Feng Shui's main purpose is to help solve whatever issue with a "cure." A cure is a balancing act which improves the situation. In the Black Hat School, perform any cure with intention. This is the secret code. In addition, memorize this Feng Shui principle: The microcosm environment—your home and office—reflects the macrocosm environment—your life in general. You use your dwelling to read what the symbols tell your conscious and subconscious mind. Change the symbols, transform your life.

Again, this does not mean that by fixing the stove, the boss necessarily sees the blunder of his ways and then promotes you to VP of the company. It could happen, and for sure the relationship with the boss will improve as you refine your surroundings so the symbols you give your mind and spirit are comparable to a proactive position about solving life dilemmas.

If the Shape of Your Building is Irregular, Cure it so that All Parts of the Bagua are Represented.

If you live in a western architecture home which is interestingly shaped, there is a good chance not all the Life Values are represented. The Feng Shui philosophy states that chi flows through an irregularly shaped building in such a way as to affect the corresponding life quality in your day-to-day existence. For instance, suppose your home or office misses the part of the building which represents Wealth/Power and Fame/Reputation. This could be the reason why you have just enough money to pay the bills, but nothing left over each month, consequently, lacking that "more than enough" quality. And, your health is okay, but certainly not great. You are far from having abundant good health. Plus, you have tried to get this new greeting card business to take off, but traders never seem to remember your name from the conversations you had with them the month before. It seems hard to get a good reputation in the profession. This is where missing Wealth/Power and Fame/Reputation sections of your house could brand your life.

In spite of having an irregularly shaped dwelling, some of my clients report a different result. After looking at the outline of their house, I have asked questions like: "I see you are missing the Love Union/Marriage area from your home. How is the relationship between you two going?"

"Fantastic."

Or, the Family/Health and Wealth/Power sections are missing, but they have "fabulous health" and clearly plenty of money and generous spirits. This doesn't mean the Feng Shui premise of unevenly shaped structures is untrue. The occupants instead experience two possible abstracts: 1: they experience great luck that the lack of chi has not yet affected those particular values in their life. They still have time to correct it before the shape starts to seriously influence their lives; or 2: the corresponding parts of their lives which they miss in the building are not being touched outwardly because a great amount of personal energy is being used to maintain the status quo.

Whether you are greatly affected or not at all, if you occupy an irregular space, a cure is in order. Addressed first is the single-family home which has an asymmetric shape. You need to anchor the missing piece(s), then make assumptions as if that section of the house existed. The anchor is placed in a corner of your lot outside just as though it completes the square, (or rectangle, or circle) of the building. See diagram A-3 for clarity.

THE CURE FOR IRREGULARLY SHAPED BUILDINGS (A-3)

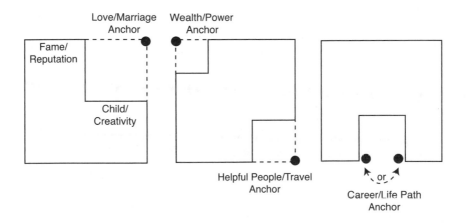

An anchor is anything heavy. So be sure to signify the completion of a missing section with something weighty. A statue, birdbath, an existing older tree, a large pot of flowers will all suffice. A small rock, a plaque, or a small pot of blooms will not. You may symbolically complete the square of several missing pieces which exist side by side with only one anchor. For instance, a heavy object in the far upper-right-hand corner of where the Love Union/Marriage area dwells could also easily cure some missing Fame/Reputation, as well as some missing Child/Creativity parts when done with intention.

CURE FOR THE IRREGULARLY SHAPED HOME OR OFFICE

1. *Placement of Object*

   Put the anchor in the appropriate outside corner of the building.

2. *Visualize/Imagine the Action Already Occurring*

   See a line of light extend along the horizontal boundary of where the structure would exist and continue this line out to meet the anchor. Then draw an imaginary vertical boundary from the existing structure to the anchor as well. See the horizontal and vertical lines meet at the anchor, completing the imaginary square (rectangle, circle).

3. *Speak Your Intention Out Loud*

   Use the missing Love Union/Marriage, Fame/Reputation areas as examples. "Now, Love Union/Marriage and Fame/Reputation qualities are represented in this home (office) and in my life. This or something better for the Highest Good, now occurs."

CURE FOR THE IRREGULARLY SHAPED APARTMENT OR OFFICE
(Where Outside Anchors are not Possible)

1. *Placement of Object*

    Suspend a faceted crystal from the ceiling about a foot inside the front door. It can dangle down on either a red cord (traditional) or fishing line (western-friendly and just as effective). Make the cord or line in odd inch increments (9-inch, 7-inch, 5-inch, 3-inch or 1-inch).

2. *Visualize/Imagine the Action Already Occurring*

    See the absent pieces of the apartment filled in with horizontal and vertical lines of light replacing the necessary Life Values which are missing (even if it is extending into the neighbor's space).

3. *Speak Your Intention Out Loud*

    Here's an example for the stated areas. "Now, Love Union/Marriage and Fame/Reputation qualities are represented in this apartment (office) and in my life. This or something better for the Highest Good now occurs."

DON'T:

Do Not Confuse Yourself by Mixing Various Schools of Feng Shui Together.

More than a few of my newer clients have been perplexed into nonaction by the science of Feng Shui. One book says this, another says that. Mirrors are no good in the bedroom; mirrors are great in the bedroom. Have your Love Union/Marriage in the southeast corner. Or, it doesn't matter where the Love Union area is, just make sure you hide the knives in the kitchen. Or, this one: Every home is compromised unless there is Lucky Bamboo placed in the center. Another book doesn't even mention Lucky Bamboo.

The problem might be that when you seek the deep knowledge of Feng Shui, you grab any book which has Feng Shui written on the cover. If you read enough of these books, and there are plenty to choose from, intellectual, emotional, and mental bewilderment is guaranteed. Why? There are presently at least three main schools in the West. The most traditional is the Compass School of Feng Shui. It relies on directions, astrology, and numerology to decipher the home and office. A compass tool is used by the practitioner to determine bearings within the structure and the appropriateness of where different rooms are located. This particular mode of thought is exceptionally difficult for the layperson to understand. Usually, a Compass Feng Shui consultant is needed. Another method is the Form School of Feng Shui thought. This focuses primary on shapes of structures in nature and determines what animal the configuration most closely resembles. The idea is to choose homes and offices which are surrounded by auspicious, protective figures. This style is subjective and perhaps not recommended for the Feng Shui beginner's insecure ways.

Enter the Black Hat Tibetan School of Feng Shui. It was brought to America by Master Lin Yun in 1982. It is also called Tantric Buddhist Feng Shui and Master Lin Yun School of Feng Shui. He spread the concepts of Black Hat on the West Coast, specifically Berkeley, California where his Feng Shui temple resides today. Although Black Hat is steeped in traditional Feng Shui guidelines and beliefs, there is an element of forgiveness in this particular school. Intention is what allows this mercy to occur.

Instead of using compass direction to determine what room should represent what value, the front door (as the architect intended) or the main door (when dealing with a room) is used as the pivot point to establish where Life Values exist in the building. The layperson can easily grasp the concepts given in Black Hat Feng Shui, as well as grow into their own interpretations within their space. This particular school is right brained, intuitive, and ultimately very empowering. It is more delightful to avoid extra exasperation and bafflement as you establish home and office balance. In the end, there are many schools of Feng Shui, and only you will know the one right for you. Find a mode of Feng Shui you like and stick with it.

Do Not Believe that Feng Shui is a Religion.

Feng Shui is an art. It is a science. It is an ancient Chinese belief system. People in China will not go to work in an office building which has not been Feng Shui treated. It is not, however, a religious endeavor. True, there are aspects of mindfulness, conscientiousness, and even reverence with the process—qualities religions applaud. Yet, Feng Shui doesn't care what you believe, in whom you believe, or if you believe at all.

Do Not Think You Have to Change Your Personal Styles or Values to Embrace Feng Shui.

Black Hat Tibetan Feng Shui is indifferent to whether your home is decorated in French Provincial or your office is filled with furniture you ordered online. Suppose your preference is antiques, eighties-era modern black and chrome pieces, the minimalist look, or, for that matter, just bad taste in general. Feng Shui has no judgment, unless something lowers your energy—yes, the evil *clutter*—then it insists the object should be removed from your personal environment. You can keep your Christianity, or (insert religion of your choice), your morals, and your standards. The Feng Shui cures used in your home and office don't have to be obvious or overtly Chinese in nature, thus clashing with your solid oak, traditional dinette set.

Here is the one condition insisted upon with Black Hat Tibetan Feng Shui: Every action and value you change because of a Feng Shui suggestion must be done with intention. This is also where the leniency part comes into play. You can keep your favorite old easy chair. But move the chair to a position more favorable so that you can see the door, then perform the Three Secrets Reinforcement Ritual after the huff and puff is over.

THE BATHROOM

When Feng Shui first originated in China, centuries ago, indoor plumbing was not a reality. The philosophies of Feng Shui would prefer the home and offices to have outhouses as separate buildings even now. There is little respect for that particular invention of modern humankind, the indoor bathroom. Why is that? Remember Feng Shui is the language of symbols. The modern bathroom is so important in Feng Shui, not because of the conveniences it provides for us, but because of the symbolic stories a washroom oozes. Water, in the right places and in the right amounts, stands for abundance in Feng Shui. The bathroom has lots of water coming out of faucets. Water hangs out in the toilet. But there are also plenty of drains. Water goes down the drains. Symbolic translation: Abundance drained. Remember the example of the Family/Health Life Value residing in the guest bathroom and the issue of low energy? What about the zero reputation at work? Fame/Reputation in the bathroom.

Not to worry. You don't need to call a contractor to build an outhouse in the backyard. However, do learn how to protect your various forms of abundance—money, health, love, and more—from symbolically going down the drain. Although a strong set of ideologies and opinions are presented, each notion should be personally experienced before integrating into any life. Incorporate every Feng Shui notion into your own mind and see what happens. Only good can come when you change the symbols in your life to support your growth and ability to thrive. When you create symbolic actions which endorse empowerment rather than reaction and victimization, the subconscious mind quits its rule of emotions. Instead, it is given signs which show strength and positive growth and all parts of your being begin to heal. Start this process. The following cures will send this message to your High Self, your subconscious mind, as well as teach you how to co-create your life.

DO:

Always Keep the Bathroom Door Closed.

The essence of this art responds to what you do in your environment and what your actions and objects "say." Closing the bathroom door deters the abundance of all things in the rest of your house from "going down the drain." Remember, too, each and every room stands for some Life Value: Love, Career, Health, and more. By keeping the bathroom door shut, you consciously stop the symbolic action of the draining of your resources, any and all of them. Don't have the bathroom door open when it is the first thing you see when coming through the front door. This can generate bad luck.

Hold Chi in the Room.

The bathroom also stands for one of the Life Values, depending on what it lines up with on the Bagua. Even though you are keeping the door closed, take steps to hold the life force inside the bathroom for whatever Life Value it represents in your home or office; whether it is Love Union/Marriage, Wealth/Power, and so on. Having a particular Life Value in the bathroom does not mean this specific part of your life is over. It means the cures recommended are a Feng Shui top priority. Holding chi, or life force in, brings attention to that Life Value, whatever it is. It also starts to bring the medicinal force of chi to whatever Life Value it corresponds to in your general life. Amazingly, whatever you bring attention to, blesses you. For instance, want the Helpful

People/Travel aspects in your life to sanctify you? Hold in the chi of that Life Value.

There is a traditional way this Feng Shui school recommends to hold in chi. Please obtain a 9-inch red cord or ribbon (or multiples of 9, i.e., 18-inch, 27-inch, and so on). Attach a multi-faceted leaded crystal to the cord. Hang this crystal suspended from the ceiling (in this case, the bathroom). Use the Three Secrets Reinforcement Ritual to keep chi from going down the drains.

Here comes the fallout...

"I'm not a crystal person!"

"Red? That is NOT going to go with my baby blue and pink bathroom color scheme!"

"Nine inches! Are you crazy? It will hit my head every time I enter the room."

"A faceted crystal is quite expensive, $4 to $25 a piece, and you suggest them in a few places. I don't have a money tree in the backyard."

I know my Westerners. If something is too complicated, too brazen, or too expensive, you will not do it. Chill, there is no need to shut the book and instead use it as mulch in the garden. Feng Shui can work for you as you are now. The power of intention is effective no matter what object you choose to use. Whatever modifications you make to any traditional cures, however, should have a semblance of Feng Shui convention in them.

Here is an alternative: Go to a bead store and get a few beads because holding chi in the rooms of your home and office is something you will do in many places. Buy glass, crystal, clay, metal, and gem beads. You can even get clear ones. But avoid plastic. Think natural. Whenever you are doing a cure in Feng Shui, benefit from the most original, energy-raising components.

Your positive results will be all the thanks you need. Then get fishing line. What it lacks in naturalness will be made up in the fact it is essentially invisible. Thread will work also. Tie one bead to a piece of this string. The string does not have to be 9" long, although nine is the power number in Feng Shui. If you have high ceilings, use the recommended 9" of cord or line, as it should be no problem. If you need to make adjustments for low ceilings, make your cord or line in odd increments; for example, 1", 3", 5", and so on. Odd numbers are more powerful in Feng Shui.

Hang this chi catcher from the ceiling, about a foot inside the door of the room. Suspend it with a thumbtack or some other hooking apparatus. See diagram B-1 for visual example of an inexpensive, virtually invisible chi catcher.

EXAMPLE OF CHI-CATCHER (B-1)

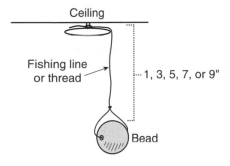

Ceiling

Fishing line or thread

1, 3, 5, 7, or 9"

Bead

Regardless of how you make the chi catcher, and creative ideas are of great value because they will raise your energy and thus the power of whatever Life Value is being enhanced, construct the chi catcher, or any other Feng Shui cure, to work for you. Otherwise, you won't do it. Yes, I live in this culture, too. It is surprisingly easy to resist an idea which is unusual or different.

CURE TO HOLD CHI IN ANY ROOM

1. *Placement of Object*

   Suspend the chi catcher from the ceiling about a foot inside the room door.

2. *Visualize/Imagine the Action Already Occurring*

   See chi (think of it as a glitter-like substance) floating throughout the room.

3. *Speak Your Intention Out Loud*

   "Now, the chi of Career (Helpful People/Travel, Family/ Health, or whatever room Life Value you are inside) stays in my life and in this room. This or something better for the Highest Good now occurs."

Keep the Lid Down on the Toilet Seat When Not in Use.

"HELLO, I live with a man. I can't get him to put down the seat!"

This point cannot be over-emphasized: The bathroom cures discourage the prosperity in your life from going down the drain symbolically. Change the symbols, and watch to see how the details in life alter also. For the discouraged who believe in Feng Shui whole-heartedly, but live with "doubt personified" in the form of your mate, a gang of children, or deal with an office full of clients who are only interested in your professional services, please know to become the Feng Shui police is not necessary.

In a classy way that stays with your personal style, attach a word sign or a symbol sign on the outside of the closed bathroom door that everyone agrees means, "Please Keep Door Closed." Likewise, inside the toilet lid, attach another agreed upon symbol, even the same one as on the door. It stands for "Please shut when done." If you are working in a professional office, the above words can go on a laminated poster attached to the door and to the inside of the toilet lid. People accommodate when asked to do something nicely. This also "tells" the symbols of your universe, your Higher Power, and your High Self, that you are aware of the potential loss of abundance and don't want such action to happen, regardless of whether people close the bathroom door or put the toilet lid down. If you have a party, don't worry. People will knock to see if the bathroom is occupied, and there are always legitimate reasons why you have to leave the bathroom door open or the toilet lid up for something really important. Exceptions with everything and anything are realistic. We live on planet Earth, not some Mount Olympus cloud where fairies magically perform every whim our minds and hearts desire. But make these bouts of transgression the exception, not the rule. Feng Shui bathroom cures require new thinking and the changing of habits. Get into these new Feng Shui bathroom behaviors. They will become as instinctive as brushing your teeth when you get up in the morning.

Put Uncooked Rice or Popcorn in a Container (With or Without a Lid) on Top of the Tank Lid.

You symbolically show a bounty with the container of grain (please keep them uncooked, thank me later). If you are resistant to putting uncooked grain on your toilet tank lid because of the possible, but unlikely, attraction of bugs or rodents, then consider sea salt as a viable alternative instead. This filled bowl becomes your object of prosperity; it symbolically states, even though you flush away your abundance (water), that you still have plenty. This shows that obligatory deeds which take place in the bathroom will not affect the affluence in your life. If you want an open bowl of uncooked rice perching on the tank lid, fine, as long as you actually feel comfortable taking such action. However, consider these options as well. Put the uncooked rice, popcorn, seeds, salt—whatever celebrates the idea of abundance for you—in a bowl which has a lid. Or, cover the grain with potpourri so your guests can't tell there is more in the bowl besides smell goodies. My personal preference for this cure is a lovely green earthenware vase filled with uncooked popcorn. No one knows a thing except that I have good taste. See diagram B-2 for clarity.

CURE FOR LOSS OF ABUNDANCE (B-2)

CURE FOR LOSS OF ABUNDANCE

1. *Placement of Object*

   Put a bowl of uncooked grain on tank lid (or appropriate shelf).

2. *Visualize/Imagine the Action Already Occurring*

   See yourself outside with arms outstretched and face up toward the sky. Glitter falls from the heavens, overflowing bounty. All you can wish for, you receive.

3. *Speak Your Intention Out Loud*

   "Even though abundance goes down the drain, I still have plenty of wealth in all areas of my life. This or something better for the Highest Good now occurs."

Provide a Cure if You Can See the Toilet When You Enter the Bathroom.

This is called, Toilet Vision, the phenomenon that occurs when you can see the toilet as you enter the bathroom. Even if the lid is down, regardless that chi is being held in the room, the chi or life force of the individual can symbolically shoot straight down the toilet. Though some toilets are placed in their own little room inside the bathroom or behind a cute half wall, most toilets are set in plain view of whoever enters. If you can see the commode when you enter, a cure needs to be implemented to hinder life force from going "down the toilet." You can use the same chi catcher that you used to hold the life force in this room to also balance the problem of chi going down the visible toilet. Just make sure the chi catcher is placed between the door and the toilet. It now has two assignments instead of one. First, complete the Three Secrets Reinforcement Ritual to hold in chi in the room. Then, return to that magnificent chi catcher with this cure. See diagram B-3 for clarity.

CURE FOR TOILET VISION (B-3)

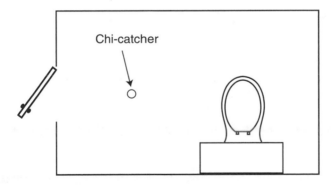

Chi-catcher

CURE FOR TOILET VISION

1. Placement of Object

Put attention on the chi catcher that already hangs from the ceiling.

2. Visualize/Imagine the Action Already Occurring

See an energetic force field between the door and the toilet which extends from the chi catcher all the way to the bathroom floor. Imagine the glitter-like substance of chi unable to escape past its barrier to get to the toilet.

3. Speak Your Intention Out Loud

"My chi and every person's chi which enters this bathroom, stays intact. This or something better for the Highest Good now occurs."

Plug Drains in Tubs, Showers, and Bathroom Sinks.

With this action, you symbolically insist, "No abundance is lost here!" as you cover each drain with a drain cover. Do not get overly obsessive about this one, however. To stop up sink and tub drains, and other such water suckers, can be next to impossible if you don't live alone. Plus, becoming the Feng Shui Police gets old if you always have to play "bad cop." Unless you like that sort of thing.

Instead, have the covers near the drain and for important occasions, like when you are going to a job interview, giving a public talk or meeting a date for dinner. Cover up the symbolic drainage of abundance. At other times, the mere presence of its existence near the offending suck hole will tell your universe plenty.

Fix Leaky Water Faucets.

By now, you get the picture on how to read symbols. That's right, abundance slowly leaks away. The same goes for shower and bath heads that dribble incessantly, and please don't forget the running toilet. The sound of water plops might as well be synonymous with the tone "ka-ching!" Each reverberation stands for Wealth spent.

DON'T:

Do Not Leave the Toilet Lid Up so Pets Can Drink the Toilet Water.

Whenever giving a workshop, I always ask for a show of hands on which pet owners do this very thing. At least a few tentative and embarrassed hands creep up from the mommies and daddies. I hear this regularly: "It's the only water Herman will drink…" (I have always assumed they mean the dog.)

I reply, "This is to show proactive symbols to your subconscious mind and emblematic universe, which reflects the loss of Wealth is not what you choose. Shut the toilet lid. Keep the bathroom door closed. Put out a bowl of water for your sweet thing in, say, the kitchen. If he gets thirsty, I swear he will drink it."

Animal activist groups may contact my publisher.

Do Not Find Excuses for Leaving the Bathroom Door Open.

You did a "happy dance" when I said we don't live on Mount Olympus. But, you don't want to live in "water funnel" alley either. Here are some solutions for your various justifications:

Many clients have the kitty litter box in their bathroom. Thus, their bathroom door must remain open for their pets.

"You mean it matters, even if I leave it open just a crack?"

I insist, "A fracture in a water bowl is all it takes. The door should stay shut all the way."

I know, I am ruthless.

Solution 1: If you own your house, a pet door can be put into your bathroom door. Then you can keep it shut and little Missy will still have full access. Solution 2: Employ the Hippie Cure. Find a piece of fabric which extends from the very top of the doorway to the very bottom. Arrange this fabric to slide open on a curtain rod placed inside the door frame. The name "Hippie" implies that only tie-dye fabric will work. Please, choose a piece of material in your own style and color scheme that raises your energy. Avoid lace, however, as it "leaks" chi through its fine threadwork. The rule here is if you can see through it, or if it is a piece of material with a pattern of holes, and if it doesn't reach from the very top to the very bottom of the doorway, then this solution is really no solution. If you have applied the proper fabric, then know the cloth door is appropriately discouraging the loss of abundance and the entrance is now soft and flexible to allow pets to enter. This also keeps the hard door open when unusual and special situations call for the bathroom to be accessible at all times. The bathroom door is still there to be closed whenever you want privacy. See diagram B-4 for Hippie Cure example.

EXAMPLE OF HIPPIE CURE (B-4)

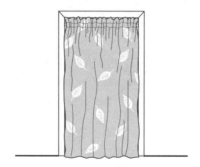

HIPPIE CURE FOR DOOR

1. *Placement of Object*

   Hang a piece of fabric or cloth (your colors and style) from the top of the open bathroom door frame. The cloth extends all the way to the floor of the bathroom opening. Arrange the fabric on a tension rod so it slides open and shut like a curtain.

2. *Visualize/Imagine the Action Already Occurring*

   See the glitter-like substance of chi from the building's Life Values unable to pass through the obstruction of the cloth.

3. Speak Your Intention Out Loud

"All the abundance stays within the building, and in my life, and cannot go down the drain. This or something better for the Highest Good now occurs."

When you enter into a bathroom that respects the above practices, there is a sanctity about the space. This is hard to create by the washroom's very nature. It is a place where we conduct our least glamorous activities. However, there is nothing more incredible than a room which holds your plenteousness intact.

THE BEDROOM

This section refers to the master bedroom, focusing on the boudoir you, and possibly a mate, inhabit. In another portion of the book, rooms of children, roommates, and guestrooms are evaluated. The master bedroom gets high rank in Feng Shui. This is the room where relaxation, restoration, and intimacy occur. It also is the space which reflects the Love Union/Marriage condition of your life, besides the actual Love Union/Marriage Bagua position in the home or office. Though sometimes they may be the same. Interestingly, when you follow Feng Shui practices and make cures in the master bedroom, this action generates the greatest impact to create movement in all areas of your life.

Ideally, the master bedroom should be located in one of the most commanding Bagua stations: the Wealth/Power position or the Love Union/Marriage position. Each one of these places is the farthest location from the front door, and therefore symbolically keeps the mate at home. It also fixes you in the most auspicious position to make decisions regarding household and life matters. A word of caution here: Some clients move their master bedroom from the Wealth/Power position on the Bagua to that of Love Union/Marriage to enhance this aspect of their relationship. Fine, if the previous bedroom, which is still in the Wealth/Power position, becomes an office, a meditation room, and so on. Keep control of the Wealth/Power room. This is supreme. The now empty area should not become a child's room.

"But our six-month-old baby, Favio, lives in there right now. He has given us no problems!"

"Wait 10 years for Machiavelli to grow up!" I promise.

Also, do not make your Wealth/Power area a guest room. The company will smell worse than fish before the three-day limit is up. Similarly, do not give this area to a roommate. Soon you will sign over the property to her. Last but not least, do not let your animals eat, rest, and play here without the presence of an alpha human (pets who sleep with you in your Wealth/Power bedroom are fine). Those cute, sweet things will run your life, perhaps in cute, sweet ways, but run it they will. Honor the Wealth/Power of every building. Know where it is. Don't turn your back on it. Such regard will compensate you tenfold.

DO:

Hold Chi in the Bedroom.

The bedroom, although it has definite references to relationships, love, and partnerships, also stands for one of the Bagua Life Values, like Helpful People/Travel, Self-Knowledge/Wisdom, Fame/Reputation, and so on. It is necessary to hold the life force in the room, just like you did in the bathroom. Bring attention and thus blessings to whatever Life Value the master bedroom stands for in the Bagua. See the cure for holding in chi given on page 54.

Place the Bed in "Empowerment Position."

Don't worry, I'm a Feng Shui consultant not a sex therapist. The Empowerment Position is when you are lying in bed and can see the door to the bedroom. A door which leads to a deck or a small study off the bedroom is not a concern. In a perfect Feng Shui example, however, the bed placement is in a position which gives a full view of all the entryways should multiple doors exist. When the bedroom is in a loft where the stairs are the "mouth of chi," the position of the bed would be so that you could see the stair landing. See diagram C-1 for bed position options.

EXAMPLES OF BED EMPOWERMENT (C-1)

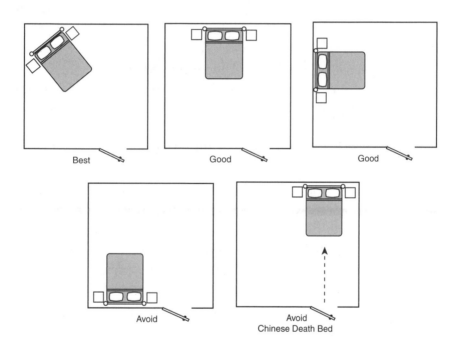

First, place the bed in the Empowerment Position. This is important. Regardless if this post grants you little conscious ease, you will release a subconscious sigh. You sleep and rest better when you can see who is coming through the door even if you live alone. Second, since the mattress is a metaphor for love in Feng Shui, there is an undeniable proactive shift which comes as you choose to empower your love relationships, whether they are current or yet to be manifested. A force is born in the choice of strength. It heals, alters, and calls to it the best options.

However, there are ample reasons why you might not be able to move the bed. The space could be too small to position the bed anywhere else. Glass sliding doors might stop a bed from being relocated so that you can see the main bedroom door; plus, at no time do you want to block a doorway, even if seldom used. In some cases, a bathroom could be directly encountered where an empowered bed placement should go. If a similar situation as described exists in your bedroom, find yourself a mirror. Mirrors are called Feng Shui Band-Aids. The suggested mirrors are without damage, dents, or cracks. Forget the mirror tile. It is not endorsed in Feng Shui. Make sure whatever mirrors you choose 1: raise your energy; and 2: fulfill the form and function test. In other words, they look pretty and are also large and practical enough to reflect the door. In some cases space, windows, and such obstruct the placement of a large form and function mirror. In these instances, self-adhesive automobile mirrors are recommended. They are small and inexpensive, plus their concave or convex construction make them perfect to reflect a large area behind them—ideal for when there is little room to hang a standard mirror. Attach the mirror on a wall so that when you lie in bed, the door to the bedroom reflects off the mirror so that you can see the door. This cure puts you most at ease when moving the bed isn't possible. This is the remedy which secures empowerment of love and life for you. See diagram C-2.

CURE FOR EMPOWERMENT (C-2)

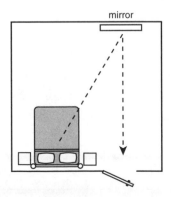

mirror

This is not, however, to be substituted for placing the bed in an empowered position when such is possible. In other words, the *cure* for the empowered bed position is not the same as placing the bed in the Empowerment Position. The differences are subtle but undeniable, and if a renovation in perception of life and love is what you seek, the latter is recommended if at all possible.

CURE TO GAIN EMPOWERMENT

1. *Placement of Object*

   Secure a mirror on a wall so it reflects the main door of the room when the position of a piece of furniture has you turned so your back is to the door or your vision is obscured.

2. *Visualize/Imagine the Action Already Occurring*

   See the mirror reflect the door to the room. Also, see yourself empowered, at ease, healed, and joyous.

3. *Speak Your Intention Out Loud*

   "I am empowered in my love and life, full of ease, grace, and joy. This or something better for the Highest Good now occurs."

Have Night Tables with Lamps on Both Sides of the Bed.

I once had a consultation with an older woman. Upon entering her bedroom and taking a quick glance around, I was then able to say, "So, you have been hurt in love relationships." She looked at me with a "How did you know?" splattered all over her kisser.

This is what I saw: a single bed, pushed up against the wall, so only one side had access. The pillows showed me the bed was not in the Empowerment Position because the head of the bed placed her in a direction so the door was behind her. There was one table beside the bed. On the wall, directly in front of the bed, was a picture of a single woman, languishing beside a water fountain. The woman in the picture looked very beautiful, but not happy. On the wall across the room was a picture of a sweet-eyed little kitten, roosting in front of an aluminum trashcan. To put the cherry on the proverbial whipped cream, the room was located in the Love Union/Marriage area of the home.

How did I come up with my particular interpretation? I read the language the symbols told me. A single bed would never be advocated in Feng Shui except for a child. There is only enough room in the bed for one person. No overnight rendezvous. No potential partners. This limitation of elbowroom in the bed is not only an actual fact, but a symbolic gesture as well. Far from suggesting a person get involved impulsively with another, a bed should nonetheless support two adults comfortably. For some people, it takes this purely symbolic gesture to make room for the heart to heal, whether this means to grieve, to address anger and betrayal issues, or even to raise low self-esteem issues regarding romance. The spare part of the bed then is reserved for the heart to soothe itself into readiness to walk the Life Path again. Thus, decisions can be made not from a reactionary, unhealed place, but from the whole being who makes choices consciously about the next step in the life story.

Part of the Feng Shui theory is you prepare for something "as if" it is already a relevant, functioning, present part of your life. Hence the omnipotence of intention includes the appearance of things in the present tense. As if they are already happening. Thus you don't wait to have a partner before you have a place for her or him to sleep. You prepare a place symbolically, complete with at least a double bed, access from both sides of the empowered position love-trundle, and a nightstand with a lamp on each side of the bed just in case Casanova wants to read a book.

If you lack the space for all of this Feng Shui love gear, consider creative options instead. The night tables do not have to be the same. They just need to be balanced. If a dresser is on one side of the bed and a flimsy, bamboo table is on the other side, who do you think is in control? That's right, the dresser partner. If having lamps on both sides of the bed is not practical, try two candles instead. They do not need to be lit to signify mate bonding and passion. Concurrently, this particular bedroom setup acts as an equalizer whether you want a mate, are recuperating from a break-up, or an operation, or just need time to heal your psyche. This arrangement is recommended whatever your circumstances are, even if you are happily involved with your soul mate. This layout will keep it that way, if the Highest Good so bids it.

Hang Pictures that Have the Representation of Pairs, Couples, or More Than One on the Walls of Your Bedroom.

This was the other sign "Ms. Love-is-a-Crock" had less than a stellar track record with romantic love. The pictures in her bedroom made me want to cry and not smoke a cigarette. Visibly, between the pictures and the rest of the symbology in her bedroom, she would not be placing a personal ad anytime soon. Pictures, art, and sculpture have an incredible influence on the mind and spirit. The messages they consciously or subconsciously speak must be brought to your awareness. Needless to say, your choices of statues and portrayals should make your heart yodel. Understand how negative art in Career/Life Path (or wherever) affects your emotional attitude about your job (or whatever). In the bedroom, the Love Union/Marriage area, especially if different than the bedroom, and also in the Self-Knowledge/Wisdom area (Opposite-Attract Law), you should only have only images which reflect more than one image. This is a requirement especially for the single person who desires a mate. Interestingly, rarely does an unattached person, desirous or not of a mate, not have an unusual amount of single objects and images in her home.

An even more remarkable study is that of married clients who feel alone in their unions. One woman client sensed her husband was not present in the partnership. Upon looking around her home, pictures of beautiful single women alone in nature shrouded the entire place. Therefore, this need for the "twosome" reflection is for the happily, and unhappily, married mates as well. Also included in this evaluation are the single clients (or unhappily married ones) who have pictures of gurus, statues of Buddha, crucifixes of Jesus, candles with the Virgin Mary on them, and such surrounding their home environment. Being enveloped in the ethereal presence of masters might seem to lend a degree of comfort. Yet, how does being surrounded exclusively by spiritually evolved beings who have no equal serve your desire to have a counterpart lover?

Pictures, three-dimensional art and sculptures do not have to reflect only human imagery. Representations of animals are allowed, as long as it is, say, a pair of rabbits that frolic in the woods, rather than just one. A vase of flowers is fine. Just make sure it doesn't reflect one lonely rose bud. Images which are double should be balanced and equal; mother/child pictures do not count, nor does a statue of a bird with a framed picture of another bird right beside it. Dimensionalities must be respected. Pictures reside with pictures. Statuary stays with statuary. If you add a statue to one which is already placed; it should be equal in size, not larger or smaller.

We create what we believe. Our small universes, our homes and offices, could display a truth to us which has no leniency towards growth. For instance, you may have one idea about your goals and who you want to become, yet the images in your environment tell another story. This has more to do with what you hold subconsciously to be true. Thus heal and envelop yourself with images which reflect more than a single.

If you must have some that are solitary, stash them out of the bedroom, the Love Union/Marriage area and the Self-Knowledge/Wisdom area. Consciously build a library of non-solo illustrations in your world. Enjoy the human experience. Take pleasure from how such attentive cooperation towards variety in your environment alters your existence in superior ways.

If a Bathroom is in the Bedroom, Hang a Full-length Mirror on the Outside of the Bathroom's Closed Door.

You already know about bathrooms and their particular role in Feng Shui. The bedroom reflects the state of relationship love. The symbolic way to deflect the bedroom (love) away from the bathroom (drainage of abundance) is to place a full-length mirror on the outside of the closed bathroom door. If you are using a Hippie Cure in your master bath, place a small, round mirror above the outside of the bathroom's door frame. See diagram C-3 for visual.

HIPPIE CURE WITH MIRROR (C-3)

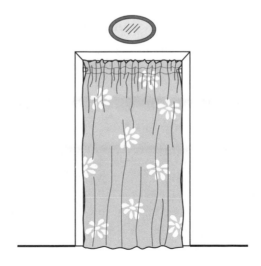

DON'T:

Do Not Have Pictures of Your Parents and Your Children in the Bedroom.

Focusing ad nauseum on images, it seems perfect to concentrate on just a few more picture rules. It is greatly advised to keep the parents out of the bedroom. You don't need the matriarch and patriarch symbolically watching you, whether you enjoy their company still or they have already passed from earth. Amazingly, more than a few clients have reported a new resurgence of passion in the bedroom when Ma and Pa hang on the hall wall, not across from the bed. Similarly, pictures of your children do not belong in the bedroom. This does not mean you love them any less. You can still place their portraits in an area which communicates great importance, but somewhere outside of the bedroom. The bedroom is your retreat—a place to heal, relax, make love—not fold the socks, prepare grilled cheese sandwiches, and help with algebra homework. When you want to allow yourself time for your individual needs, separate from being the ideal nurturer, the bedroom offers the perfect refuge. You can close the door and magically transform yourself from the nose-wiping, waffle-making mother of three to a human being who has dreams, aspirations, and passions. In your refuge you can be an adult with grown-up needs. What a concept. By the way, pictures of parents love to be near pictures of their grandchildren.

Do Not Settle for a Used Mattress or a Mattress From a Previous Relationship for Your Bed.

The bed, specifically the mattress, is symbolic for relationship love. The mattress also stores patterns, belief systems, and energies in its very fibers. Amazingly, keeping an old mattress can actually stop you from attracting a new mate. It can also influence you to bring old patterns from an ex into a current love affair. Thus, have respectful awareness of your particular mattress' history. This mattress philosophy does not affect the couple who purchased a mattress together over 20 years ago. The patterns which exist in the bed's filament are their own. Likewise, don't be nervous with the overnight fling or affair which lasts just a few days. You do not need to get a new mattress every time you have sex on it. However, be conscious with connections that have an emotional component to them, whether the relationship lasted for years, months, or just a few weeks. Be honest with yourself. If an affair really horsewhipped your heart, purchasing a new mattress is sound advice. Otherwise, those same heavy patterns could repeat themselves.

Consider this synopsis: You are single and desire a mate. The double mattress you currently sleep on was given to you by Cheryl, your friend from yoga class, who recently got a divorce and has moved into a smaller apartment. In the divorce, she got the bed. Then she gave it to you. What a wonderful friend, right? Perhaps a lovable confidante, but when she gave you her old mattress—one with disharmony, anger, and Heartbreak Hotel patterns—she ultimately did not strengthen your desire for a lover. Not that Cheryl did this deliberately. She tried to help you out by giving you a comfortable, expensive mattress for free. But after gaining comprehension of what a mattress can truly bring, way more than a good night's sleep especially if the historical patterns are negative, spring for a new mattress which offers a clean slate regarding your love journey. Here's another situation: A client was desperate to attract a lover. In the consultation, we eventually arrived at his bedroom. Though there were many symbolic problems which contributed to his lonely nights, there was one in particular that took the lead.

"Tell me about your mattress," I asked.

"It was my grandmother's," he sheepishly admitted.

Obviously, the mattress was not exactly giving off the stud-magnet vibe. I recommended he purchase a new one. To become the Don Quixote of his dreams, he needed to sleep on a mattress with his own patterns and energies, and not Grandma Kettle's. A different client resisted my advice, but after a few mental and emotional processes, she let go of an old mattress she and an ex-boyfriend had shared. She literally threw the old mattress in the garbage outside. Ten minutes later, she took a walk down her neighborhood street looking for the house cat when she met a hot, younger man, who soon after became her lover.

Although the mattress truth is primarily for adult-love relationship health, this same issue plays a role when a young child is afraid to sleep in her or his bed at night. If you wake up each morning with a cute, little snuggly human between you and your beloved, it becomes imperative to remember if the child's mattress is used. More often than not, a child sleeps on a single bed. If the mattress was bought at a thrift store—admittedly for a great price—it is at least plausible that the mattress could have been donated by an elder-care facility, because it was no longer needed. Whoever slept on it previously has now died. Thus death, struggle, and illness could easily exist in the character of the bed. Who needs a monster in the closet when such horrors live right under the sheets?

Obviously, the purchase of a brand new mattress might not exist in the monthly (or annual) budget. In such a case, go to a bedding store and purchase a complete set of new sheets, pillowcases included. The new bed linens are intentionally programmed to neutralize any used mattress intensity plus support patterns and energies unified with your objectives. Like the Empowerment Position of the bed, this is the *cure* recommended for used mattresses. The purchase of a new mattress is solidly advocated when you can afford it. A futon, cut foam, or an air mattress can be an inexpensive, yet valid, alternative to the expense of a new standard mattress.

CURE FOR USED MATTRESS JUJU

1. *Placement of Object*

   Make your bed up with a set of new sheets and pillowcases purchased with the aim of being a part of a clearing ritual.

2. *Visualize/Imagine the Actions Already Occurring*

   See the sheets provide a protective barrier against the patterns, energies, and belief systems of the used mattress. See your peaceful sleep and loving relationships.

3. *Speak Your Intention Out Loud*

   "My love relationship patterns are my own, harmonious, nurturing, and empowered. This or something better for the Highest Good now occurs."

If you have a used mattress, this does not absolutely guarantee your relationship(s) are or shall be horrible. It is when the ideologies of Feng Shui are integrated into your being, your environment, and thus your universe, that not only will the life force energy increase in all aspects of your body and life, the support you feel from the Higher Power will be evident. Flow is guaranteed. When struggle occurs in some dimension of your life, you are supported by your consciously created environment to recognize this struggle as a familiar remnant which no longer needs to be nourished. The breath of vitality can then move through your life.

Do Not Store Objects Under the Bed.

Because the bed is the token of love, you want the chi to freely revolve around it. Unfortunately, many rely on this extra space under the bed for storage. The bed, however, is too important a symbol to use as a clutter storage area. Please see the chapter on mirrors to create storage areas in garages, basements, attics, and closets. A favorite story is of the woman who had three objects under her bed—a baseball bat, running shoes, and a suitcase. She was not feeling great about her relationship with her husband. The articles were representational of the internal process she was undergoing at the time in regard to him. These items were hardly symbols that reflected satisfied, peaceful love. Following my advice, she took the things out from under the bed to establish a positive alternative pattern which occurs with healthy chi flow.

If you have a bed which has compartments on either side for storing blankets, panties, socks, and toys, obviously there is no area "under" the bed. In fact, the trundle usually goes all the way to the floor. This is where mirrors and intention promise you freedom of chi. See diagram C-4 for visual clarity.

CURE FOR THE FLOWING BED CHI (C-4)

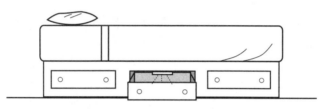

Mirror position under bed with
reflection facing into drawer

CURE FOR THE FLOWING BED CHI

1. *Placement of Object*

   Attach a self-adhesive automobile mirror to the bottom of the bed frame or whatever creates the "ceiling" for the drawer. Have the reflective part of the mirror face into the drawer. Place one mirror on either side of the bed inside the top drawer.

2. *Visualize/Imagine the Action Already Occurring*

   See the mirrors reflect all the clutter and objects in the drawers away from where you lie on the bed. See the one mirror affect every drawer on its particular side. Then visualize or imagine chi (glitter-substance) revolving around your bed.

3. Speak Your Intention Out Loud

"The chi of love flows around my bed. This or something better for the Highest Good now occurs."

Do Not Have Mirrors Hanging on the Bedroom Walls Unless You Understand Their Nature.

One use of the mirror is to achieve the Empowerment Position cure with the bed. The other is to deflect the bedroom back unto itself when a closed bathroom door is involved. Black Hat Tibetan Feng Shui allows mirrors in the bedroom, but is cautiously aware. Consider these reasons: 1: you might wake in the middle of the night, sit up to rub your eyes, see a shadowy figure in the room, and have a panic attack. All the time it is your own reflection in the mirror. Freaking out in the bedroom is not good Feng Shui; and 2: mirrors have a very active chi. In Feng Shui, it is believed that mirrors never sleep. Imagine having a little kitten playing in your bedroom all night. Your sleep is more than likely disturbed. Maybe a little, maybe a lot. In other words, mirrors may agitate the quality of your shut-eye. Insomniacs, please enter the hall now. Get your cure here. Mirrors may not alter the condition of your nighttime slumber, but, if the caliber of your dreamtime is at all compromised, do the following treatment.

CURE FOR PUTTING A MIRROR TO BED AT NIGHT

1. Placement of Object

Choose a piece of fabric, one which raises your energy and is large enough to cover the mirror you tranquilize. Drape the cloth over the mirror's reflective glass so it is completely screened. This action is to be repeated nightly, or as needed, when you have a hard time falling asleep.

2. *Visualize/Imagine the Action Already Occurring*

See the cloth as a shield which stops busy energy, like a barrier, from entering the room.

3. *Speak Your Intention Out Loud*

"The mirror is put to bed. Peaceful, healing energy now fills the room. My sleep is deep, restorative, and nurturing. This or something better for the Highest Good now occurs."

If your closet doors are sliding mirrors which extend across part of or an entire bedroom wall, substitute a curtain on a curtain rod to act as a bedtime elixir for the quality of your sleep. Use the above cure to enhance its function.

Do Not Have the Bed and the Toilet Sharing a Common Wall.

If the bed emulates love, and the toilet reflects injury to abundance, the Feng Shui symbolic story tells us the ending is not happy. Love is going down the toilet. The following cure can be employed whether the bed shares a common wall with the toilet, or for those who apply Feng Shui treatments more conservatively, the bathroom in general. See diagram C-5 for clarity.

CURE FOR TOILET-BEDROOM COMMON WALL (C-5)

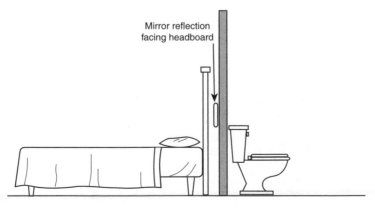

Mirror reflection facing headboard

CURE FOR TOILET/BEDROOM COMMON WALL

1. *Placement of Object*

Attach a convex mirror to the common wall with the reflection side facing the bed's headboard. If the room which shares the common wall with the bathroom is the kitchen, then place the reflective side of the mirror toward the stove. The mirror is secured below the visual line so it is not observable.

2. *Visualize/Imagine the Action Already Occurring*

See your relationship love chi (or your prosperity chi if in the kitchen) stay within its boundaries as the mirror reflects back the love (or prosperity) so it doesn't ever reach the toilet (loss of abundance).

3. *Speak Your Intention Out Loud*

"My love (or prosperity) stays intact. This or something better for the Highest Good now occurs."

Do Not Have Too Much Furniture in the Bedroom.

The bedroom is a place for relaxation, rejuvenation, and intimacy. Please don't make it activity central. It is very customary to enter a bedroom which has a sewing machine piled with mending, a work desk heaped with bills, plus a treadmill whose intended purpose has long since been forgotten. If nothing else, avoid having a work desk in your sanctuary, even if it just holds a computer where you only check emails. The symbol of the desk still stands for labor in the subconscious mind. Put the desk in the home office or in some other appropriate place so it does not affect the ambiance you create for this room. Likewise, do not have sewing projects, paint easels, or exercise equipment stowed in the bedroom. Sure you can sew, paint, even work on your abs there, but keep the room your sanctuary for only your special activities. Don't have them waiting around in the room for you to get inspired. If space absolutely requires that you have a desk, a sewing machine, or something else sharing the same air space as the bed, find a creative way to hide the exercise equipment from view when you first wake up in the morning. Following are a few ideas for how to keep the bed separate from the other bedroom objects which are less than Feng Shui favorable. Choose one which reflects your own style: 1: something similar to a Chinese folding screen; 2: hang a bamboo window covering (or Hippie Cure) which continues from ceiling to floor between the bed and the items being blocked so the only thing you see is the makeshift curtain; or 3: come up with a Hippie Cure for covering the object, say the desk. See diagram C-6 for visual clarity.

When the first thing you see in the morning raises your energy, and the symbols of work are not initially imposed upon your consciousness, the day starts harmoniously. Beginning anything—your day, your work, fixing breakfast for the family—in a centered way, gives you much more strength, clarity, and higher wisdom for all of the challenges which might arise. Feng Shui has quite a few standards for the bedroom. However, the importance of this room is given equal standing with the bathroom. The bathroom takes. The bedroom has the potential to give. Know the places in every building which bestow energy and those where depletion occurs. Such discernment will serve you in countless untold ways.

EXAMPLES OF CURES WHEN BED AND DESK
MUST OCCUPY SAME ROOM (C-6)

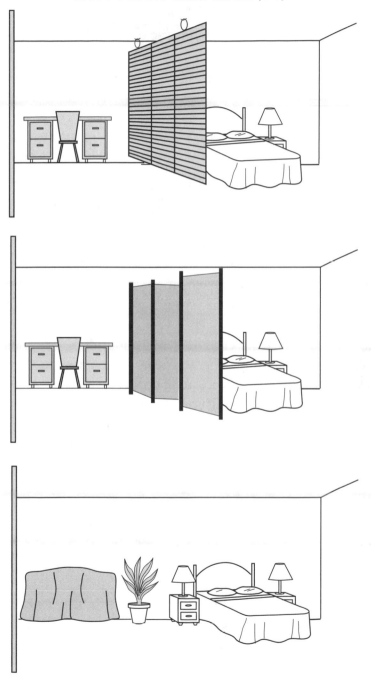

THE KITCHEN

Recipe for Health and Harmony:

30 minutes	clutter-clear per day
1 made-to-order	chi catcher
1 pinch	Intention

Add Empowerment and stir well.

Enjoy the fruits of your success with a cherry on top.

In Feng Shui, good food is good health is good wealth. Unfortunately, you are not hired to cook the meals for your family. It is an essential task of survival, whether for just you, you and a beloved, or the entire family. Some folks hire a cook to make their meals. Some of you are that chef. Some of you work in a restaurant kitchen. Whether you cook for yourself, for six, or for 600, according to the laws of Feng Shui, such a post is a place of power. This concept goes beyond the "you are what you eat" slogan and enters the realm of "you are what emotions and mindfulness are used in the preparation of the edibles." Whenever you eat a meal prepared with love, it is this love force which directly affects you, and, by osmosis, the world around you. Likewise, when your omelet is prepared by a "wish I was not here, I'd rather be drinking a beer" short order cook, make no mistake, such apathy goes directly into the cracked eggs and straight into your hungry mouth, stomach, and consciousness. Thus to make your food palatable on every level, perform these Feng Shui kitchen cures.

DO:

Hold Chi in the Room.

Remember the kitchen stands for one of the Life Values of the Bagua. Hold in that life force, symbolically and actually. See the cure for holding in chi on page 54.

Place the Stove in the Empowerment Position.

In order to be empowered when you cook on the stove, you need to be able to see the door, or at least behind you, while you stir the pot of delectables. Stoves built into wooden islands which sit in the middle of the kitchen usually deliver the cook a clear view of the door to the kitchen. Such is an example of an empowered stove. However, most stoves are fabricated into the kitchen counter, stuck in a corner, and are stationed such that the chef has his back to the kitchen door when preparing a meal.

Here is the story (call me Confucius). One mate arrives home after a long day at the warehouse. The other mate is preparing a delicious soup for both of them. Mate A enters the kitchen to give his love muffin a hug. He wraps his arms around the chef's waist from behind. The chef never heard him come into the house. Supposed affection has instead scared the daylights out of the cook. This fear goes into the pot of soup being stirred. Later that evening, they both devour the soup, hungry and vulnerable to its pleasing flavors. Yet the elements of the soup are much less palatable. The negative feelings are consumed as well. Both partners are influenced by them. The next day at their various jobs, it is apparent the less-than-favorable qualities of the soup have seasoned their professional relations with coworkers and clients. Both are less confident. That innocent hug, presumed to be loving, was hardly harmless. Don't let this scenario happen to you. Empower that stove. See how fabulous your cuisine becomes then. Not only will the food have the proper ingredients, but it will give off the spirit of the right invisible substances as well. Watch your own health, as well as the health of those you cook for truly thrive.

To place the stove in the Empowerment Position, secure a large mirror to the wall behind the stove so you can see behind you when you are using it. Options are to use the automobile self-adhesive mirrors if space or finances are at a premium. Their small circular shape can reflect a large space. Though it might seem like a funny design to attach a large mirror on the wall behind the stove, it is actually chic looking. Just make sure glass cleaner is your friend. Amongst other things, the mirror, by its placement, naturally adds authority to the spot reserved for the chef. See diagram D-1 for visual clarity.

CURE FOR STOVE EMPOWERMENT (D-1)

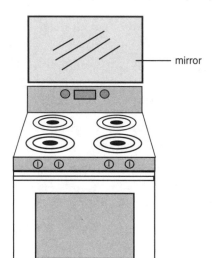

CURE FOR STOVE EMPOWERMENT

1. *Placement of Object*

   Attach a large mirror on the wall behind the stove. Make sure you can see in back of you. Having a view of the kitchen door is recommended, but not necessary as long as you can see behind you.

2. *Visualize/Imagine the Action Already Occurring*

   See the reflection in the mirror show the area behind the stove when you cook, making the position of the stove empowered. Then imagine what it feels like symbolically to be empowered in your life and love. See yourself peaceful and nourishing yourself and others as you prepare any meal.

3. Speak Your Intention Out Loud

"I am at peace and healthy on all levels. The food I prepare is infused with love, well being, and joy. This or something better for the Highest Good now occurs."

Make Sure All the Burners on the Stove Work and Use All the Burners.

Just as the bed symbolizes relationship love, the stove in Feng Shui is the symbol for prosperity. The stove is a very important token in your home. It becomes meaningful to keep it clean and working properly. It doesn't matter whether you prepare food at home often or eat more meals at the corner coffee shop each week. The stove is still the symbol for prosperity in your home.

Important as well, make sure the burners function, as this is necessary to reflect prosperity. Get in the habit of working all the burners frequently. For example, use the front right burner to heat the water for the morning coffee. Make the lunch meal on the left back burner. Cook dinner on the front left burner. Finish the night with tea made on the back right one. This practice ensures chi is stimulated throughout the symbolic representation for prosperity, thus firing up the possibilities for abundance. You can do this even if you are about to meet a friend for a spaghetti meal at a restaurant in an hour. Turn all burners on at once gently. A few seconds is enough to ignite the potentiality of opulence symbolically in everything you do. It is not essential to do this lighting of the flame every day. However, it is a worthy rite to complete, at least once in a while, especially when you feel poverty-consciousness about any Life Value.

Mirror Stove Burners to Increase the Number of Burners Symbolically.

Because Feng Shui is the language of symbols, and the stove is the depiction of prosperity, when you light the fires of the burners, this ignites affluence. Doubling the burners becomes logical. It magnifies the chances for thriving in your life. You can mirror the burners in a few ways. If your stove is a flat model, without a back brim, your empowerment mirror can be programmed symbolically to double the number of burners on your stove. Perform the Double Your Pleasure Cure after the ritual for Stove Empowerment.

If a back rim does exist, measure the length and the width of the space. Measure below the control dials if they are located on the back panel. Take your measurements to a glass and mirror shop. Quickly and inexpensively, they can produce a safe, made-to-order piece of mirror you can attach to the back of your stove with intention and Velcro. Automobile blind spot mirrors will also work. Just make sure each round mirror reflects two of the burners, so two turns into four, and four into eight. Of course, there are various situations where putting a mirror up to reflect the burners will be impossible. In such cases, substitute a polished metal teapot to sit on one of the back burners. It reflects the other three burners from its base and the doubling effect is realized. You then perform a mathematical dream and magically multiply the quality of your life in all areas. See diagram D-2 for examples.

DOUBLE YOUR PLEASURE CURE (D-2)

DOUBLE YOUR PLEASURE CURE

1. Placement of Object

Attach properly sized mirror (auto mirrors will also do) to back rim of the stove (or appropriate place to maximize reflective qualities). If a mirror is not possible, a shiny teapot situated on one of the back burners will reflect the remaining burners.

2. Visualize/Imagine the Action Already Occurring

See the actual doubling of the burners in the reflection. Imagine the increase of prosperity in all areas of your life.

3. Speak Your Intention Out Loud

"The potentials for prosperity increase in all areas of my life. This or something better for the Highest Good now occurs."

Avoid the Stove Sharing a Common Wall With the Toilet.

The bathroom is like a chronic skin rash. If you ignore it, far from going away, it spreads to more places on your body.

Translation: Even though the amount of regard you must have for the washroom is preposterous, it is strongly advised to treat the symbolic drain with great discernment. If you disregard it, far from disappearing, it will permeate your life. Do not let your prosperity get washed down the drain. See diagram D-3.

**CURES WHEN THERE EXISTS
A COMMON WALL WITH TOILET/STOVE (D-3)**

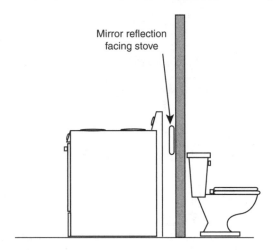

Mirror reflection
facing stove

DON'T:

Do Not Let the Kitchen be the First Thing You See When Entering the Home.

Whether you, a group of friends, a stranger, or even the celebrated life force chi sees the kitchen first when coming through the door, this arrangement might negatively influence the goals in your life. The story goes like this. A young woman artist tried unsuccessfully to get known for her paintings. She had already made the typical adjustments in the Career/Life Path, Fame/Reputation, and Helpful People/Travel areas. Then she received advice in a Feng Shui consultation to screen the visual of the kitchen and the dining room table from anyone who entered the front door. People then started coming for her art and not her food.

If you plan to climb the corporate ladder, write a novel, or get your handprint on the Walk of Fame, do not have your arrangement such that you view the kitchen when you first enter your home. People, as well as chi, will take you less seriously. It can also lead to eating disorders and weight problems. What you initially see captures your attention first.

Women, especially, are warned about the kitchen view. It is the female portion of the culture which has been trained to nurture, give ceaselessly, and yes, cook the meals. This is not always the case, but it is taught on a regular basis to the majority of women.

"But wait! I happen to love the fact that my friends and family can come into my house and know they will be fed and nurtured!"

One client emphatically resisted my recommendation for the arrangement of her kitchen in accordance with the most frequently used door. Friends came regularly to the back door, which invited them into a lovely kitchen. This particular client was a grandmother past her fierce professional days. Her friends and family were her satisfaction. Her particular needs dictated a contrary opinion rather than the typical Feng Shui laws. "Then don't change a thing," I said with an air of "I was going to say that anyway." (True brilliance is about having flexibility under duress!) In fact, if you are a stay-at-home mom, have a catering service, a day care center, or any other vocation that relies on the values of nurturing and aid for its success, please do not worry about the kitchen being the first thing you see when you come into the house. However, for the career-minded 9-to-5 types trying to get ahead, if the kitchen is indeed the first thing you (or chi) sees when entering your home, please consider these options:

Place a Chinese screen, or one which represents your style, between the kitchen and the front door so the kitchen is concealed. Nice tall plants can also visually block the view. If your kitchen is one where a half wall separates it from the entrance to the home, hang a bamboo window covering that visually divides the door entrance from the kitchen. Use a Hippie Cure on a kitchen opening which has no door. For you who enter the kitchen from a door which leads to the garage, and you can't hide your view of the kitchen, hang a picture on a wall directly in front of you as you enter the door to draw your attention. The objective is to direct your focus to something such as a piece of art rather than to the kitchen and the values it represents, whether conscious or subconscious. See diagram D-4 for examples.

IDEAS TO CONCEAL THE VISION OF THE KITCHEN (D-4)

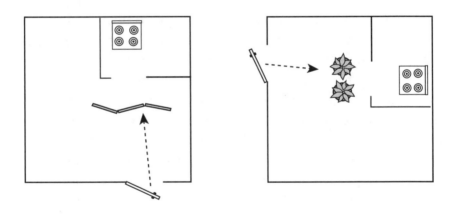

Do Not Allow the Kitchen Sink to Drip Unnecessarily.

If your kitchen sink drips, abundance slowly leaks away. Each drop of water is like a withdrawal in the opulence bank account of life. Fix the sink. Show the Higher Power, the High Self, and your subconscious mind that lack is not the pattern you want in your world.

Do Not Wash Dishes with Your Back to the Door.

With Feng Shui applications, think Mafia. Avoid having your back to the door in any room. Some people might call this behavior paranoid. I call it proper chi management. Use this same mentality in all facets of life. Keep yourself in a commanding situation. If you can't physically change the location of an object so you can easily view the door to the room, study the Cure for Stove Empowerment and adjust it accordingly. In this instance, you need to be able to see behind you while at the kitchen sink. Usually, the kitchen sink resides in the kitchen counter and has a window above it which looks out to the backyard, side yard, or into the neighbor's bad-taste living room. If this sounds like your kitchen sink, then use a blind spot automobile mirror to affix somewhere on the window or wall around the window. Just make sure its placement gives you a healthy view of the room behind you. With the mirror's convex qualities, this is guaranteed. Of course, if you have a wall behind the sink, it is recommended to have a mirror which not only serves the function, but also has a nicer form. Be at ease when you are soaping up the dishes.

Do Not Keep the Kitchen Knives Visible.

This indicates "sharp edges." What if you had the Life Value of Love Union/Marriage in your kitchen? Communications with your beloved could be edgy, less than healing, and sharp. Such a figurative gesture might create a feeling in the kitchen, one which is not nurturing. Showing the knives does not automatically create a harsh environment for communications or any other such outcome. But quit working against the flow. Hide the razor-sharp edges! Knives should be stored in a drawer, out of sight, when not in use. Magnetic strips which display them, wooden holders, and other such exhibitions are not recommended.

The kitchen is not only the room where multigrain pancakes and strawberry smoothies are made. It also contains potent situations where life makeovers can occur, careers are made or broken, and the lasagna cooking in the oven boasts layers of possible nourishment, either positive or negative. The kitchen giveth, and the kitchen taketh away. Direct the Feng Shui cures so this place only bestows.

THE OFFICE

The office resonates with an air of importance, even if what you say before entering this work place is, "Now leave Mommy alone for a while. I am going into the OFFICE!" Hence, the office referred to in the following do and don't list includes both the home office and the separate workplace. Know that you apply Feng Shui values to offices in separate buildings as you would your home.

DO:

Hold Chi in the Room.

The office in the home stands for one of the Life Values, for instance, Helpful People/Travel, Family/Health, and so forth. Bring attention to the particular Life Value by holding in the chi. It is not necessary to change around the rooms in your private dwelling to fit the Feng Shui Bagua model. In other words, the bedroom is not necessarily more suitable in the Love Union/ Marriage area of the house. The children don't need their rooms in or near the Child/Creativity section (do avoid Wealth/Power for them, however), and the office doesn't have to grace the Career/Life Path room. You may set up your home to align with the Bagua layout of your house, but this is not required. Just be sure that whatever room your office or bedroom and so on is in has been treated with the proper cures.

In an office outside the home, one chi catcher can be used with intention to hold in every Life Value of the Bagua inside your private office or workspace. If you share the space with many others, remember the chi catcher is virtually invisible. Far from suggesting you hide such intentions, communicate with your office mates assuring them that the holding in of the life force would be an advantage for everyone. In spite of that, the overall visual of the office, including what hangs from the ceiling, would practically remain unchanged—a definitive plus. Regardless of whether you work in your home or in a separate building, hold the chi in your office. May it surge. Good things come to those who flow. See Cure for Holding in Chi on page 54.

Place the CEO and/or the President of the Company in a Commanding Room of the Building.

This is for separate office situations. Head honcho decision makers should have their offices in the Wealth/Power section of the building. Do not give up the Wealth/Power area for an employee coffee break room. The time-outs will consist of members of the staff talking mutiny. If you situate a patient or client waiting room there, expect dissatisfaction with the quality of your work by the patron, even if you feel your service is above average. The next in status, such as a Vice Big Cheese, should have an office located in the Love Union/Marriage position, the second most commanding area of a building.

Work life goes easier for everyone when it is clear who is boss. Such is determined by the layout of offices. Authority is given to the one who inhabits the Wealth/Power position, consciously or subconsciously. Companies fair better, economically, structurally, creatively, and spiritually when everyone is in her or his proper place. With the advent of new paradigm thinking, and consequently the avant-garde business which is structured more as a cooperative company with no official CEO or president, it is still recommended that the Wealth/Power position as well as the Love Union/Marriage area hold offices and meeting rooms where the primary tasks are decision-making, financial affairs, as well as employee and customer relations.

Place the Desk in the Empowerment Position.

The desk is in an empowered position when you sit behind it and can see the door to the room. See diagram E-1 for clarity.

EXAMPLES OF THE EMPOWERED DESK (E-1)

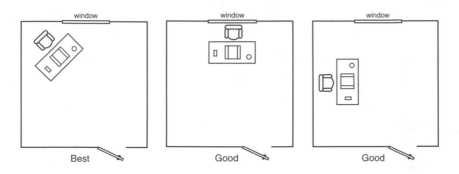

If your back faces the door, there is a symbolic implication you could be "stabbed in the back" by partners, employees, and such. This is true whether you sit in a home office or go downtown every morning to your employment. There are countless stories of people who merely turn their desks around to the Empowerment Position and then get promotions, enjoy more positive relationships with employees, as well as gain more respect for themselves and from those around them. This is also a treatment for the procrastinator. A person tends to take action, take care of less than favorable tasks in a timely manner, and other such behavioral shifts. People who work at home and make all their connections with current and potential clients by phone should still make the calls from an empowered place. It is amazing how intonations change, interviews are enhanced, and sales are clinched when you face the door.

Sometimes, however, it is impossible to shift the desk. It may be a permanent structure built into the architecture of the room. You may also work in a maze of cubicles, in which case moving the desk is out of the question. If this is your situation, please see Cure to Gain Empowerment on page 65 and adjust accordingly for dealing with various kinds of work stations.

Comfort zones arise in working environments as well. The computer desk, for instance, towers above you. While it conveniently holds all the necessary modern paraphernalia, it is unfeasible to see the door. You may think, "Why bother then?" I say, "Bother." Does the desk actually raise your energy? If it doesn't, then you work in the middle of clutter. If it does make you go pop, then experiment. Take the towering shelves off the top of the desk. Put them beside the desk or in some other practical configuration. Be in an empowered work condition. This positively affects your entire existence. Another scenario is when the desk is simply too big to turn around in a room because the room is small and space does not allow the empowered position. Do the clutter check to see if this bulky desk raises your energy. If it does, proceed with a Cure for Empowerment, a less effective choice, but nevertheless valid. If the desk is clutter, give it to a friend or your local used store and then search for another one at a garage sale or furniture storeroom. Acquire one which is appropriate in size to the office room. Get present to the now of your life. An important consideration in desk placement is the view. For instance, if you turn the desk to face the door, you lose sight of the incredible garden with blooming roses. Regard the visual examples for different ways to place the desk in an Empowerment Position. Perhaps you could view both the door and the garden. Also consider hanging a form/function mirror on a wall across from your empowered desk which reflects the view outside.

With the same philosophy as the bed, I promote the idea of placing the desk in the Empowerment Position whenever possible, not just curing an unfavorable situation. There is nothing like the abilities, the confidence, and self-esteem it can give you. Some cases are unchangeable, however, so the Empowerment Cure is needed. However, don't make excuses for why you can't place the desk in the Empowerment Position, if such placement is at all possible. Here is the following catchphrase to encourage you to implement the Feng Shui empowerment models at all times, whether or not they threaten your comfort zones. Former emotional blueprints will be replaced with positive, validating prototypes which help your life in every way. Whenever you are tempted to ignore the Feng Shui rules for empowerment, say these letters: WWTGD? What it means is quite simple, but very persuasive: What Would the Godfather Do? Clearly, the Mafia Godfather would not insist on a window view in his office if it meant he could not see the entrance to the room. He would want to see the door, both to command respect and to know if a bullet sandwich was being delivered for lunch. The Godfather would not sit behind a computer tower which hides the view of the door. He also would not confess, "Oh, my desk is too big for this room and only fits against the wall, but it was given to me by my favorite uncle. If I get bumped off by the afternoon, at least my dead uncle, God rest his soul, will be pleased with my desk choice." Sure, the Godfather was suspicious. However, his insistence on having a commanding point of view gave him respect from others as well as the ability to make offers that no one could refuse. This simply would not have been the case if he had lived his life with his back to the door.

Choose a Stable Desk.

Make sure your desk has a secure structure. A shaky desk which quivers when you write on it or a glass desk you can see through translates as a person who is translucent and shatters easily in work situations—not very good Feng Shui interpretations. Desks represent livelihood. It doesn't matter if you never use the desk, make use of it occasionally to pay a bill, or just enjoy sitting at it while reading, meditating, or looking outside. The desk is still the Feng Shui illustration of labor. With this rather significant role, work symbols you create in your environment affect the ease of your Life Path. Thus, select a solid, well-footed desk to signify your intentions with regard to your profession, whether mother, artist, or corporate lawyer.

Choose a Chair with a Solid Back.

Personal chi can leak through the rear of a chair if it does not have a back continuous from the seat to the top of the chair. What is wrong with the following picture? Donald Trump enters his office, waves at his personal assistant, and belts, "Hold all my calls for an hour. I have an important task to do!" The assistant nods at the multi-billionaire. Trump enters his office. He strides across the room to his empowered desk. He gingerly sits down in a secretary swivel chair and adjusts the height so that he can tower over his work space to see clearly. He opens his briefcase and pulls out a magazine. He grabs a pen, looks at an open page, then mutters to himself, "Hmmm... 2 down, a five-letter word which means the head of a corporation."

You guessed it. Donald Trump, or any person of power and authority, would never choose to sit in a secretary chair. Potency seeps out the back. Instead, a wise person would manage chi by choosing a chair which supports focus. Now, imagine the executive chair. It concentrates all intellectual and creative energy toward the desk and the goal-oriented achievements of the smart individual. There is no way for life force to escape out the back of the chair. All the energy remains present to create and manifest true success. Want a promotion at work? Whether in your home office or separate office, show the executives you can relate to their lifestyle and dedications. Promote yourself with a chair which symbolizes accomplishment and commitment. The five-letter word which means the head of a corporation: Chair. See diagram E-2 for clarity.

GOOD CHAIR CHI (E-2)

Good Chair Chi

Ding! Ding! Ding!

Have "Protection" Plants if Necessary.

Botany lesson 1: Protection plants are hardly ever needed in the home office. Botany lesson 2: It is not necessary to employ the services of Venus flytraps and other such carnivorous plants to protect you. Botany lesson 3: Susie, at your job downtown, will absolutely despise this cure, especially since she exists to upset you.

Protection plants can be any potted plant you desire except cactus. Cacti represent prickly, hard-to-touch boundaries. You may have guessed by now—no rough edges or open bathroom doors. Choose two plants which are upright and look like they are standing at attention, like a couple of armed guards. Protection plants do not have to be very tall. The best height would be about nine inches to start. If taller or shorter, odd-inch increments are preferred. Place them on the front part of your desk, with you in your chair behind and between them. Then add the power of intention. Watch how you are never again affected by the negative oomph directed your way. See diagram E-3 for visual clarity.

THE BOTANY CURE (E-3)

THE BOTANY CURE FOR PROTECTION

1. *Placement of Object*

   Choose two similar plants which raise your energy and are upright in height about nine inches to start.

2. *Visualize/Imagine the Action Already Occurring*

   See negative energy (see this as dark spirals) stopped at the space between the two plants. Nothing harmful and depressing can infiltrate their invisible blockade.

3. *Speak Your Intention Out Loud*

   "I am protected and safe in my public workplace. My job brings me only positive, healing vibes as I work efficiently and effectively. This or something better for the Highest Good now occurs."

DON'T:

Do Not Put the Office in the Bedroom.

The bedroom is a place to relax, regenerate, and make love, not the room to call the supplier in Ohio to see where in the hell last Friday's shipment is. The whirl of the fax machine is not the sound you want to wake you up from an afternoon nap. By the same token, it doesn't serve the function of the office if it resides in your sanctuary. An unmade bed, a pile of dirty clothes, a dresser with stacks of old magazines on top of it, all suggest a less than serious regard for how you perceive your work, whether it is as a parent, performance clown, or professional. If space is the issue and you must have the office share the love nest, separate them, both symbolically and actually. Give each part of your life—the reveler and the realist—a clear boundary which suggests seriousness and commitment to both sides of you. Get ideas by studying ways to divide the office and bedroom in the Bedroom section.

Do Not Let the Home Office Be the First Thing You See When Entering the Home.

When you, or the life force of chi, see an office, or any symbol for work upon entering the home, this image can promote workaholic tendencies. The psyche will go where it is led by the symbols in your surroundings. Thus, if the mind (or chi) sees a kitchen, you are not taken as seriously by the outside world. If the mind (or chi) sees symbols of work, you will find yourself at the desk, pen in hand, even before you uncurl the local newspaper. Ironically, true success comes when you are in balance, not when work is the only focus. The home should reflect poise through an arrangement which symbolically welcomes you when you enter. Demonstrate awareness of your value and function in society. Shut the office door or conceal a living room desk behind tall plants or a stylish screen. These actions will raise your confidence on the physical plane.

Maintain equilibrium between your personal and professional life. Only then can authentic achievements—with your occupation, relationship love, and self-growth—truly be realized and show their profound influence. Having a proper desk in its empowered placement, as well as an impressive chair, means you can watch the patterns of insecurity change into designs of competency. This office design assists you to possess the capabilities the world respects. Whether this is to soothe screaming kids or complete a report on time, your expertise is represented by alignments made in your office and thus your world in general.

THE LIVING ROOM

Unwind! Take your shoes off and put your feet up, anywhere but on the coffee table. The living room exists as the breathing space where you let go, play games, and maybe even watch some television. You can relate with your children, have a nice conversation with your mate, or even spend some quality alone time. You might have a very formal living room with plastic wrap protecting the furniture. For you, I am then referring to the den. Regardless of the title you give this place, complete these Feng Shui do and don'ts.

DO:

Hold Chi in the Room.

Remember the living room stands for one of the Life Values found in the Bagua. Hold in its life force. Bring attention to this part of life so it may pay homage to you. See instructions on how to hold in chi on page 54. Don't forget the value of a modern chi catcher, inexpensive and virtually invisible. Because the living room is customarily about comfort and entertainment, people tend to be protective when anything might change its character. Don't worry, a chi catcher will not clash with your American Heritage patterns.

Arrange Furniture so it Welcomes the Guests (and Chi) to Sit Down.

A few years back, I consulted a client whose front door opened at the Self-Knowledge/Wisdom area. Immediately, the front hall revealed symbology which challenged her and her family's life. As soon as I entered, I was met on the right side of the entryway with the back of a couch. In order to sit down, it was necessary for me to walk around the set of sofas and chairs, as they basically made a defensive square around the television. Although this stance felt safe to her and her family, it also blocked the fluid chi from circulating into the Career/Life Path section. This impasse also affected the rest of her home. The barricade of furnishings assured that. See diagram F-1 for examples.

EXAMPLES OF GOOD LIVING ROOM SETUP FOR OPTIMAL "CHI IS WELCOME" FLOW (F-1)

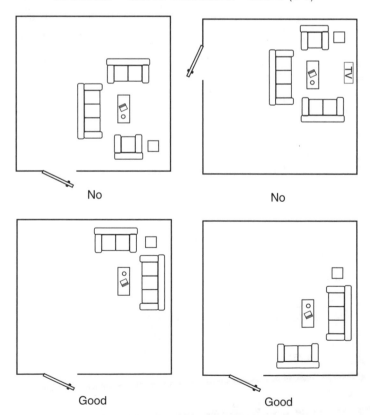

No   No

Good   Good

I advised, "In order for chi to bless the rest of your space, it must feel welcome when entering the front door, the Mouth of the Chi. What you have now is a situation called blocking chi. Move the couch so its back is not facing the door. Then when chi comes in, it doesn't have to go around anything to sit down or to enter other areas of your home. When the flow is there, blessings can occur."

She nodded and then we proceeded to the kitchen. Later, after I left, her husband came into the house and said, "So, what did she say?"

This client wanted to focus on her job opportunities, so she stated, "She wants us to move the couch against the wall so the back of it isn't to the door. It will open up the room. Help me, please."

She started to pick up one side of the couch. The husband shook his head and laughed.

"That is the craziest thing I ever heard. I'm not going to help you move that couch. I'm going out to get a drink instead. Work was hell today."

This was also a man who had a Samurai sword hanging on the wall by his side of the bed. You can bet I had something to say about that symbolism! The client wheezed and panted, but repositioned the couch by herself. Her motivation was that strong. Rewards tend to follow such commitment. Her husband came through the door hours later. Literally blown away by the new receptive feeling in the room, he asked, "What else did she say to do? Let's start…"

I have never received a testimony other than incredible delight when clients open up a room. Chi is a powerful force if allowed to surge and is strongly felt when the adjustment of the furniture frees up jammed circuits. Because living rooms and dens tend to have the most furniture, I have reserved the idea of "blocking chi" for this section. It can, however, happen in any room, so be on the lookout for it. If you can't easily enter a room to sit down, to reach a desk, or to lie on the bed, inspect for objects which could be obstructing your passageway.

If opening up an area seems unworkable because of the need to rearrange furniture in the space allotted, be receptive to the idea of getting rid of some of it. Perform a clutter test. Some of the furnishings might be there for convenience only. Understandably, you want to make sure your seating is arranged so guests can sit facing each other or in such a way that conversation is encouraged. But realistically, how many spaces do you need in general? When doing a clutter test and not judging a section merely for handiness sake, you might discover you actually despise a piece. The science of Feng Shui believes that the room, home, or building you currently inhabit is never too small for your things. Thus, if your objects overflow inside a dwelling with less space than where you lived or worked three years ago, it is time to do a clutter-clear to get present with life as it is right now. Realize, too, whenever there is a stoppage in your home or office, the path of chi is being thwarted. Liberate the energy gridlock created by your stuff. Sensational things can occur by simply repositioning a chair.

Cover the Television with Fabric or Have it Located Behind Console Doors When Not in Use.

A home feels marvelous when you don't know where the television is as you walk in. The television has become a huge center of attention and distraction in our society, a concentration which is not always a positive focal point. Celebrity importance is screwy in the Hollywood world of fantasy. Our sheroes and heroes are people who pretend to be somebody else. Its value systems are strange. The image of beauty is demonstrated by a small screen culture who augment, diet, and skin tuck their way to an idealized splendor. We are constantly marketed to: commercials between, before, after, and sometimes during the programs we watch by way of product placement in the show. We are told partial truths by the evening news and accept them. We are given half-hour, mass therapy sessions with talk show hosts who bring on a noted psychotherapist to lecture us about depression. We observe while others take part in a staged version of their lives during a reality-based television program which tells us this is "the real thing," and it is all entertaining as hell. Pass the popcorn.

Because Feng Shui is a language of symbols, the television decrees these peculiar ethics twenty-four/seven, regardless of if it is on or not. When the television is no longer the focus, families talk and children play board games. Marriages have been saved in the bedroom when the television is covered. Mates actually communicate, vocally and intimately. Because the television no longer publicizes its peculiar messages at every moment, your home feels revered.

Not to worry, you can still watch your television. However, the television screen should be concealed when not in use. Unveil with awareness when you want to watch it, whether this means you open the wooden media center doors or move the front part of a fabric to the top of the television. Be sure to pick a fabric, or a media center, which raises your energy. See diagram F-2 for clarity.

EXAMPLES OF TV CURES (F-2)

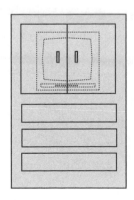

The concealment of the television forces you to engage actively with the choices you make. You must walk across the room to ready the set for ignition with the conscious intention to watch a few hours of mystery, comedy, or adventure. The stroll also makes it easier to inform the mind that chimera is about to enter the room and your consciousness. Take control of your environment. Don't let the symbols in it tell your involuntary awareness that your looks, your occupation, even your very existence is anything less then normal, meaningful, and healthy. Study the Hippie Cure and the Cure for Putting a Mirror to Bed at Night. Become familiar with both. Those cures will help you to create a treatment which keeps your television in check. The television is a tool for amusement only. Do not let it become a fantastical looking glass that relates to you, metaphorically, that your life is robotic and pointless.

DON'T:

Do Not Have a Fireplace Without Properly Curing It.

Imagine sipping tea in a darkened room where just the light of the flames dance on the walls. The crackle of the blaze. The heat of the glow. Oh, so lovely, yes?

Yes, but not until Feng Shui basics are applied to it.

You sigh. "Can't I just have a @#%& fire in my fireplace without this Feng Shui tradition putting a damper on it?!?"

Cool your ashes and consider these Feng Shui facts:

The fireplace is an exquisite object, both symbolically and actually, especially after correct curing has occurred. Surprisingly, a treatment is highly recommended whether the fireplace works or not, whether the actual fire pit is boarded up, whether there is merely an indication of where a hearth used to be and now is a concrete block, and most important, whether you use it often and had a roaring fire in it just last night. Elements will be discussed more thoroughly in the next section of the book; however, it is relevant at this point to mention the two specific Element representations which need to be balanced when you have a fireplace. Most obvious is the Element of Fire. It is urged, therefore, you balance this Fire energy with Water energy. Extraordinary is Fire medicine when mediated by Water so that it does not crackle the air around you but nurtures the atmosphere.

You can hang a large mirror above the mantle of the fireplace and give the mirror the intention of Water. The mirror should be as large as the fire pit, so the representation of both the Fire and the Water Elements are equal. Although a mirror above the fireplace looks quite tasteful, if a form/function mirror is out of the interior design question, a large picture or painting of a water scene, like a beach or a lake, can be substituted instead. If you have a woodstove so that a walled mantle does not exist, get an iron teapot—one which raises your energy and is sturdy enough to be on a lit stove all day. Fill it with water (and even a few drops of essential oil), and let the steam cool the Fire's jets. See example of fireplace cures in F-3.

EXAMPLES OF FIREPLACE CURES (F-3)

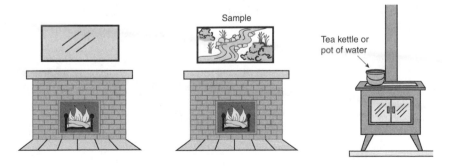

COOL THE BURN CURE

1. *Placement of Object*

   Hang a large form/function mirror (or water picture) above the mantle of the fireplace. If you have a woodstove, an iron teapot full of water can be placed on top of the stove.

2. *Visualize/Imagine the Action Already Occurring*

   See the Water Elements of the mirror (or picture or teapot) come down into the Fire and mix with its Elements. See the stabilization of these fundamentals take place. (Imagine red merging with blue, twist dancing.)

3. *Speak Your Intention Out Loud*

   "The flame is a perfect balance of yin and yang (Mother/Father God or Divine perfection). It heals, glows, and blesses this space and everyone in it. This or something better for the Highest Good now occurs."

But don't clink the wine glasses yet. You are not quite done.

By now, you are familiar with the life force of chi and the Feng Shui philosophy which strongly suggests you keep it inside your home and office. Yet the fireplace has a chimney which leads to the outside of the home. This is a perfect way for chi to escape, especially in the summer when the fireplace is not being used to warm and relax. During the summer season, place plants or other energy popping objects, for instance, a pair of dancing flamingo statues, to protect the space in front of the fire grid so that chi does not escape up the chimney. A combination of the Botanical Cure for Protection and the Cure for Holding in Chi is called for here. An example of what this balance might look like is in diagram F-4.

FLASH DANCE MUMBO-JUMBO CURE (F-4)

FLASH DANCE MUMBO-JUMBO CURE

1. *Placement of Object*

   Arrange two or more plants on either side of the fireplace opening during seasons when the hearth is not in use. Two objects, like statues, one on either side of the fireplace cavity, can be substituted.

2. *Visualize/Imagine the Action Already Occurring*

   See the chi (glitter-like substance) within the room of the home or office unable to pass through the plants (or objects) which defend the passageway.

3. *Speak Your Intention Out Loud*

   "The chi of this room and home (or office) stays intact. This or something better for the Highest Good now occurs."

Clearly, a fireplace can exist in any room of the home or office, bedroom, kitchen, study, and more. Perform these cures with dedication on each fireplace, except fireplaces which exist in the Fame/Reputation Life Value. The explanation to this reasoning shall be given in the Elements section of Part II. Without a doubt, there is nothing like a roaring balanced fire to heal, nurture, and cleanse you. Symbolically, however, it doesn't matter whether you ever burn a fire in the fireplace or not. A fireplace still signifies the Element Fire. Elementally temper the blaze, keep the chi in, and the flames, real or representational, will restore you.

The living room is a place to take it easy and to let yourself be who you are. When you master the mission of the living room, the world becomes an enjoyable play, and you star in it.

LIVING WITH MATES, CHILDREN, TENANTS, AND GUESTS

Often other people share your living spaces, either on a short-term basis or for many years. Much of the time, they can add qualities of joy, ease, and helpfulness. Other times, however, it seems like they are pure demonic tornados whizzing out of control and messing up what you hoped would be their carefully laid out clutter-free rooms. They might leave the bathroom door open and the toilet lid up. Plus, don't they realize the space they occupy represents the Family/Health area of the Bagua and their finances, health, and connection to the elders are being disturbed by the chaos in their chambers? Not to mention how it disrupts yours as well. Don't they care? Sigh.

The answer is: Probably not. To them, the bathroom is a bathroom—a place to relieve themselves with little concern for how it affects your bank account. Then they proceed to the living room to see what's on television and rifle through the paper, neatly stacked on the coffee table, as they look for the circular containing the program guide. So what if a pile is left all over the place. In addition, the couch is not comfortable to lie on unless they throw the pillows on the floor. Besides, pillows on the floor are great for the cat and dog to play in with the earsplitting television as the backdrop for their chase scene.

I'm sorry. Did you not hear the answer to the question of *don't they care*? The answer is: Probably not.

Case in point, children are children. They play for a living, complete homework, eat chocolate-chip cookies, and watch cartoons. They don't care if the chi is being held in their room, and they care not if the abundance of anything is going down the open-lid toilet. If fact, keeping the lid open is kinda cool because then you can watch the water funnel twist down into a spout. Neato. That is why little Jimmy keeps flushing the toilet over and over. Roommates pay rent to share the space with you. There is nothing on the lease about shutting the bathroom door and certainly nothing about keeping their rooms clutter-free. Sally, your renter, puts up with the mirror behind the stove, and although she can't tell that her stir-fry tastes better, she kind of likes that she can watch the television in the mirror while she cooks.

When guests come to visit, you can't wait at their bedroom door each morning. "How was your snooze on that new mattress? You haven't placed anything under your bed, have you? Would you like me to throw out that ratty old sweater of yours?" You also can't request "to please sit in the Empowerment Position of the room," whether you offer them such a seat of honor or ask for such placement for yourself. Your guests might excuse themselves and the next time you see them, they are at the front door with their packed bags muttering soft excuses about "leaving the iron on in their house" thousands of miles away.

It does seem discouraging, but not everyone believes in the science of Feng Shui, much less knows what it is. On the other hand, when it comes to mates, children, tenants, and guests, not all are averse to Feng Shui. Some clients' children are the ones who bring enthusiasm to this art. For instance, there is the story of the six-year-old who clutter-cleared his room, and coming into the den with his purple Barney dinosaur, admitted, "Don't go pop no more, Momma!" Another example is the roommate who found a very creative way to conceal the view of the kitchen when the occupants of the home entered. He worked in a plant shop and brought home tall, elegant foliage to compose a beautiful visual wall. Also many clients tell me about how when house guests do come to stay, they often rave about the good feelings, jot down a quick memo with the words "Feng Shui" on a piece of paper, and promise to apply this science to their own home when they return. Ahh, now there's an optimistic vision of the Feng Shui cosmos.

But life is a slide show. Prepare for both positive and negative Feng Shui image snippets. Complete these do and don'ts in every room that has another life form living in it. Even if you think you have dominion over your youngster, it is not appropriate to insist their behavior patterns enhance the Helpful People/Travel aspect because her or his room is in that area of the house. Likewise, a roommate is not a pawn for your Love Union/Marriage area because that Bagua Life Value lands right in her room. Breathe and relax. Do not employ *Fear Shui*. Your Feng Shui will not be ultimately affected by whether your child, roommate, or house guest leaves a banana peel or gum wrapper on their bedroom floor, especially after you complete the Feng Shui cures which follow.

DO:

Hold In Chi.

It doesn't matter if you have little influence over one of the Life Values of the Bagua because it lands in the room of a child or a roommate. For instance, you want to work on Career/Life Path but your roommate, Harry, occupies the room which represents it. Harry is a roommate who likes to create art with dried rice and mung bean noodles. Then he hangs them on his walls as a kind of ongoing homage to Denot, the exiled leader of Zare, in the Kan galaxy 50 light years away. Woe is your career.

Even though you'll learn the Feng Shui habits to employ to work around this situation, Harry's room still symbolically stands for

Career/Life Path and chi should be held in the room. Remember the magnificence of the chi catcher, small, almost invisible, and non-obtrusive. Hang it from his ceiling, about a foot in from his bedroom door, suspended by a 1-inch piece of fishing line. Do not secretly dangle it there when he is off at one of his Star Trek conventions. Instead, show him how invisible it can be and how non-invasive it is to his particular dried noodle style. Then you can be like Captain Picard and "Make it so."

Children can be much easier when it comes to this type of thing. Oftentimes their minds and spirits are more wizened to the Universal Truths than adults' are. They can accept this Feng Shui science as easily as choosing a flavor of ice cream. For this reason, it's not necessary to slip an unnoticeable chi catcher in when they are at the skateboard park. In the case where the child is "down with" Feng Shui, a chi catcher extraordinaire can be used—big, showy, obvious. It could even be an airplane mobile, a fairy goddess, or a big shiny silver ball. Chi is being held in whether the catcher is unseen or as visually loud as a siren flashing. Whatever is used, be sure to use the Cure for Holding in Chi on page 54 to add the glue of intention (metaphorically) to your masterpiece.

Place a Mirror on the Inside Wall Above the Bedroom Door.

The idea here is to reflect the "stuff" which happens in the privacy of their room, even when it's not so private. Think heavy metal punk music screaming from the stereo reflecting back onto itself and away from the Feng Shui of the rest of the home. This is easily accomplished with a form/function flat mirror which has been measured to fit above the inside of the door. Or you can use a convex, self-adhesive automobile mirror for the job of deflection. With intention, either kind of mirror will work. See diagram G-1 for the visual.

THE LOOKING GLASS LOCH NESS MONSTER CURE (G-1)

Mirror above INSIDE of door facing INTO room

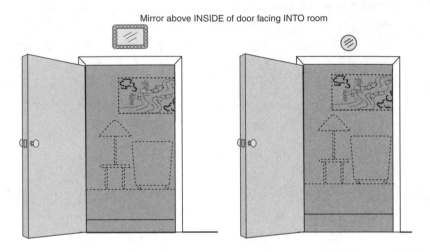

If you are worried the roommate might balk at such an idea, remember, the mirror can be placed so it is a creative centerpiece for, say, a dried noodle prism or other such works of art your roommate wants to present. Not to mention that a mirror can easily simulate the Kan galaxy. In other words, it can assume the fashion of any taste—a mirror being such a neutral, forgiving object. Therefore, this should be an easy sell. The child is usually fine with the concept of a mirror above the door. If not, make it creative and fun, a wishing pool or a gift from the Fairy Godmother. It could also be a sunflower with the mirror as the pollen center. Yet another idea is to make it an extra special, magical looking glass, which is reserved for only superheroes and sheroes. Anything goes. Just be sure the mirror reflects into the room. If your incredible ideas are stepped on and rubbed into the dirt with a heavy-booted foot, consider this option. Above the outside of the delinquent's door, place a flat mirror with the reflection part of the mirror facing into the wall. See diagram G-2 for example.

(G-2)

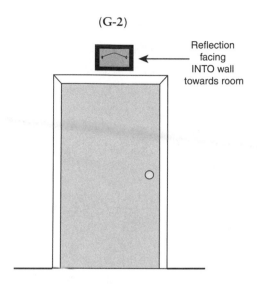

Reflection facing INTO wall towards room

The back of the mirror faces the rest of the house and can be covered with a picture or left as it is. The idea here is to be sure the reflective part of the mirror is deflecting all bits and pieces from the unpleasant space back onto itself. Thus it faces into the wall. This action is merely symbolic, of course. A flying pizza crust will still make its tomato mark on the living room wall when thrown in frustration by your angst-ridden teenager.

THE LOCH NESS MONSTER CURE

1. *Placement of Object*

   Attach a mirror of your choice, in the creative flair of your child or tenant, above the inside of the bedroom door of a child, roommate, or guest room. Make sure the reflective part of the mirror is facing into the room. If it isn't possible to affix a mirror inside the space, attach the mirror above the outside of the bedroom door. Make sure, in this case, the reflective part of the mirror faces the wall into the room.

2. *Visualize/Imagine the Action Already Occurring*

See all negativity, mental processes, anger, sadness, grief, boredom, and such being caught by the mirror and deflected back into the room. Imagine these emotional processes as shadow-like circles. The mirror acts as a protector from any and all emotions being thrown unintentionally into the rest of the house, whether the bedroom door is open or closed.

3. *Speak Your Intention Out Loud*

"All energies are being redirected back onto themselves. This or something better for the Highest Good now occurs."

Far from injuring your child or roommate, this cure keeps their development and tendencies "close to home" as it were. Focus is enhanced on all things, positive and challenging. When something is in your face, you tend to deal with it. Consequently, evolution is born with this remedy.

Place a Polite Written Sign or Agreed Upon Symbol on the Outside Door of any Bathroom Being Used by a Child, Roommate, or Guest, Requesting it be Kept Closed. Do the Same on the Inside of the Toilet Lid.

Obviously, I have ruined it for those of you who wanted a career in Feng Shui law enforcement. To spend your spare time making sure the toilet lid is shut and the bathroom door is closed is a worthy, satisfying, and challenging pastime. Unfortunately, the Feng Shui police are not hiring right now.

If a child doesn't read yet, or a sign which hangs on the outside of your closed bathroom door is not your style, teach her or him the habit of shutting the toilet lid and the bathroom door with an agreed upon symbol which represents "containment" to you both. Examples might be the symbol of a spiral, a harvest scene, or even the Chinese letter which means prosperity. Place this symbol on the door and toilet lid in place of the words. As she learns her ABCs, she will at the same time learn proper bathroom protocol. Remember, too, that placing these signs or symbols makes a statement to your subconscious, universe, and High Self you are aware of the role bathrooms are given in Feng Shui and refuse to be part of such a draining reality. See diagram G-3.

THE SYMBOL OPTION FOR TEACHING
PROPER FENG SHUI BATHROOM PROTOCOL (G-3)

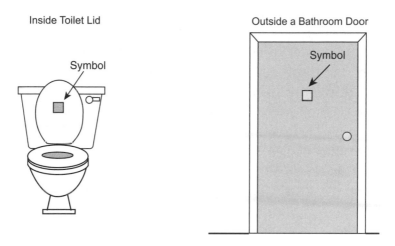

Have Children's Beds and Homework Desks in the Empowerment Position.

This is not for the benefit of anyone other than the child. Story time: I had a client whose teenage son was sent home from school for fighting. When we arrived at his bedroom, I peered in, and without surprise, saw his bed was not in the Empowerment Position.

"I strongly recommend that Larry's bed get moved so that it's in an empowered position. This happens when Larry can lay his head on his pillow and see the entrance to his room."

"But he doesn't need any more power. He already gets in too many fights at school!" She crossed her arms and shook her head.

I persisted. "When one is empowered, one does not act out. Larry behaves in violent ways because he feels helpless in his life. Empower him, and then see what accomplishments are revealed."

Likewise, when a child's homework desk is in the Empowerment Position, study is not only done in a timely manner, but grades tend to be higher as well. Although it may not seem possible to turn the desk around in a child's room, be aware that comfort zones are a sinister force. There might be the physical ability in the room, but the mind is too undersized for the change. Crack it open! If indeed this furniture shuffle is truly impossible, employ the Cure of Empowerment. Give your children the gift of self-confidence in their rooms. Their development, grace, and self-esteem on this planet will be gratitude enough. The Godfather will be pleased as well.

Teach Receptive Mates, Children, and Tenants About the Clutter Test.

It is possible for a child to easily clutter-clear their bedroom when they are open and aware of whether an object raises or lowers their energy. The action of clutter-clearing teaches the child many things:

1. Good things occur when space is made, which could mean cooler toys, a glowing report card, better relations with the parent, higher self-esteem, or all of the above.

2. There is a Law of Abundance to respect, which promotes giving as a means to receiving.

3. When a child learns clutter-clearing from a parent, they inherently understand the parent "trusts" that all is well and naturally adopts this as their own approach to life.

4. The child learns to share, to give, and to let go. These are great skills to master on Earth.

Roommates can be interested in clutter-clearing as well. Maybe instead of a house meeting, you suggest a clutter-clearing party when you seek a shift in the household energy. Benefits in everyone's lives will no doubt manifest as well. Be creative with this game and have fun.

DON'T:

Do Not Overly Concern Yourself about the Feng Shui Life Values Which Fall in Children's, Tenants', Guest Rooms, Bathrooms, or Garages.

Why? Because you will learn how to set intentions, create dreams, and to solve issues regarding Life Values whether or not you control that area of your home or office. This is achieved with a clever little device you set up called a Sacred Space. Feng Shui is a problem solving tool, not a tool that creates more problems because the recommended cures generate more concerns. Here is a prime example: How do you work out an issue of grief if your Self-Knowledge/Wisdom area falls in the ridiculously junky garage? The messy garage might be the metaphoric reflection of obsession with the past and, sure, cleaning out the garage might be the first step to developing a blissful, present existence. Most of the time the garage, however, is an out-of-control cesspool of stuff and not something you want to take on just so you can look at yourself in the mirror without seeing anguish in your eyes. Relax and breathe. Thankfully, there are easy solutions to anything. Impossible situations are merely a dilemma waiting to be solved with Feng Shui. Even if you want to enhance your creativity but the dark, depressed Bride-of-Frankenstein happens to rent a room (morgue) in your Child/Creativity section of the house, put your feet up, exhale, and read on. Follow the signs by the road which say, "No *Fear Shui*, instructions on dealing with frightening Feng Shui situations ahead!"

VARIOUS OTHER ROOMS WITH A FENG SHUI VIEW

This section is about pantries, dens, dining rooms, spare bedrooms, studies, screen rooms, breakfast nooks, maid's quarters, and so on. Remember the Bagua divides into nine equal sections over your floor plan. Sometimes two or three rooms will stand for one Life Value. Other homes will have a Life Value (for example, Fame/Reputation) that falls between two rooms, so it resides half in, say, the kitchen and the other half in the guest bathroom. Still, other homes will have more than one Life Value represented in one room. The layout of a trailer, for instance, might be such that the Love Union/Marriage, Child/Creativity, and Helpful People/Travel each fall within the confines of a bedroom. See diagram H-1 for example.

HOW THE BAGUA SUPERIMPOSES ON A TRAILER (H-1)

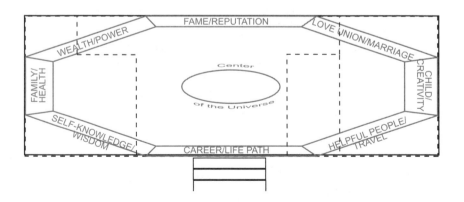

Regardless of your particular circumstances, it is strongly advised to do these few things in each room, especially if what you call a room is not already mentioned in detail in this book. Bring to mind the need to add the Three Secrets Reinforcement Ritual to every action you take. Also, remember whatever Life Value the room stands for must be acknowledged in your intention ritual.

DO:

- Hold chi in the room.

- Perform proper cures in any bathroom.

- Avoid blocking chi.

- Place in the Empowerment Position, or Cure for Empowerment, any bed, desk, stove, or sitting chairs.

- Perform a clutter-clear.

DON'T:

- Do not worry about repeating cures in these extra miscellaneous spaces which have already been handled in specific rooms: like the kitchen, master bedroom, or children's/roommates' rooms. Exceptions would be attached apartments.

THE MIRRO-MATIC TOOL

Mirrors have reflective qualities, and because you speak the language of symbols, you can easily use a mirror symbolically to divert what you don't want to affect you. They are amazing little creatures when coupled with intention. Following are suggestions for the home or office which put the mirror in a starring role.

GARAGES

Get four blind-spot automobile mirrors. Discount stores usually sell them for cheap. Place one on each of the four inside garage walls, including the garage door, facing each other. Use the Three Secrets Reinforcement Ritual to intend that all the garage clutter, as well as the car angst, stays inside the space. Now it does not affect the Feng Shui of your house. The garage can then be used as a storage space for all the clutter you remove from the house. When the garage is attached to the home or office, be sure to hang a chi catcher to hold in the Life Value essence it represents. Also place a Sacred Space somewhere inside your house to work on the issues and situations which exist in that particular Life Value. Your garage becomes *the garage*, rather than the reason why you don't have a great relationship with your clients (a Helpful People issue). Even if your garage is as clean as the Army's kitchen floor, and you can eat off it, this cure is still recommended. See diagram J-1 for visual.

MIRROR MIRROR... TAKE THE FALL GARAGE CURE (J-1)

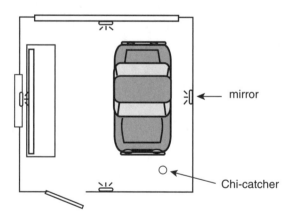

MIRROR, MIRROR TAKE THE FALL CURE

1. Placement of Object

Attach four blind-spot automobile mirrors—convex, concave, or flat mirrors are all equally effective—one on each inside wall. They do not have to be directly across from one another, but if possible, have them attach at the same place on their respective walls, both at the same level and approximate distance on the wall.

2. Visualize/Imagine the Action Already Occurring

See the mirrors send back the clutter, car exhaust, and poisonous chemical energies to their source. The four mirrored walls act as a protective shield against all negativity passing into your house.

3. Speak Your Intention Out Loud

"My home/office is peaceful, healthy, and nurturing. All negativity and clutter stays in the garage. This or something better for the Highest Good now occurs."

If an apartment exists over the garage, place another mirror on the garage ceiling. Do the above cure, including the power of deflection from the garage ceiling, so no undesirable energy can infiltrate the apartment.

STORAGE SHEDS

Pretend the garage and the storage unit have the same messy parents. Clutter is clutter, even in buildings which are officially created to stow untidiness. Be sure each inside wall has a mirror on it facing the others. Intend the mirrors to keep all the confusion inside the building. Then the energy won't seep out and affect the Feng Shui of your land or home. Adjust the Mirror, Mirror Take the Fall Cure for storage units.

CLOSETS

Realize the closet is the place where even the perfectionist can be a bit human, yet closets do count in Feng Shui. Perform the following cure, whether falling boxes bruise your cheek on their way down, or whether each coat hanger is aligned with a straightedge ruler. Use one small mirror above the inside of each closet door(s). You can apply a convex, concave, or flat mirror. It makes no difference as long as the reflective side faces into the closet. Intend the mirror to reflect the closet clutter back inside itself. Then the larger room Feng Shui is not affected. Do this cure with every closet in the home and office. Allow for your humanity, even if you are compulsively neat. See diagram J-2 for visual.

CLOSET CAPERS CURE (J-2)

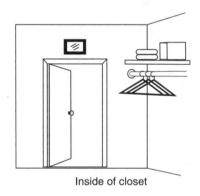

Inside of closet

CLOSET CAPERS CURE

1. *Placement of Object*

   Attach a blind-spot automobile mirror (convex, concave, or flat) above the inside door(s) of the closet. Make sure the reflective side of the mirror faces into the closet.

2. *Visualize/Imagine the Action Already Occurring*

   See all the closet clutter reflected back to itself by the mirror.

3. *Speak Your Intention Out Loud*

"My room Feng Shui is peaceful and unaffected by the state of the room closet. This or something better for the Highest Good now occurs."

ATTICS AND BASEMENTS

Cure all basements and attics. Don't let the stuff which is stored in the loft or cellar affect your Feng Shui efforts in the living space. The basement represents the foundation of a building. It therefore has the potential to affect every level in your space and in your life. So treat it. Place a mirror, any kind will do, on the ceiling of the basement, reflective side down, and visualize/imagine one mirror has enough authority to keep the jumble in its place. No more basement woes. This cure also perfectly creates a storage space for your various pieces of unsightliness. See diagram J-3 for example.

BASEMENT CURE (J-3)

Basement

The attic is the top position of a house. Imagine the home as a body. The attic is the head. Is your noggin full of mind mess or sharp focus? It is simple to repair, regardless of its condition. For an attic, just place a small mirror, any kind will do, on the floor in the corner where it won't be stepped on or disturbed. Imagine/visualize this one mirror, with its reflective side up, keeps the attic stuff in the attic. No more attic afflictions. This cure is for an attic used as storage, not as a bedroom. See diagram J-4 for visual example.

ATTIC CURE (J-4)

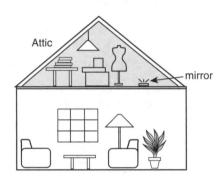

APARTMENTS, CONDOS, AND OFFICES

Take Feng Shui control of your individual space in the overall building of any apartment, condo, or office. Use mirrors to reflect back all pessimism from your neighbors on all sides, including from the floors above and below you. The self-adhesive blind spot auto mirrors are easy and effective to use. However, any flat mirror can be used and is just as successful. The use of these mirrors does not have to be a visual compromise in your home and office. Attach this mirror to the back of a picture which hangs on a common wall shared with a neighbor. The reflective aspect of the mirror faces toward the wall, in the direction of the neighbor. With clear intention and a few "raise your energy" images, you can easily reflect all negativity back to its source. See diagram J-5 for visual clarity.

GOOD WALLS MAKE GOOD NEIGHBORS CURE (J-5)

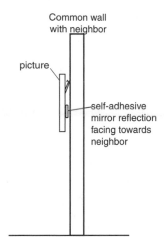

For neighbors who live below you, attach a mirror, reflection side facing down under a shelf in a closet and with intention, make sure the mirror returns any yuck from your entire space. See diagram J-6 for clarity.

MORE CURES FOR DIFFERENT NEIGHBOR SITUATIONS (J-6, J-7)

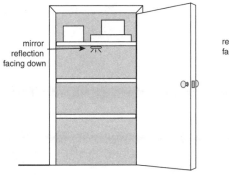
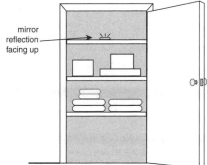

For residents above you, use the same or another closet, but this time attach a flat mirror, reflection side up, toward the floor of the above occupants. Again, with your intentions, make sure the mirror keeps all negativity from the above spaces away from your dwelling. See diagram J-7 for clarity.

GOOD WALLS MAKE GOOD NEIGHBORS CURE

1. *Placement of Object*

   Attach a mirror, the reflective side towards the neighbor, on each of the four walls where there are occupants on the other side. Be sure to include floors and ceilings, if necessary. There is no need for more than a total of six mirrors.

2. *Visualize/Imagine the Action Already Occurring*

   See each mirror act as a barricade as it completely keeps all negativity from entering your space. It fully returns anything which does not belong to you, whether this is energy from outside neighboring dwellings or anything which does not positively serve you.

3. *Speak Your Intention Out Loud*

   "All negativity from the outside is reflected back to its source. This or something better for the Highest Good now occurs."

SINGLE-FAMILY DWELLINGS

Perform the same cure as above, but adjust it accordingly if you live or work in a completely separate space from others. This is strongly recommended whether your neighbors are across the street or miles away. You create a protected space with this cure so your building is no longer vulnerable to the emotional, physical, and mental whims of drive-by passengers, argumentative families, and ill people. Because you have access to four outside walls of the house, attach a small mirror on each outside wall, reflective side facing toward the neighbors. Even if the view from the house is lovely, for example, beautiful mountains, still use shielding mirrors on all four sides of your dwelling. A mirror, when attached to the outside of a building, can be as small as 1-inch x 1-inch. You don't need a big symbol on your exterior to make a powerful point. See diagram J-8 for visual.

MIRROR CURE FOR THE OUTSIDE
OF A FREE STANDING BUILDING (J-8)

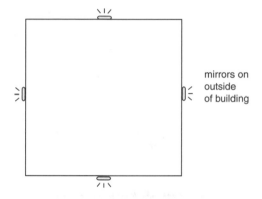

mirrors on
outside
of building

This cure will not affect the dwelling's ability to receive the positive experience of living across from the good energy majesty of a canyon, a forest of trees, or even a best friend who resides across the street. You program the mirrors to avert negative energy only.

PROBLEM SPACES

Study the situations and solutions given in the child, roommate, and guest room section. Make the Loch Ness Monster Cure your best friend. You will be amazed by the results. Any unruly room, one which has become an unsightly mess, can benefit from this cure. Examine how when you contain the chaos of your life, radical improvements naturally happen in your world.

You have already learned many uses of the mirror in Feng Shui. In addition to the situations above, you have also gained the knowledge that mirrors can put you into empowerment stances and more. Mirrors do a lot more than just reflect back whether or not we look smashing.

A MIXTURE OF FENG SHUI INITIATIONS

This segment deals with ideologies not associated with a particular room, but should be included in an omnipotent way—everywhere, anywhere, all the time—similar to when you are first in love. This particular do and don't list easily is applied to each room in the house or office since it translates to your life. By now, you already know this.

DO:

Have an Owner's Mentality.

This is easy to say, but harder to do. Whether you own or rent, it can be difficult to change patterns and comfort zones which appear standard when moving into a house, apartment, or office. Countless clients have compromised their criterion of living. For example, a room might need a new coat of paint. The landlord refuses to get it repainted. If the room represents, for instance, your Family/Health area, and you struggle with an emotional issue about your childhood, it is strongly suggested you spring for a new can of paint and hold a painting party with your friends. Healing on all levels, with all issues, is made simpler when any room is lifted up by attention placed on its Life Value placement. This is the most inexpensive therapy imaginable; you beautify a room and put healing energy into that Life Value. Pay attention to how this feat positively renovates that aspect of your life in general.

So try this: Imagine you wear a jeweled crown on your head. Envision throwing a purple cape over your shoulders. You are royalty, regardless of whether you pay a mortgage or rent each month. Walk through your living space or office with this "entitled" sight while saying this mantra over and over in your head, "I am a Queen (King)! I deserve everything!"

Such a belief system goes far to solve issues around your home, office, and life creatively; and even helps if your bank account is feeling a bit low. You don't have to spend lots of money to enjoy the rewards of Feng Shui. Still, if your sense of worth is depleted, and you don't believe you deserve anything, such a conviction is emotionally expensive. It's a belief you can't afford to keep. The Queen or King walk invites this positive shift. When you optimistically alter your self-worth, a new paradigm takes place in your life. You become responsible for the possession of your place, whether it's your home, your office, or your very being. Give yourself permission to take up space in the universe. Start with the creation of a home or office you are proud to be in. Now that is owner's mentality!

Fix All Home or Office Maintenance Needs.
The dripping sink equals abundance plopping away. The stuck door says opportunities can't open easily. The leaky roof may mean you experience too much emotion. The burnt-out light bulb signifies not letting chi fully into the situation. The old couch you hate causes clutter in your life. A used mattress means you are satisfied with old, repeated patterns. Begin to fix one thing at a time, or where appropriate, insist your landlord repair the building ills. A happy home is a cared-for home. This is evident in the aura around every dwelling, or anything, alive or inanimate, which receives nurturing, love, and concern. This symbolic gesture also reflects connection and awareness about your life. The home or office replicates the condition of your

reality. May it be in mint condition. If a space doesn't merit fixing up, it is more than likely not worth staying in. Be certain, however, your resistance to transform a house into a home is not some deeper psychological resistance to change. If you have a suspicion this might be the case, start small. Step-by-step, refurbish the building which reflects your life.

Make Sure Chi Can Find Your Front Door and May Enter into Your Dwelling Easily and Effortlessly.

Your front door, as the architect intended, is also called the Mouth of the Chi. Chi must be able to find your home or office and the front door easily. In addition, for chi to bless your entire building, it must also feel welcome. When following directions to a client's house for the first time, I always see whether I get lost. If directions are clear, chi can easily find its way. But if I do get lost, chi is also unsure how to get to the home or office. This also includes dwellings which are not clearly marked with numbers on their buildings or on their front curbs. There are numerous clients who use another door to enter their space, so they never acknowledge their formal front door, even though it is the official door for the Bagua diagnosis. On top of that, many front lawns border the front door without a walkway or have walkways which are blocked by something, like a moveable basketball hoop with a backboard.

If the chi can indeed find the path to the front door, there is still the front porch to contend with, complete with steps which might need repair or are so steep it isn't safe to ascend. A place might even boast a porch which has become a trash receptacle for everything which no longer fits in the dwelling. Too bad, because a less than beauteous porch is the first thing everyone sees. Chi has the same sensibilities. If a place is not clear, safe, and welcoming, chi will find the spaces down the street, across town, and so on, which are.

Regardless of your particular entrance reality, you don't need to start using your front door as your main source of passage into your house. It does mean, however, that regardless of use, your front door should be in good repair. There should be a clear path to the entrance, a pathway which leads up to a welcoming, clutter-free front porch which has stable, safe stairs with handrails, if appropriate, and a door which opens and closes easily. Imagine chi as an honored guest, your mother-in-law, your homeroom teacher, or that good looking person who you want to impress. Make the front door what it is—the most important symbol in your home and office—whether you use it regularly or not.

It's very simple and inexpensive to create a symbolic trail which leads to the front door even if you don't have a sidewalk. Gather many good-sized stones and place them on top of the grass or ground to create two edges of a pathway with enough space between the two rows for two people to walk side by side comfortably. Make the lane a meandering one, like a stream, instead of a straight shot arrow which goes right towards the door. Chi is very powerful. It will serve your space better if it is gently called to you, not pulled into the home or office like a Tasmania whirlwind. See diagram I-1 for ideas.

EXAMPLE OF HELPING CHI FIND THE FRONT DOOR (I-1)

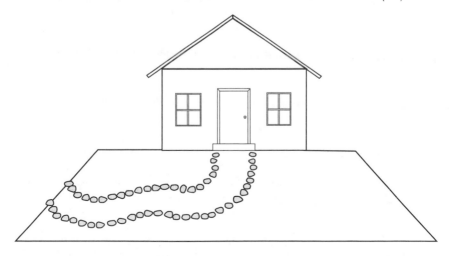

Place a Bagua Mirror above the Outside of Your Front Door.

The Bagua mirror can be traditional, which is made of wood and formed into eight sides with a small circular mirror in the center. Or, you can get a very inexpensive, beveled octagonal mirror at a craft store if your personal style is more subtle. See diagram I-2 for visual clarity.

THE BAGUA MIRROR POSITIONED
OVER THE OUTSIDE OF FRONT DOOR (I-2)

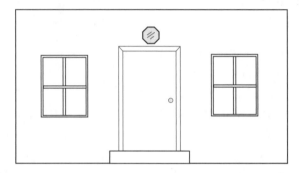

The Bagua is a very powerful icon in Feng Shui. Whenever you live across the street from a cemetery, power lines, extremely dysfunctional neighbors, and such, a Bagua mirror is the defensive item which keeps such gloomy tendencies out of your personal domain. Even if the pessimistic influence lives beside or behind you, a Bagua mirror can be used instead of a regular mirror to reflect away strong influences (see chapter on Mirro-Matics). Regardless, the Bagua mirror is always placed above the outside of the front door as well. Perform the Protection Reflection Cure, described below, with its placement.

PROTECTION REFLECTION CURE

1. Placement of Object

Attach the Bagua mirror of your choice above the outside of your front door.

2. *Visualize/Imagine the Action Already Occurring*

    See all forms of negativity turned away from your home or office. Imagine positive energy (a glitter-like substance) entering through the door.

3. *Speak Your Intention Out Loud*

    "All negativity is reflected away from this home or office. Luck and good fortune happens for all who enter. This or something better for the Highest Good now occurs."

Because the Bagua image is so forceful, it is not recommended inside the space. Exceptions to this rule are if you live or work in a multi-dwelling unit. In such a case, the Bagua mirror of protection should be placed above the outside of your individual door even though your individual door may reside inside the building in general. However, it is not recommended to use a Bagua mirror for empowerment cures and so on. Think of a Bagua mirror as a jungle lion—independent, powerful, loving in an unattached way—and totally inappropriate for the domesticated nature of the interior of your home and office.

Learn the Feng Shui Definition of Clutter and Follow its Philosophy.

If something lowers your energy, promise yourself to get rid of it. A garage sale, a give-away, or a second hand store are all ways to transform your clutter into the contributions promised by the Higher Power. Know that clutter which exists in any Life Value affects how that particular value translates into your daily reality. When you have an issue, identify the Life Value it fits into and locate it in your home. Clutter-clear that area. Also, clutter-clear the room(s) in your building which are in the opposing position to that Life Value. The Opposite-Attract Law is an important principle to remember. Then notice the sensational occurrences in your life on the physical, emotional, mental, and spiritual levels.

Clutter-clearing does not involve the mind. In fact, the more intelligent you are, the harder it can be. Determine clutter with your heart and gut, not your head. Establish whether an object makes you go pop instantaneously. If a client gives me a snivel story, or her eyes get starry as she explains why she needs to keep the roses given to her by her prom date 20 years ago, this is over-romanticized confusion masked as beat up, dried botany.

Clutter is not about sentimentality or caretaking. It is a physical manifestation of what exists on every level of your being. For example, if you have a lot of stuff in your sewing room, in fact, it teems over with so much junk you no longer know what is in the room, and it is your Self-Knowledge/Wisdom area, you can bet you have just as much stuff around boundary, growth, and self-worth issues on the emotional and mental level.

Remember—no thrill, just spill—the stuff out onto the curb for somebody else to take. In Feng Shui, except with stove burners, less is more. When every object in your environment makes you pop, then your surroundings serve you. Amazing feats occur when you are supported by the ambiance around you.

I am especially impressed by one client's testimony. This man was very motivated, followed the clutter-clearing rules, and used his heart and gut rather than his mind, to clear out his home. Hours later, he had bags and bags of objects which were no longer motivators in his present life. He removed almost 40% of his comfort zone articles. By the end of the day, he lay in a fetal position, in the middle of his newly opened home, sobbing, his body releasing grief, anger, and fear. Such a story might seem scary to relate. You might be concerned and end up rushing over to your neighbor's house to get back the pasta maker you gave her a few hours ago. What if you lose your cool as well and turn into a bawling mess? You have to pick up the kids from school at 3:00.

Not to worry, clutter-clearing is an emotional and spiritual release but usually does not affect a person so dramatically, unless great amounts of stuff are excavated and removed from the premises in a very short time. Regardless, I told the story to convey how powerful a clutter-clearing can be. It is a great tool for true healing. If you want the self-improvement rate with your therapist to move at quantum healing speeds, ruthlessly clutter-clear your dwelling. Watch the curative powers take place then. To get to the core of any recurring theme quickly, systematically get rid of the items which bore you. You will be fascinated by the end result.

Perform the Three Secrets Reinforcement Ritual with Every Cure.

Intention should always be capitalized whether it begins the sentence or ends it. It is that important. Intention should get a reserved space, up front, in the Feng Shui parking lot of life. Intention should get an award of honor for making all things happen, whether your aim is to go to the store or move your bed into the Empowerment Position. Intention is what makes Feng Shui miraculous. Intention is what crafts you into a powerful, magical organism. Want to be a force to reckon with? Intention is your magic secret weapon. You've heard the phrase: In the beginning, there was the Word. My own expansion on that is: In the beginning, there was Intentional Word. It is a creative power incomparable to anything. Harness it.

Designate Nine Different Areas in your Home or Office to Maintain a Sacred Space for Each Life Value Represented in the Bagua.

Reread the informational section of this book which focuses on the qualities of a Sacred Space in more detail. It will help you understand the purpose and importance of the Sacred Space, which holds mysterious power, very much like intention. A Sacred Space assures determined, contemplative focus in every area of your domain, even when your teenager's hormones occupy a bedroom in the Family/Health section or the Creature of Id pays rent to ruin the Fame/Reputation bedroom. Employ the Sacred Space, for instance, when your garage is in the position of the Child/Creativity area and the bathroom challenges your Wealth/Power position. Clearly, none of these examples are idyllic to have in these Life Value places. Many a paranoid client has come to me with teary eyes, head hung, and feelings trounced.

"I don't have to include my garage, do I? Or, my teenager's room, or my tenant's room whom I barely ever see?" They lift their head ever so slightly so that their water-logged eyes can see my mouth.

"Is it attached?" I ask.

Nod.

"Then the garage, or any of the other rooms, are included." I know—ruthless.

Now the tears fall. The garage is piled high with boxes of books, old furniture, and greasy, messy tools. Rubert, your teenager, is an angry, silent, chaotic muddle. In addition, the roommate makes the Wicked Witch of the West seem like the Fairy Godmother. Repeat after me:

"Sacred Spaces are doses of medicine for the Feng Shui heartburns in my existence."

Once again:

"Sacred Spaces are doses of medicine for the Feng Shui heartburns in my existence."

Amazing. Don't you feel improved, stronger, more empowered? It does not matter if the Love Union/Marriage laundry room has enough animal fur on the floor to make a coat, a kitty litter box which smells like old shoes, and a dryer which sounds like a dying car when it runs. You still have a good chance of attracting the perfect partner in this lifetime. Be aware, however, of the symbolic implications you reveal to the universal mirror with a Love Union/Marriage room in such disarray. Keep to the attitudes of Feng Shui, perform the necessary Feng Shui cures, as well as making the room a pleasant place for you, your cats, and your imagined mate. But such a makeover is overwhelming and it might take some time. Meanwhile, your biological clock is ticking. You haven't had a date in months. After apparent Feng Shui treatments are added, ones like holding in chi, consider the power of the Loch Ness Monster Cure. Next, appoint a place for the Love Union/Marriage Sacred Space somewhere outside of that room. It could even reside in your bedroom. You decide. Just remember a Sacred Space can be vertical, like a lovely picture (energy-raising, more than a single image) you hang on a wall. Or, it could be horizontal, like a small table perhaps the size used for an altar or an entry table. See diagram I-3.

EXAMPLES OF SACRED SPACE (I-3)

Horizontal sample   Vertical sample   Hanging Sculpture sample
(or anything in your style)

The role of any Life Value Sacred Space is to focus on the particular concerns of that Life Value. For instance, a Love Union/Marriage Sacred Space would deal with lovers, passion, resolve of partner conflicts (the kind which magically appear when two people live or work together), and other related subjects. The Love Union/Marriage Sacred Space has a wondrous role. It lets you work out issues which pertain to the blessed union without the worry of whether or not the Feng Shui of the Love Union/Marriage is in an appropriate place in your house, like in your teenager's hate shack. This is true for each Sacred Space which represents a Life Value. You don't have to be controlling. Your teen may play torment music. You can still attract a loving and respectful partner because you have placed such intentions on your bedroom's Love Union/Marriage Sacred Space. Your Highest Good companion is carefully, and with perfect timing, summoned.

In case you live alone, or have an accepting partner who respects your Sacred Space's placement, each Life Value Sacred Space can rest in the room where it has its Bagua representation. For instance, a Career/Life Path Sacred Space can operate somewhere in your Career/Life Path living room. Or, it can reside in a hallway alcove near the living room, if that feels more appropriate. Or put each one of your Sacred Spaces in your bedroom. If you have multiple floors, treatment of Feng Shui formulas on each level is still recommended, but one Sacred Space for each Life Value (a total of nine) is all which are required. You decide the floor level to keep each Sacred Space on. Regardless, it is imperative a Sacred Space for each Life Value is indicated somewhere in your home/office. Be sure you know where each Sacred Space is and which Sacred Space stands for which Life Value. Being acquainted with such specifics will change your life. It is worth the organization necessary.

Thankfully, the Sacred Space does not have to be obvious to everyone else. You do not need a neon sign above a table that flashes, "Sacred Space for (fill in the blank) Life Value. Do not touch." The Sacred Space is for you, and you alone, and a mate if the synthesis of philosophies exists. If small, exploring fingers constantly alter the placement of power objects on a table which have been assigned an intention, make your Sacred Space a picture on the wall instead. In fact, Sacred Spaces created from art pictures are great for tiny homes and offices, as well as for the person who cringes at the idea of having funny little altar-like things all around her or his house. The power of Sacred Spaces, however, claims its effectiveness when the picture (or table) raises your energy and follows other Feng Shui qualities. Have pictures represent more than just single images. Also do not mix sacred with secular. If your Family/Health Sacred Space consistently has a little hot wheel roadster on it because the shiny surface of the table makes for a great racetrack, decide on a wall picture for it instead. Yet if it is clear you want a horizontal Sacred Space for one of the Life Values but you only have room on the top shelf of a bookcase, for instance, use this cure to keep the Sacred Space just that way. See diagram I-4 for visual.

HOLY SPACE KEEPER CURE (I-4)

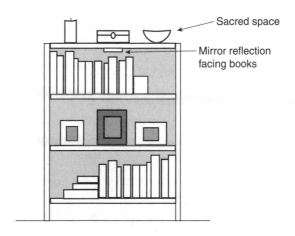

HOLY SPACE KEEPER CURE

1. *Placement of Object*

   Attach a small flat mirror (or a self-adhesive blind-spot automobile mirror) on the underside of the top shelf of a bookcase, or the underside of the lid of a bureau of drawers, and so on. The reflective side should face the books, articles of clothing, and other such material items.

2. *Visualize/Imagine the Action Already Occurring*

   See the mirror actually deflecting the secular, worldly items away from the Sacred Space. This prevents the secular from affecting the Sacred Space as a hallowed, problem-solving tool.

3. *Speak Your Intention Out Loud*

   "All worldly energies are now deflected away from my (insert Life Value) Sacred Space. My Sacred Space is now kept pure and helpful so my issues are easily solved. This or something better for the Highest Good now occurs."

It is simple to alter the Holy Space Keeper Cure to fit your various placement needs whether you would like a Sacred Space to be on a lower shelf, a window sill, or wherever. Make sure you attach any mirror so the reflective side is placed away from the Sacred Space symbolically discouraging the energies from all the neighboring shelves and drawers which might infiltrate it.

Plainly, Feng Shui remedies are powerful, effective, and life-changing when applied throughout your home and office. They are also general balancers to ensure beneficial flow and problem-solving in your space. Notice the differences, however, between Feng Shui treatments for general problems and the focus of Sacred Spaces on specialized issues in an area. Both are essential and valuable. So how do you employ the services of a Sacred Space? The use of power objects and power images needs to be discussed so a complete understanding of the function of Sacred Spaces is realized. Let's stick with the example of the Love Union/Marriage Sacred Space. Once you have chosen where the Sacred Space will be located, place the "power object" which raises your energy on it. For instance, a red candle molded into the shape of two people intertwined, symbolically representing passion in your relationship, could be placed on this table. With Intention, visualize or imagine whatever specific action you want (for instance, a resurgence of excitement in your relationship with your mate). Next, speak your intention for the purpose of the candle, "(beloved's name) and I now enjoy passion to new heights. We thrive in our connection. This or something better for the Highest Good now occurs." The candle becomes the symbolic container for this desired intention. Different objects can be added, at your discretion, to create dream desires as well as to address specific roadblocks which exist that offer solutions to both your love union and work relationships.

Using an example of a vertical Sacred Space which focuses on Wealth/Power issues, designate a picture, either one already hanging or one bought especially for this purpose. Make sure the picture gives you the poppers. Let's say it is an image of a beautiful waterfall cascading into a pool of turquoise water accented by a bank of flowers. The river bank is also graced with lovely, big trees. Next, choose an aspect of the picture to represent a power image, for instance, a lovely, big tree. Place your attention on the tree, even touch the image. Visualize an action you want to occur, for instance, sitting in a red sports car with mounds of money in the passenger seat. Speak your intention out loud with your focus on the image which retains this desire. "I now have more than enough money after I pay the bills to buy a new sports car. This or something better for the Highest Good now occurs." Like the horizontal Sacred Space, you choose images in the vertical Sacred Space to help establish, support, and unravel issues related to whatever Life Value a particular Sacred Space maintains.

Clients often ask, "Is it necessary to infuse power objects and images with intention daily? Another thing, do you have to remember which object (image) has which intention?"

"Done once in a faith-filled manner is enough," I admit.

However, when you have a central concern which infiltrates all aspects of your life to the point where your joy of living is compromised, you can benefit from repeating the affirmations you establish with your power icons. New subconscious configurations are then established which support a healthier outlook. Health on all levels is wealth on all levels. Just remember, a power object is merely an object or image until, with the magic of intention, you infuse it with the potential to positively alter your existence. Pay attention to what comes to pass. Here is an example of how you would perform a Three Secrets Reinforcement Ritual on Sacred Space power objects or images to set them up as specific problem-solving tools. In Part II of this book, the colors, as well as the Elements to be added or avoided on each Sacred Space, will be discussed. For now, however, concentrate on the perfection of this intention ritual.

INTENTION RITUAL FOR SACRED SPACE POWER ICONS

1. *Placement of Object*

   Place the item you've selected to be your power object (which raises your energy) on a horizontal Sacred Space, such as a table. In the case of a vertical Sacred Space, such as a picture, choose an image within the picture as your power object.

2. *Visualize/Imagine the Action Already Occurring*

   See the movie you create, with whatever issue you are dealing with, become clear and resolved. Be sure to "see" the action in the present tense, as if has already happened.

3. Speak Your Intention Out Loud

State with clarity and forethought, the issues you want to resolve or what you desire to create, and then add: "This or something better for the Highest Good now occurs."

See Feng Shui as a Problem-Solving Tool and Yourself as a Powerful Person of Intention.

In case you have been using this book as a face shield up to this point, here are a few points to reconsider. Feng Shui makes your home and office feel extraordinary. It is the art of placement, which with intention, encourages the energy of the chi life force to flow throughout your dwelling and also your life. This ancient Chinese science can be aesthetically pleasing in any building while keeping your styles and values. Finally, the most exciting part of this Feng Shui philosophy: It is a magnificent problem-solving tool. Not to mean that your problems will magically disappear as you apply Feng Shui values to your environment. However, Feng Shui does assist you in solving any and all of life's little setbacks and, at the same time, lifts the average existence to one of excellence.

Use your Sacred Spaces unfailingly. Can't pay the bills this month? Intend a resolution with a power object (image) on the Family/Health Sacred Space. Need more recognition at work? Intend this with a power object (image) on the Fame/Reputation Sacred Space. Want to stop procrastination? Turn your desk around. Want a date? Hold chi in the Love Union/Marriage area and buy a new mattress to replace the used one. Get in the habit of using Feng Shui principles to put your life into proactive status. Victim patterns pass right by when your eyes are on the prize, not on the ground. Wear the jeweled crown and purple cape all the time if necessary, and carry out whatever actions remind you that you're mighty. Your intention is an elixir with great influence. Miracles, simply the manifestation of what you conceive, occur when the intention switch is turned on.

DON'T:

Do Not Give Your Power Away to Anyone Regarding Feng Shui, Especially Feng Shui Consultants.

Forget the impressive business cards. Feng Shui consultants are information givers only. When I give a personal session, my goal is to look at the symbols in your environment with a trained, objective eye and to communicate these views to you. However, the power, the magic, and the ultimate effectiveness of the Feng Shui treatment to your home and office depends on the intention you put into the applications of the cures. I give objective ideas. You take such understanding and turn it into enchantment.

Do Not Get a Feng Shui Consultation Unless You are Ready for Major Life Changes.

If there's a part of you which doesn't believe, turn your work desk around, clean out a corner in your junk room, reposition your bed into the Empowerment Position, then get out of the way. Your world shall quake, clatter, and rotate. Still don't trust? Clutter-clear a whole room. Hang chi catchers in a few designated areas. Keep the bathroom door closed.

You think none of this will change you? Try switching your single image pictures to equal images of more than one. Hide the knives and avoid blocking chi. No, you're still not there yet? Buy a new mattress. Place the stove in the Empowerment Position. Move your child out of the Wealth/Power area.

Okay, *now* you are a fan.

SOUP FOR THE SOUL

It is true soup can be quite tasty when you add a few onions to the pot. One of the keys to success when addressing the Feng Shui model in your home or office is the willingness to peel the layers of the onion without discouragement. As you add curiosity and bravery to this process, you begin to get to the truth that resides at the core. Triumph is assured in the end. Your life is guaranteed to be spicy. Whether you like it mild, medium, or hot is up to you.

Proceed to Part II; it travels deeper still. It is multifaceted and promises to bestow upon the seeker more of the glory of Feng Shui knowledge. It will take patience and courage to understand and apply its principles, but valor is always rewarded ten-fold.

PART II

DEEPER FENG SHUI IMPLEMENTATIONS FOR THE REST OF US

THE CORE OF FENG SHUI

Congratulations on finishing Part I. Do you sense the power of the basic treatments and have excitement by the potential you see before you? In Part II, we will go deeper into understanding the Elements, the use of Sacred Spaces, and other techniques which will address how to work with more complex issues associated with your home or office space. Keep your mind open and harness the information to direct to your space. Be strong in pursuit of your objectives, yet receptive to all possibilities. Then watch and see what happens.

THE NEXT STEPPING STONES

A Feng Shui treatment to your home makes miracles something that you anticipate. Employ the multiple layers of Feng Shui principles in your dwelling, then observe the mind-boggling things which happen on a regular basis. Countless clients' testimonies confirm it! For instance, a woman clutter-cleared her office and, by the next day, discovered a passionate path regarding her job where before only boredom and clock-watching existed. Another example is the man who merely altered the atmosphere of his dining table, located in his Love Union/Marriage area, to have a sensual ambiance and months later shares his meals with his live-in mate. The stories go on.

Admittedly, I have had a few clients who claim they have done the countless things recommended, but nothing has happened in their life. One woman said the only difference was a cleaner house. When people are fully aligned to create change in their lives, however, it is virtually impossible not to experience at least some of the effects of Feng Shui. As clients motivate for positive reflection to transpire, Feng Shui never disappoints. In fact, the uninvolved client often notices changes in spite of themselves. Still, it's true many of the ideologies of Feng Shui are unusual. It's hard to admit when a desk gets turned around and a used mattress replaced that noticeable improvements are produced. Yet Feng Shui follows the Laws of Nature and the universe. Imagine if the Law of Gravity took on an unpredictable behavior.

Besides being a science, Feng Shui is clearly an art and appeals to those with an artist's sense. In addition, it focuses on chi and how energy creates invisible but noticeable shifts in a dwelling. Those who have a feeling sense of energy appreciate its gifts. Regrettably, many people have detached from this sensitivity to survive in a world that can be a painful challenge. However, make the adjustments recommended by the Feng Shui doctrines. This will provide a container for healing and empowerment to your life, even when it is not at first evident. Here are some theories on how a person's lack of response to a Feng Shui treated environment are created:

1. The person embraces a victim role (or martyr role, which is a victim who wears a jeweled crown), and when the Highest Good does occur, they can't accept the gifts which ensue. A proactive position is never taken. Thus, one believes nothing at all has occurred.

2. Feng Shui outcomes can be subtle. Sometimes they are like a bugle. Other times Feng Shui results come as a soft breeze. If the client waits for drama, the more subtle occurrences are missed altogether.

3. Patience is a virtue for a reason: first-class miracles arrive in their own time. The person should carry on as if it has already happened. It will.

If the results you get from the Feng Shui treatment of your home or office are understated, don't assume you've done something wrong. A lightning strike can be too powerful. It can leave once beautiful trees burned and scarred. As Americans, we tend to want this type of quick result. Yet, spectacular changes can be hard to integrate into a sustained way of being. Practice witnessing subdued movements in your life. Useful also is to look at Feng Shui results in terms of the force expressed by time and a river against a rock. Slowly, with gracefulness, the shape of the stone is molded by the river's consistent flow. Thus, lightning and the river are both undeniably potent. One is brash, the other, persistent over time. Believe in the capacity of Feng Shui, for it can have both of these attributes.

DO:

Do Remember to Breathe.

My true profession on this planet seems to be a breathing coach. Here's an example of a typical scenario:

"I recommend you rearrange your living room furniture and put the couch over there against that wall. This action will open up the chi flow and can drastically amend your life."

The client nods, but there is a silence.

"Are you okay? You seem a bit stressed."

Nod.

"Can you say you're okay, or is it you're just stressed?"

Nod. I let the client process like this until a 911 phone call becomes necessary. The blue tinge of the client's face is my first clue. Then I reach for the brown paper bag brought to every consultation and begin to encourage gulps of air to move again through the client's body. As the hyperventilating client gasps into the bag and her breath becomes more regulated, I decide whether or not to share my impressions of the laundry room.

Feng Shui goes right to the nucleus of one's personal life. When a trained eye begins gently but firmly to perceive patterns, uncover subconscious messages stored in the arrangement of things, and asks you to alter your world in order to create a "better" tomorrow, it can be emotional, threatening, and more than a bit discouraging. Thus, the suspension of breath is scarcely a mystery. Any time fear enters the equation, a person's first response is to constrict breathing. In a weird, purposeful way, when a client turns a different shade, advancement happens. However, true evolution requires breath.

DON'T:

Do Not Let Feng Shui Overwhelm You.

You say, "Oh, don't worry about me, I *love* this stuff! I can't wait to start to change things around!" Famous last words. What happens is this: The client, hopeful about altering the love symbols in her world, attempts to remove the exquisite, but tragic, picture of a single woman resting under a dead oak tree looking up at the storm-threatening sky. Somehow the framed image feels like it weighs 1,000 pounds. The motivated client grunts and moans, and finally the picture is unhooked from the wall. Now, it leans against the baseboard. This is normal behavior for many as they challenge comfort zones. Excitement turns into non-action as they contemplate what all these Feng Shui changes mean. Who has the energy or the time to move furniture or remove unhelpful pictures? Plus clutter-clearing any space means you have to figure out what to do with all the unwanted stuff.

Here is a possible outcome to this kind of thinking. Fast-forward three weeks with the energized client. The once wound up Feng Shui fan has collapsed into an inanimate object. She sits on a couch, which she had considered moving to the side wall, but instead it rests in the center of the room with its back to the door. The room is filled with half-packed trash bags, framed prints inclined against the walls, and piles of possessions dotted across the floor. Erratic flickers of light indicate the incessant flipping of television channels, a sure sign of Feng Shui overload.

This is an example of overwhelm.

Feng Shui seems straightforward enough; move that, place this over there, get rid of that thing, and so on. Simple. Well, it may be on the surface, but experiences on the emotional, mental, and spiritual planes are quite the opposite. For instance, you might remove a picture, but this feat challenges a comfort zone. Every shift you make with your furniture for Feng Shui reasons touches upon patterns of resistance, victimization, and apathy which have taken residence in your cells. Change the symbols, transform your life. When clients begin the arduous task of transformation, those words get engraved on a stone. It is also at this point in the Feng Shui process most crises are born—the Feng Shui emergency. Here are suggestions for keeping off the Feng Shui emergency call sheet:

1. Promise yourself to do at least one Feng Shui task a day. For example, buy the necessary supplies for chi catchers one day, move the couch on another day, clutter-clear a drawer, and so on. Consistency of Feng Shui action will win the Feng Shui game.

2. Remember Feng Shui is a process, not an overnight improvement course.

3. Have a like-minded friend assist you. Clutter-clearing the guest room which has been used a storage unit is not quite as crushing when a good friend and oatmeal cookies are part of the plan. Friends are also great gauges to check out your Feng Shui handiwork. For example, very common is replacing a single image which used to hang on the wall with another single image. Subconscious patterns are pitiless. An objective observer with a heart can see the issue and nudge you to evolve.

4. Be gentle with yourself. Feng Shui is hard work. Not because you might have to move the heavy bed across the room, but because as you shift the symbol of love (bed), different thought patterns, belief systems, and esteem values are promoted. Healing crises can easily happen after Feng Shui treatments are practiced in your space. At the same time, these modifications bring an upbeat feeling to you, your environment, and your universe. It is well worth the tears and days of quiet ponder. Treat yourself like a fragile butterfly during the process. It is awkward to grow wings.

MORE FENG SHUI TANG:

Getting Intimate with the Elements.

This next section takes a few more layers off the Feng Shui onion. The burn is more intense, but so is the tang. Review the

Element Plunge in the informational section of Part I, so that you know which Elements are important in what areas of the Bagua. If you're one of those people who starts to nod off at the mention of Elements, remember they are your friends.

DO:

Become Skilled at Where Each Element Resides in Your Home or Office.

This is a fascinating study! As you understand the use of Elements, you can tweak any Life Value area to serve you. When you know your Career/Life Path is represented by Water, you are free to create the Life Path of your dreams. In this case, know also Metal is the Creative Element and Earth is the Destructive Element associated with Career/Life Path. If a less than favorable elemental relationship exists in a certain room, a cure is simply applied. For example, there is always going to be Fire in the kitchen because of the stove. What if the kitchen happens to fall in your Family/Health Life area? Fire is destructive to Wood. No problem, learn how to cure it!

Learn the "Make My Day, Everything's Okay" Cure to Solve Situations of Elemental Uncertainty as Well as to Balance Elemental Obstacles.

You may think this Element stuff is a bunch of gibberish, so the cure at the end of this section will make your day because: 1: it allows you to use the power of Elements in your home or office, even if you are confused about them, and 2: it fixes any elemental issues which you can't change, like Water in your Fame/Reputation Fire bathroom. Use this cure whenever you are unsure about what Elements are strongest in a certain area and not as powerful in another, or when you're unclear if there is an elemental representation at all in a zone. Also use it when you are unsure about the Creative and Destructive Element Cycles. And, of course, it is very practical when you physically can't move an object, for instance, a fireplace, and its Element depiction harms the Life Value Element indicated. An example is a bathroom which resides in your Fire, Fame/Reputation area. From the chart in the Element Plunge section of Part I, you can see Water puts out Fire. However, the bathroom cannot be moved. This is where the Make My Day Cure is exceptional. It promises when equal amounts of all five Elements are intentionally represented in a chosen area, the Destructive Element Cycle no longer exists.

Although this cure is fantastic at resolving issues considered untreatable, please use it with respect. More is not necessarily better in Feng Shui. This cure is not an excuse to disregard the power and placement of an Element in its true habitat. It is, however, a tool to serve you. Employ it as a specialty instrument. The sample cure here will make use of a bathroom which has an unsavory elemental relationship. Use this example to help you create other appropriate cures for any elemental relationships which need to be fixed in your dwelling.

MAKE MY DAY, EVERYTHING'S OKAY CURE

1. *Placement of Object*

   Choose or attach a shelf you've designated just for this cure. Place equal amounts of the Elements necessary to void the negative effects of Water in the Fame/Reputation bathroom whose Element is Fire. Suggested examples are a large candle (Fire), a rock the size of approximately three closed fists (Earth), a tin jewelry box (Metal), and a wooden statue about as tall as half of your forearm. The Water Element already exists naturally in the pipes of the bathroom.

2. *Visualize/Imagine the Action Already Occurring*

See all five Elements swirl around in a circle—balanced, harmonious, powerful, and peaceful together.

3. *Speak Your Intention Out loud*

"All five Elements are equally represented in this (fill in) Life Value. They work together to create my dreams, resolve my issues, and fulfill my goals. This or something better for the Highest Good now occurs."

Freaked out? Don't be. See example of Make My Day Cure with a fireplace, the most common use of this cure, in diagram K-1.

MAKE MY DAY EVERYTHING'S OKAY CURE
(EXAMPLE USING FIREPLACE) (K-1)

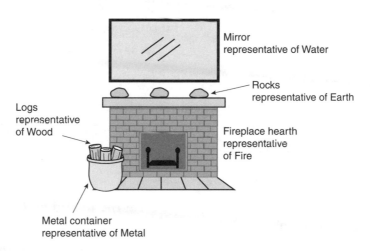

Next is the Elements Are My Friends Cure. It is much simpler to do than the previous treatment and is designed for the person who completely understands the Elements. Both cures effectively eliminate any and all disagreeable elemental relationships. It is recommended, therefore, to trust your intuition and proceed with whichever cure seems appropriate.

ELEMENTS ARE MY FRIENDS CURE

1. *Placement of Object*

Determine which Element weakens a harmful Element in a particular Life Value. For instance, in the Career/Life Path, Earth is a harmful Element. So you then use Wood to weaken Earth. See the chart in the Element Plunge in Part I. Choose an adequate representation of the Element which cancels the harmful effects of the Destructive Element. In this sample, a nice piece of driftwood makes a nice choice. Be sure the object you are choosing for this "rescuer" Element raises your energy. Place this object (or image) near an offending Element representation. The driftwood, for example, is placed in the flower pot of the bushy spider plant which sits by the window.

2. *Visualize/Imagine the Action Already Occurring*

See the chosen Element do its intended task. For instance, see the Earth dam the Water, the Wood pierce the Earth, the Water douse the Fire, and so on.

3. *Speak Your Intention Out Loud*

Say what action has occurred since the introduction of this new Element. For instance, "The Wood pierces the Earth so my Career/Life Path Water can flow. This or something better for the Highest Good now occurs."

Be assured that whatever Element you use to neutralize the impact of the Destructive Element of a Life Value will not harm that particular Life Value in any way. With any new activity, the first movements and actions are less graceful. Such is the case as you master the Element study. Learn the particulars of the Elements. They are a crash course in self-improvement. Put these values into practice. They can only positively enhance your existence—a great motivation. Oh, yes, keep breathing.

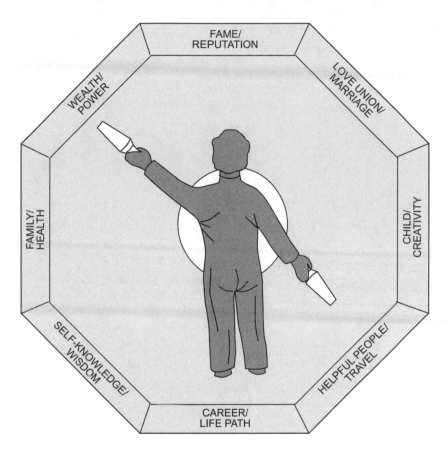

WORKING WITH THE LIFE VALUES

In addition to the standard function of each room in your home or office, such as a living room, bedroom, bathroom, or kitchen, each room also has a Life Value representation. Sometimes, depending on the size or shape of the dwelling, a room might have three Life Values represented in it. For example, a living room may include Helpful People/Travel, Child/Creativity, and

Love Union/Marriage, whereas other buildings may have a few smaller rooms which all fall in one Life Value. Determine which Life Value a room stands for in your home then work with the do and don'ts for that kind of room, for instance, a bath or bedroom. In addition, go to work on the details for each Life Value, which includes colors, Elements, and Sacred Spaces. When you apply the combination of the two inventories, be assured of a shift to your dwelling in marvelous, life-altering ways.

CAREER/LIFE PATH

Color: black
Element: Water

CAREER/LIFE PATH

This information is about your home and office Career/Life Path Life Value. May the river of life flow smoothly. Your universe will be grateful.

DO:

Use Black for Color Enhancement.

It is unnecessary to paint your walls black to reap the benefits of this guidance, unless you are currently in a Gothic phase of life and black serves such a mood. Instead, try a black frame around a picture, a black cloth on a horizontal Sacred Space, or the ever-popular black table. All of these examples are persuasive when given the intention that black increases the power of the flow of Career/Life Path.

Realize the Career/Life Path Area Affects the Fame/Reputation Area.

Remember the Opposite-Attract Law. It is influential and effective. Whenever you apply the Feng Shui values specified for an area, but are not satisfied with the results (Career/ Life Path in this sample), then journey to the room(s) which represent the opposite Bagua Value. Go to the room(s) and see what exists there. Fame/Reputation would be the opposite Value in this example. Make everything Feng Shui savvy in this area. Here is an example: You've completed the suggested cures for your Career/Life Path dining room. Yet, you still haven't realized your stated objective, a promotion at work. Before you use this book's pages to line the birdcage, go to the Fame/Reputation area of the home and office. This room is filled with boxes of things you're storing for the garage sale. Plus, you neglected to hold chi in this area. You figured it was just an extra room for stashing worthless, old stuff. The lack of Feng Shui treatment here affects your Career/Life Path region as well.

Know the Career/Life Path Area Symbolically Represents the Water Element.

In classes and workshops, raised hands rarely pop up when I make the above statement, a testimony to my clear, concise teaching style.

Use Water and Water Imagery.

A bowl of water, an aquarium, and a table fountain are all examples of Water. A mirror, a picture of a pond, and a frog are also Water imagery. Water and the image of Water are equally as potent. You may use either one or both. You do not need an ocean motif with fishes painted on the walls. If this raises your energy, however, get the paintbrush! If not, remember this Feng Shui interior design tip: Less is more. You could have a picture which features Water imbued with the intention to enhance your Career/Life Path. Another option is to choose a water fountain for the space with the intention that great things occur with your job. Or, you can simply focus your Water Element oomph on the Career/Life Path Sacred Space. Use of three-dimensional objects or images on this sacred area can ground your proposed goals into the physical. Some examples of Water Element expressions which would work well are a pair of seagulls, a small photograph of your favorite beach, or even a mirror.

Use Metal and Metal Imagery.

Metal is the Creative Element of Water. Its presence makes Water grow bigger. The symbolic abundance of Water helps every action you want to manifest in Career/Life Path. Metal examples include a copper vase, a silver necklace, money coins, and even a hunk of ore. Metal imagery might be a picture of a train or a metal building. Anything metal goes, just make it pop. Then Metal can perform its Element magic show. It makes Water larger and vast Water creates a big splash in your Career/Life Path.

Use the Wood Element to Weaken the Earth Element, if the Earth Element is Necessary in this Area.

Maybe you like having your gem collection in your Career/Life Path living room. It adds an ambiance. Besides, the minerals happen to raise your energy, even though the stones represent the Earth Element here. Earth dams Water. Given this is blocking the flow of Water in Your Career/Life Path, your favorite stones are hardly desirable here. You have three choices:

1. Move the rocks to a place in the dwelling where the Earth Element is represented or enhanced (Center of the Universe or Child/Creativity areas). Many clients prefer just to eliminate or move the offending Element. Sacrificing the precious stones for the good of your Life Path may not get

you any humanitarian awards, but it can produce the desired movement in your life. But is it mandatory? No.

2. Study the Make My Day, Everything's Okay Cure. Add an equal representational amount of the rest of the Elements to your rock collection. Into the living room comes your three-part photographic Water series. Next, in come your two fake palm trees. Wood and Water, check! Next, your armored knight statue. Metal is now accounted for in full gear. Finally, you add a few well-placed candles which represent the Fire Element. Now, you have atmosphere and proper Feng Shui Element relationships. But how does it rate on the mandatory scale? This scene has not yet been rated.

3. A final option to resolve this Element puzzle is to use your understanding of the Destructive Element Cycle to find a creative solution. Hence, the Elements are my Friends Cure. In this case, what weakens the Element Earth? Wood. Pay close attention to the simplicity here.

Acquire a piece or an image of Wood. One representation of the particular Element, used with intention, carries enough authority for a needed cure. Make sure, of course, the chosen piece of Wood, even a branch from an outside tree, makes you pop. Set your intention and place the Wood Element object near the Earth Element gem collection. Then perform the Elements Are My Friends Cure on page 156. Now, how does this rate on the "Feng Shui doesn't have to change my life completely to work meter?" Ding-ding-ding! Folks, we have a winner!

Avoid Death Imagery.

Feng Shui is unmistakable on this point. Do not have mortality images in the Career/Life Path vicinity. You don't want the demise of your career or your life journey. Instead, you want to support its growth with ease. Subsequently, the obvious death-by-funk items must go: the glow in the dark skull and cross bone wall picture, the collection of cool caskets, and the amazing, combination plastic tombstone and telephone. On a more serious note, many clients still hold on to the ashes of a loved one. The urn brings them comfort. This type of clutter symbolizes grief. Huge emotional releases are experienced by many who liberate their loved one, both figuratively and symbolically. This includes beloved pets. Spreading ashes of their adored encourages discharge of core sorrow. As a result, there is often emotional and spiritual rebirth.

However, such suggestions hardly make me popular. Here is the compromise. If the urn of ashes resides in the Career/Life Path area, or any other Life Value in the Bagua, move it to the Helpful People/Travel section. This advice does not apply when you have a Helpful People/Travel master bedroom or if a child or roommate occupies that space. In such a case, please use your intuition on the best placement of both the urn of ashes and the Helpful People/Travel Sacred Space. Helpful People/ Travel includes many things, one of them being the presence of Invisible Helpful Beings, Jesus, Mary, Quan-Yin, gurus, guides, angels, and so on. This area also includes your deceased beloved ones. Move the ashes to this section. This will symbolically place the dearly departed in a position of a guide and an aide. As assistance from the other side is given, profound healing occurs and catapults you into a higher emotional and spiritual level. Peace, then, brings the courage to let go further.

Next, become aware of the metaphors of death which are not so evident. Here is a scenario: Your Aunt Agnes, God rest her soul, died after a long, slow struggle with dementia. During her life, she was known for her iris gardens. For her funeral ceremony, your family invested time and money to fill the casket and to cover the gravesite with irises. In addition, every attendee was given a lovely iris. A beautiful send off, but now, hard as you try not to, whenever you see irises you think of your Aunt Agnes' funeral. That is death imagery. In such case, it would be unwise to plant irises outside a Career/Life Path window.

"But irises don't mean death to me! They make me think of new beginnings, spring, hope…"

Then plant them in containers to sprinkle your Career/Life Path kitchen with purple majesty. Make sure, however, the Earth is pierced by Wood. It is interesting to note how whatever the item, its effect on you is subjective, just like clutter. If Joe Blow also attended Aunt Agnes' funeral, and irises now make his skin crawl, he too needs something else to decorate his Career/Life Path. Since irises are a favorite item for Sara Sue, however, and they definitely raise her energy, the choice to have them becomes obvious. Whatever brings you down and makes you associate with mortality, whether it is a skeleton head or a stuffed toy kitty, it has no place in the Career/Life Path section of your home or office. Move it. Everything will be easier then.

Solve Job Related and Life Path Related Issues with the Career/Life Path Sacred Space.

The Sacred Space's purpose in every Life Value is to assist you with specific themes related to that particular part of your life. It is also the metaphoric antacid for Feng Shui situations which are giving you indigestion. You may feel a certain Life Value area is out of control and, consequently, so is that part of your life. The Sacred Space arrives to save the day.

Everything which has to do with work, be it parenting (labor of love), work in a fast-food chain, or some big wig corporate gig on the 30th floor of a high-rise, is dealt with in the Career/Life Path Sacred Space. In addition, anything to do with your Life Path, the desire for more ease, the resolve of a particular life challenge, or even the search for a purpose, is addressed here. Once again, the Opposite-Attract Law is both far-reaching and vital here. You may put your various intentions for Fame/Reputation into the Sacred Space of the Career/Life Path. Notice how this action increases both standards.

Because the Career/Life Path Value's elemental representation is Water, capitalize on this fact when you create this Life Value's Sacred Space. Use Water and Water imagery for power objects and power images. Avoid the use of Earth objects (rocks, crystals, or clay pottery) and Earth imagery (a picture of a desert or a Native American peace pipe) for power objects or images. Items which represent the Metal Element are good. Fire and Wood are neutral and, therefore, fine to use on this Sacred Space.

What follows are some statements for you to work with for your power objects and images as holders of your intention. With practice and confidence, you will soon create your own commanding visualizations, declarations, and intentions. Thoroughly reread everything in regard to the Sacred Spaces in the various sections of Part I to understand its character and use completely. Here are some affirmation guidelines which will help to create dreams, solve problems, and motivate positively whatever Life Value a Sacred Space represents:

1. Focus affirmations in the present tense (I am now feeling fantastic…) as opposed to a futuristic vision (someday I will feel fantastic). The latter goal is, consequently, always out of reach. Prepare as if it has already occurred.

2. Avoid negatives (I am not smoking anymore). Reword this with an optimistic angle. The subconscious mind does not acknowledge negatives so instead try, "I am now free of harmful substances."

3. Always add, "This or something better for the Highest Good now occurs," to the end of every statement. This power

punched proclamation is the instant barometer which takes away any manipulative tendencies as you create affirmations. (Joe loves only me forever. This or something better for the Highest Good now occurs.) If indeed Joe is your Highest Good true love, you can be confident of a soul mate. If not, be ready for the face to change.

4. When you are unsure of what or how to state your request, try this: "The Highest Good (Career...Reputation...Helpful Person, and so on) now comes to me." Since you already requested the Highest Good, it isn't necessary to add the barometer proclamation.

5. Remember all affirmations need to be backed up with visualizations to be truly effective. See yourself smoke-free, as well as state it. Give this focused energy to a power object or image on your Sacred Space.

6. Keep affirmations short and clear. A sentence or two is allowed. Long, drawn out affirmations confuse the subconscious mind. Such complicated concerns are better addressed with an outside source, such as a therapist.

SAMPLES OF CAREER/LIFE PATH SACRED SPACE AFFIRMATIONS:

• The Highest Good career now comes to me.

• My career of (insert here) is easily and effortlessly greater than ever. This or something better for the Highest Good now occurs.

• I am now promoted in my job at (insert here). I am loved and perceived as being hardworking, creative, and brilliant. This or something better for the Highest Good now occurs.

• Parenting progresses easily and effortlessly. The children mind and respect me. This or something better for the Highest Good now occurs.

- I now enjoy a pay raise and my boss, (insert here), finds my services invaluable. This or something better for the Highest Good now occurs.

- The Highest Good Life Path comes to me now.

- My Life Path is unfolding easily. This or something better for the Highest Good now occurs.

- I am remembered for having an easy life. This or something better for the Highest Good now occurs.

- I am famous in my career. This or something better for the Highest Good now occurs.

Clearly, the last two affirmations applied more to Fame/Reputation in honor of the Opposite-Attract Law.

DON'T:

Do Not Let Doors Stick in this Area of the Home.

If doors do not open easily in your home, then the "doors of opportunity" can't function without difficulty. In Feng Shui, doors which stick are equated with possibilities ground to a halt. Especially in your Career/Life Path, you want the doors of opportunity, favor, and blessings to open easily for you. Make it so with properly maintained doors. Careers take off when the door access into this area is fixed. In addition, if you happen to have a Career/Life Path front door which sticks, chi is discouraged from ever entering your space. The Mouth of the Chi is limping. Fix it. Open to the gifts which await you on the other side of the entry.

The Career/Life Path Value makes your universe expand in massively positive directions. It is a power spot, especially if it is also the front door. When the river of life flows and the doors of opportunity stay well-oiled, the sky is the limit.

SELF-KNOWLEDGE/WISDOM

Color: black, blue, green
Element: None

SELF-KNOWLEDGE/WISDOM

The following information is given to assist you in making the Self-Knowledge/Wisdom part of your home and office serve and heal you. Remember the Self-Knowledge/Wisdom has its own function in the house, whether it is used as a bedroom, kitchen, bathroom, or other. Be sure, consequently, to augment this area with the proper Feng Shui cures given in Part I. This is the place in your home where anything with the identity of self is addressed. Keep your Feng Shui detective vision razor-sharp. The more symbols you identify which limit you and which you subsequently remove, the more self-growth is assured.

Realize the Self-Knowledge/Wisdom Area Does Not Represent Any Element.

An Element representation does not exist in this area, even if you use colors here to remind you of an Element (such as red for Fire). Perhaps you place a mirror with the intention to symbolize Water, or use stones or crystals as a representation of Earth. You may use anything in this area as long as it raises your energy and follows the recommended Feng Shui treatments for the particular room in which this Life Value resides.

Know the Self-Knowledge/Wisdom Area Affects the Love Union/Marriage Area.

Here it is again, in town for an extended stay, the famous Opposite-Attract Law. If your addiction to chocolate-covered strawberries is not getting better and you have done all the recommended cures to the Self-Knowledge/Wisdom Life Value, including addressing the addiction issue on the Self-Knowledge/Wisdom Sacred Space, check out the Love Union/Marriage section of your dwelling. Your answer could be found in the condition of the room(s) which represents Love Union/Marriage—chi management, clutter check, Empowerment Positions, and so on. Make sure both Life Values have passed the Feng Shui litmus test.

Use Green, Black, and Blue for Color Enhancements.

As stated in the Career/Life Path portion of this book, it isn't necessary to paint your walls, in this example, vertical stripes of green, black, and blue. It is merely beneficial to know the color vibrations to add to the Self-Knowledge/Wisdom sector if you desire. You might choose to decorate with throw pillows which are blue, a floor rug which has green in it, and a black vase filled with flowers. Or, you could integrate these colors on the Self-Knowledge/Wisdom Sacred Space. Be sure every color you use in each Life Value makes you go pop. If you have a shade of green in the wall paper of a Self-Knowledge/Wisdom dining room which reminds you of a regurgitated salad, you are hardly bettering the self.

Solve Self-Esteem, Self-Image, Self-Worth, Study and Test-Taking Habits, Grief, Addiction, and All Spirituality Issues with the Self-Knowledge/Wisdom Sacred Space.

The deeper your understanding of its purpose, the more a Sacred Space can help you. Learn the Sacred Space principles! Because the Self-Knowledge/Wisdom area doesn't have an Element representation, there is no parameter on what you may use for power objects or images on this Sacred Space. Make sure, however, each object or image passes the clutter test. Remember any Love Union/Marriage objectives can also be placed on the Self-Knowledge/Wisdom Sacred Space. For the intentions vested in the power objects or images to be effective, you must also include the visualization or imagination component. Review, if need be, the affirmation guidelines given in this section under the Career/Life Path discussion for complete clarity.

SAMPLE STATEMENTS FOR SELF-KNOWLEDGE/WISDOM SACRED SPACE:

- The Highest Good wisdom now comes to me.

- My self-esteem is fantastic. This or something better for the Highest Good now occurs.

- My self-worth grows stronger every day. This or something better for the Highest Good now occurs.

- I easily study for my test in (insert subject here). I know the material well and my confidence is very high. This or something better for the Highest Good now occurs.

- My test-taking abilities in my (insert) classes are impressive. I score well and the test questions are easy for me to answer. This or something better for the Highest Good now occurs.

- I am (smoke, alcohol, drug) free. This or something better for the Highest Good now occurs.

- I eat nutritious, healthy foods for my body. This or something better for the Highest Good now occurs.

- I enter into only healthy, nurturing sexual relationships. This or something better for the Highest Good now occurs.

- I am now completely healed related to (insert name of person or situation that caused grief in body). This or something better for the Highest Good now occurs.

- I now have the Wisdom to understand why (name of mate) does what she or he does. This or something better for the Highest Good now occurs.

- The Highest Good Spiritual Path now comes to me.

DON'T:

Do Not Waste Mental Energy Trying to Figure Out the Element Laws When There Isn't an Element Representation in this Particular Life Value.

In this case, save your perplexity for another Life Value. The Self-Knowledge/Wisdom (Wealth/Power, Love Union/Marriage, and Helpful People/Travel) locale does not have any Element relationships to process during your weekly Feng Shui support group. Instead, discover the ease with which the Self-Knowledge/Wisdom area can accelerate your growth on every level. Development can be as simple as holding in the chi and creating a Self-Knowledge/Wisdom Sacred Space. It is an inexpensive adjunct to therapy sessions and countless times more effective than chocolate-covered strawberries at fulfilling your cravings.

FAMILY/HEALTH

Color: green
Element: Wood

FAMILY/HEALTH

With an understanding of this area, expect ancestor relations, health on all levels, and foundation money issues to transform positively. Find where the Family/Health area is located in your space. Perform the necessary treatments suggested for specific kinds of rooms and then follow up with the ideas listed below. Your family tree will thank you.

DO:

Know the Family/Health Area Represents the Wood Element.

In this Life Value, Wood is king. It relates to deep ancestral roots, deep pockets, and being deeply grounded.

Know the Family/Health Area Affects the Child/Creativity Area.

Your teenager is spending your savings and peace of mind because she insists, "If I don't have new clothes for school, I will, like, die." Keep the Opposite-Attract Law closely monitored to ensure ultimate success.

Use Green as a Color Enhancement.

Make sure the green you choose raises your energy. You want your spirit to revel in joy because you selected a shade which makes you feel fantastic.

Use Wood and Wood Imagery.

As you make Feng Shui adjustments to your home or office, you'll find that this is one of the easier Elements to work with. Any tall, pleasing to the eye plant which reminds you of a mini tree is a great representation of the Wood Element. In Feng Shui, the plant doesn't have to be real. If you have a brown thumb, find some high-quality silk plants. Feng Shui practitioners are fearful and don't like anything dead. So keep us happy. Furniture can also be made of wood, but keep your focus more on the accessories. Wooden sculptures, wooden frames around pictures (with images of more than one, please), and the wood branch collection are all great. A picture of a forest of trees, a wooden sculpture of two lions, wooden plates, and baskets are also examples of Wood imagery. Please remember to add the intention these Wood objects enhance in the Family/Health area. Otherwise, you might as well throw them outside to the birds. They will be more useful to them.

Use Water and Water Imagery.

Water feeds Wood—the effect water has on any living plant. It makes the plant grow. Water fountains, vases of water, pictures of rivers, ponds, and oceans are good here. Bring in the frogs, the wooden fishes, the sea gulls. Also invite the mighty "intention" into the vicinity, then keep an eye out. Your Family/Health world will be revolutionized.

Use the Fire Element to Weaken the Metal Element When it is Absolutely Necessary to Have the Metal Element in the Family/Health Area. Then Douse the Fire Element with the Water Element.

This concept is more complicated. Scenario 225: You have a lovely brass bed in your Family/Health bedroom. This love nest raises your energy, is placed in the Empowerment Position, and the mattress is only six months old. Perfect except... your money situation is not as good as it could be and you have a huge piece of Metal in your Wood bedroom. Metal cuts Wood. Regard closely the three choices listed in the Career/Life Path again. With a bit of detail modification, the selections would look something like this: You may move the bed to another room and buy a new bed elementally congruent with Wood (the "sacrificial wallet" decision). Or, you could apply the Make My Day, Everything's Okay Cure and bring a balanced representation of all five Elements into the room (the "I really don't know this Element stuff, so I better just be certain" decision). Or you could weaken the Metal with the Fire Element. Remember: Fire melts Metal so your Wood can grow. Employ this Element relationship knowledge with an adapted Elements Are My Friends Cure. Give a candle (or a Fire image) the intention of the Fire Element which weakens the Metal. This way, the bed may stay. But don't relax into that romance novel yet. Although unofficial, and not listed as a part of the Destructive Element Cycle, Fire burns Wood. Great if you are feeding the Fire. Not groovy if Wood is the main Element of an area. Think about ancestors, well-being, and foundation money eaten away by the blaze.

Here's an easy fix. Place a form of Water (or the image thereof) in the room near the Fire Element representation. Now comes the fancy Element tango: First, apply the Elements Are My Friends Cure, and then make the statement, "Now Fire melts Metal, so my Wood can grow, this or something better for the Highest Good now occurs" (cha-cha-cha). Then reapply the same cure; however, this time give intention power to Water and state: "Now Water douses Fire so my Wood can grow. This or something better for the Highest Good now occurs" (cha-cha-cha).

It is complicated but highly effective to go to this trouble to secure health on all levels, bring peace to your ancestral relationships, and have enough money to pay the bills. What these remedies will do for your heart, your wallet, and your genealogy is obvious to those who are dedicated to the science of Feng Shui. The results will speak for themselves.

Solve Ancestor, Health, and Foundation Money Issues with the Family/Health Sacred Space.

Take into account that a Sacred Space may function in the room which represents its Life Value or it can reside somewhere else in your home or office, especially when the Family/Health area, or any other Life Value, falls in a bathroom, a garage, a storage room, or a roommate's or child's room. Decide where you want it located and what you want on it. Make sure each Sacred Space you create respects the various Element representations of the Life Value it is created for as well as its Creative and Destructive Cycles. With a Family/Health Sacred Space, the more powerful choices are Wood and Water (and their images) as power objects. Avoid Metal and Fire Elements on or near your Sacred Space. You may place objectives which deal with Child/Creativity issues as well on this Sacred Space (Opposite-Attract Law). You have been introduced to intention; make it your lover.

SAMPLE STATEMENTS FOR THE FAMILY/HEALTH SACRED SPACE:

- I am healed and completely at peace with (insert family ancestor here). This or something better for the Highest Good now occurs.

- I have all the money I need. This or something better for the Highest Good now occurs.

- I am completely healthy on the physical, emotional, mental, and spiritual levels of my being. This or something better for the Highest Good now occurs.

- My relationship with my mother is excellent. She listens to my pain over the past and says the right things to help me let it go. This or something better for the Highest Good now occurs.

- My (insert physical or emotional ailment here) gets better and better every day. I am completely healed. This or something better for the Highest Good now occurs.

- I am at my ideal weight. This or something better for the Highest Good now occurs.

- I have enough money to pay for rent, food, and (insert name of bill here). This or something better for the Highest Good now occurs.

- The Highest Good Creativity is now here.

- My emotional health is at peace with (insert name of teenager or child here). This or something better for the Highest Good now occurs.

- My physical health easily allows me to get pregnant. This or something better for the Highest Good now occurs.

- My relationship with (insert name of child or pet) is healthy. This or something better for the Highest Good now occurs.

DON'T:

Do Not Have Fire Imagery, Candles, Incense, Matches, and Such Burning or Stored in the Family/Health Vicinity.

If you are uncertain about which Element an article represents, just ask yourself, "When I look at this (insert object here), I think of the (blank) Element." Here are some examples: A wooden fish? Water. A shiny, colored crystal? Earth. A locomotive train painted on a piece of tree bark? Metal; and so on. This same trick can be used when you enter a room with the walls painted a certain color. What Element does it make you think of? Given the Element for the Family/Health area is Wood, do not have a picture which depicts Fire (like a bursting volcano) or store all of your inferno supplies here, like matches and candles. Otherwise, you symbolically burn up your Wood stability.

Do Not Have too Much Metal in this Area.

I am really quite accommodating and believe in flexibility. But, my elasticity only stretches as far as my fuddy-duddy conservatism tolerates. After all, Metal is the Destructive Element of Wood.

You have been given a long leash in this Element gig. In return, please respect your Wood. Limit the Metal or cure it.

Do Not Keep Guns in this Area.

The language of symbols is not happy with a gun. Besides being made of Metal and called a Fire(arm), both of which are Destructive Elements to Family/Health, the meaning behind a gun, whether loaded or not, is counter-productive to loving family values, though protection and fear are valid issues. If you must have a gun, follow the cure below and keep it out of the Family/Health area.

SON OF A GUN CURE

1. *Placement of Object*

   Put the gun inside a wooden box, which is large enough to contain it easily when the lid is closed. Have four mirrors, one on each inside wall of the box, reflect back on each other. Also attach a mirror to the inside lid of the box to reflect down on the gun. Finally, attach a mirror on the bottom of the box, reflection face up.

2. *Visualize/Imagine the Action Already Occurring*

   See all gun vibrations being deflected back onto itself by the barrier of mirrors.

3. *State Your Intention Out Loud*

   "All sensations caused by the presence of a gun reflect back on itself. No unpleasant feelings escape from the box. The whole room where the gun box is kept is calm and peaceful. This or something better for the Highest Good now occurs."

The Family/Health Life Value has the potential to make your world a lot easier. Imagine: No parental stuff, great health, and enough money to handle all needed expenses. Does this guarantee your phantoms are gone and you reside on cloud nine? No, but Feng Shui brought into your Family/Health section provides you with a foundation to deal with the skeletons.

WEALTH/POWER

Color: red, blue, purple
Element: None

WEALTH/POWER

Any negativity in this world is because of a concurrent feeling of some sort of poverty-consciousness which surrounds such pessimism. Whether it is a dramatic act of violence like murder or rape, or a subtle transgression such as a statement misspoken toward a loved one, all deeds crafted without love also lack the feeling of abundance. This is not just about material possessions. To have more than enough of anything is a concept many do not truly believe or feel. This world overflows with non-abundant words, feats, and emotions. Consequently, it is imperative that you pay tribute to the Wealth/Power location in your home and office. It is the most dominant position in your entire dwelling. If it is not controlled by you because a roommate or child resides there and to move them to another location is not an option, perform the necessary cures covered in Part I in the section titled Living with Mates, Children, Tenants, and Guests. Also create a Wealth/Power Sacred Space to encourage your need of control in this area.

It is the Wealth/Power zone where all abundance is experienced. Sure, love is shaped in the Love Union/Marriage area and is

important, but the abundance of Love is found in the Wealth/
Power Life Value. You certainly claim your health in the Family/
Health section, but the abundance of health is located in the
Wealth/Power Life Value. Whether it is time, friendship, creativity,
a good reputation, and more, all feelings of more than enough of
any qualities can be found here. Don't take this place lightly. It can
transform your cosmos. Complete the functional room Feng Shui
cures suggested in Part I, then make use of the list below:

DO:

Know the Wealth/Power Life Value Does Not Represent Any Symbolic Element.

No Element hangs out here officially. Relax and breathe.

Know the Wealth/Power Area Affects the Helpful People/Travel Area.

Opposites attract and all that jazz. This particular connection is
a forceful duo. Have a clear current that runs between these two
places in your home or office. This can create dramatic, hopeful
enrichment.

Use Purple, Red, and Blue for Color Enhancements.

I once ordered a tropical dessert in Mexico. The contents boasted
mostly purple, red, and blue layers of Jello with whipped cream.
On the very top was a cherry. At the very bottom was a thin layer
of warm, semi-sweet chocolate. I ate the whole thing. It made me
sick. Translation: Sometimes, in a moment of flamboyance and
greed to have it all, we believe our gluttony is good. But multiple
colors will most likely make you ill, so avoid the use of such. It
is absolutely fine, however, to use these colors in tasteful, stylish
ways. More color does not bring in more prosperity, however.

If such was the case, I would be dyed purple from head to toe, wearing red long johns and flaunting a blue hair-do.

Know the Wealth/Power Life Value Responds Greatly to Moving Water.

Water, in the right places and in the right amounts, represents abundance in Feng Shui. Running water denotes plenty is always coming in—a lovely metaphor to embrace in the Wealth/Power area. Consequently, a table water fountain or a picture of a waterfall is strongly advocated for this area. Make sure the Water (or image of Water) has distinct moving water patterns. In other words, a picture of a pond is not as influential as a rushing, raging river. An image of a placid stream will not elicit the same results for your Wealth/Power section as a likeness of a Waterfall. May your Wealth/Power make an immense spray.

Consider your Wealth/Power Sacred Space as a similar example of running water. A poster of a scenic waterfall or of a wild torrid river is a great model of a vertical Sacred Space. Similarly, water fountains which reside on the floor, a table, or hang on a wall, are all perfect samples of objects which easily represent the Wealth/Power Sacred Space. When a fountain choice is made, it is best (in good taste, of course) to pick a metal fountain, since you know Metal easily conducts the continual flow of Water, the very thing you strive to create in symbols. However, if a metal fountain is hard to find or economically not possible, choose any fountain which raises your energy and has a pleasing, consistent water flow. Then use appropriate Elements to weaken less than stellar relationships. For instance, clay water fountains are very common, yet Earth dams Water. To easily remedy this, add a piece of Wood to the fountain landscape, visualize the necessary action and then state, "Wood weakens the Earth, so my abundant Water can flow. This or something better for the Highest Good now occurs."

Avoid Death Imagery.

The same ideologies presented in the Career/Life Path area also go here. You don't want the demise of your wealth in all things. If Egyptian archeology is your passion, and you just happen to have a collection of mummies, keep them out of the Wealth/Power section as well as the Career/Life Path region.

Solve All Prosperity Issues Including Money, Health, Time, Love, Creativity and Such, as well as Work Out All Authority Issues With the Wealth/Power Sacred Space.

The Wealth/Power Sacred Space is inarguably the most powerful Sacred Space. When guiding your life from a place of generosity and plentitude with all things, choices, decisions, even partners, both romantic and business, are selected from a more relaxed, evolved position. This is the Sacred Space where a balance between authority and power can be achieved, whether the opponent is a child, a pet, a roommate, or an unreasonable boss.

Because the Helpful People/Travel area is affected by the Wealth/Power section, it is also sound to place some of the Helpful People/Travel intentions on this Sacred Space. Although there is no Element representation in this area, incorporate the presence of running water. Have a figurine or picture of running Water, either as your Sacred Space or included in it. Similar to the developments of other Sacred Spaces, know your affirmation guidelines well (page 164). In addition, always put in the Three Secrets Reinforcement Ritual visualization for every assertion you place on a Sacred Space.

SAMPLE STATEMENTS FOR THE WEALTH/POWER SACRED SPACE:

- I have abundance in every area of my life. This or something better for the Highest Good now occurs.

- I deserve everything and get it easily and effortlessly. This or something better for the Highest Good now occurs.

- I have more than enough (insert anything here: money, time, self-esteem, love, helpful people). This or something better for the Highest Good now occurs.

- I have abundant (health, love, creativity). This or something better for the Highest Good now occurs.

- I attract (money, friends, wisdom) easily, effortlessly, and abundantly. This or something better for the Highest Good now occurs.

- I have the proper authoritative position with (name of child, pet, employee, roommate). This or something better for the Highest Good now occurs.

- I am fully self-empowered. This or something better for the Highest Good now occurs.

- I am abundant with Helpful People in my life. This or something better for the Highest Good now occurs.

- Because I attract so much money, I can easily afford (the trip to Hawaii, a new car, the down payment on the lovely house). This or something better for the Highest Good now occurs.

DON'T:

Do Not Let Poverty-Consciousness Rule Your Life.

The number of zeroes, or lack thereof, which appear after that initial figure in your bank account makes no difference. Poverty-consciousness does include the feelings of never having enough money, but it hardly stops there. Some clients have plenty of money, but don't believe abundant health, passionate equivalent love, or unbridled creativity is their Divine right. Thus, they entertain the ungracious guest named poverty-consciousness. In small enough workshops I have everyone express one thing which makes them feel wealthy in their lives.

"My children!"

"Health!"

"Incredible friends!"

"Free time!"

Hardly ever does an attendee express money abundance. Such awareness comes from a shift in perception. Genuine wealth is invisible to the eye. Never does the workshop end without everyone in the room, even if for just one moment, feeling truly rich.

Do Not Believe Anyone Can Take Away Your Abundance.

Ring! Ring!

"Hello?"

"Gabrielle, I can't finish my Wealth/Power Sacred Space! I wanted to put my jewelry box, which looks like a treasure chest, on a stand in my bedroom. I also thought I could keep the lid open and have my pearl necklaces spill out of it to show prosperity."

"Sounds good to me." I said to the client I had consulted with the previous week.

"…but I am afraid if I leave my jewelry accessible, my roommates might steal it."

"It's pretty unlikely your roommates or some other person who is visiting might rob you. Anyway, if they wanted it that badly, they could find where you had it hidden. The more important point is that no one can take away your true abundance or affect the source of that abundance. It isn't a finite thing. Generosity of spirit can't be stolen by anyone or anything."

There was a quiet, "Thanks," on the other end and then—Click!

Apparently the client got what she wanted. Abundance is a state of mind. Bigheartedness is free. If you do nothing else, tear out the Wealth/Power pages. Put them under your pillow. May osmosis move these ideologies through your skull and into your brain matter.

FAME/REPUTATION

Color: red
Element: Fire

FAME/REPUTATION

The Fame/Reputation Life Value is also a significant area. Each Life Value has the ability to renovate drastically the particular features it represents in your life. The Fame/Reputation section of your home and office determines your claim to celebrity as well as your character or, specifically, what you are remembered for in life. Examples are: always on time, a hard worker, or a good parent. Amusingly, even the less flattering chronicles are here. Perhaps you're remembered as: a self-centered pill, a brash, loud bore, or a lousy employee at work. For positive enhancements as well as improving negative repute, this is the area of concentration.

Market a business, product, or service here. Accordingly, both personal and business goal setting converge in this segment. Time travel and the art of time manipulation are also possible in this section. For instance, you want to be remembered for a great, long-term relationship with Ms. or Mr. Right, but you haven't even gone on a first date. In fact, you haven't even met this ninth wonder of the modern world. Use the Fame/Reputation Sacred Space to bring the future recognition of this liaison. You will find sample statements in this Sacred Space section. Be sure to employ the functional room cures listed in Part I, then apply the Fame/Reputation principles below.

DO:

Know the Fame/Reputation Life Value has the Symbolic Element Representation of Fire.

Fire is an aggressive, in-your-face Element. Not cuddly. Certainly not the type you'd take home for Mom to meet. It is perfect, however, for marketing a business and goal-setting and just the thing when you want to burn a path for the future. It also transforms the bad karma you picked up last week when you cut in line at the coffee bar.

Know the Fame/Reputation Zone Affects the Career/Life Path Area.

It is nice to get self-confident and say to yourself, "I know about the Opposite-Attract Law by now." Have a strong sense of self. This will take you far in your Feng Shui endeavors.

Use Red as a Color Enhancement.

Nothing about this area is shy. Even the color is bold. Choose subtle variations if fire-engine red shocks your chartreuse dining room. When used with intention, the red tones in pink can be a gentler way to introduce this color.

Use Fire and Fire Imagery.

Fireplaces, candles, and incense are examples of this hot, sexy Element as well as matches, lighters, and fondue warmers. Pictures of volcanoes, campfires, and other such blazing stuff are also celebrated in this area. It doesn't matter whether the candle is lit, the fireplace glows, or the incense smokes. All of these items represent the Fire Element. Use them. Then do a survey on how your Fame/Reputation results intensify.

Use Wood and Wood Imagery.

Want the flame to grow bigger? Here's your basic Girl or Boy Scout campfire lesson 1: Add Wood. The blaze increases and so does your reputation. You can use anything wooden to feed the Fire, including, but not limited to, branches, bamboo curtains, and such. Images of forests, statues of wooden creatures, and so on will work with intention. However, avoid driftwood, as it is Wood which has floated in Water.

Use Earth to Dam the Water in Fame/Reputation Areas Where Water is Unavoidable.

When Water hits the Fire flame, although the sound of sizzle is elegant, energy transfer happens, and the hiss turns into a messy white-black ash. Girl and Boy Scout campfire lesson 2: How do you put a Fire out? Pour Water on it. Water is destructive to Fire. Your marketing efforts, goal manifestations, and time travel dreams are stopped with the tiniest bit of H2O. Everything you want to accomplish, including how you are perceived by others, is determined in the Fame/Reputation section. Thus, it is very important to keep the flame eternal.

Ironically, the Fame/Reputation Life Value, which is located toward the rear of the house, is often times a host to various Water influences. Many clients have pools in their backyard right outside the Fame/Reputation back door. Others have hot tubs located in this area. Some people have bathrooms in this section. Water abounds. Fire sputters.

It is not practical, or even an option, to move the Water Element swimming pool, hot tub, or bathroom. ("Honey, we must drain the pool, fill it in, and plant Fireweed.") So the Sacrificial Wallet decision (you spend enormous amounts of money because of some obscure Feng Shui principle) is out. If you're not so sure about this Element stuff, your inclination might be to turn to the Make My Day, Everything's Okay Cure. It ideally should only be used when you actually understand the nature of the Element relationships. Intuition tells you a balanced representation of all five Elements is what is needed. Only then should you ever use this cure. Since you know that Earth dams Water, try this: Dam the Water so the Fire of Fame can burn. One raise-your-energy rock offsets the magnitude of Water in a pool. Place the boulder between your home and pool. You can use a raise-your-energy rock or other representation of Earth that is a bit smaller in scale for a hot tub. Place it somewhere near the tub. Finally, one small gem can sit next to the bowl of rice, corn, or salt on your toilet tank lid. For each example, visualize or imagine the action as if it has already occurred and say, "Now Earth dams Water so my Fire of Fame can burn. This or something better for the Highest Good now occurs."

Solve Motivation for Celebrity, Reputation Issues, Marketing, Goal-Setting, and Future or Past Time Travels in the Fame/Reputation Sacred Space.

Because a direct line exists between Career/Life Path and the Fame/Reputation Life Values, it is fine to place an intention related to a career issue on its Sacred Space. However, you must place the career intention on a power object or image which enhances the positive Elements for the Fame/Reputation area (for instance, your career intention is assigned to a candle—Fire). Always value the Element of the Sacred Space you are working with even if you focus on issues regarding the Opposite-Attract Law Life Value which honors a different Element. Thus candles and incense (or their images) are great power objects as well as Wood representations (actual or image). Any Water (actual or image) is destructive in this area. The Fame/Reputation Sacred Space works out integrity problems you experience at work or home. This Sacred Space also directs your goal expressions, marketing aspirations, and your (desired or real) celebrity status. Furthermore, you fashion dreams you want to see manifest or heal situations in your past which are less than favorable.

SAMPLE STATEMENTS FOR THE FAME/REPUTATION SACRED SPACE:

- My Highest Good fame is now here.

- I am famous. This or something better for the Highest Good now occurs.

- My reputation at work is fantastic. I am seen as a hard worker and an invaluable team player in the company. This or something better for the Highest Good now occurs.

- I easily manifest the goal of (insert here). This or something better for the Highest Good now occurs.

- I am remembered for being (a good friend, a respected parent, a dedicated athlete and so on). This or something better for the Highest Good now occurs.

- I am remembered for (put future aspirations here). This or something better for the Highest Good now occurs.

- I am remembered for (put past situations you want healed. Make sure they are stated from a perspective which creates what you wish had happened). This or something better for the Highest Good now occurs.

- My reputation is so awesome the Highest Good career comes to me now. This or something better for the Highest Good now occurs.

- I am remembered for having a flowing, easy Life Path. This or something better for the Highest Good now occurs.

DON'T:

Do Not Attach a Mirror Above a Fireplace which Exists in the Fame/Reputation Area.

Because the Fame/Reputation has the symbolic Element of Fire, no Water or its imagery should find its way into this vicinity. If you have a fireplace in this section, avoid the use of the Water-intended mirror or picture as it hinders the positive value of the flame. It is the flare of Fire which creates stability in this section. Perhaps even make the fireplace your Fame/Reputation Sacred Space.

Do Not Use Water or Water Imagery to Douse Symbolically the Flames of Fire.

The Water Element can very deceptively put out your Fame/Reputation Fire. Use your Feng Shui detective vision to find the objects and reflections which either remind you of, or absolutely represent, the Water Element. Eliminate them. If their removal is impossible, dam the Water with Earth.

The Fame/Reputation Life Value has the potential to motivate and manifest new, confident visions. The Feng Shui treated Fame/Reputation area assures this.

LOVE UNION/MARRIAGE

Color: red, pink, white
Element: None

LOVE UNION/MARRIAGE

This section in your home and office, in addition to the master bedroom and the Self-Knowledge Life Value area, is where you analyze your blessed love relationships. Because relationship love places high on the "pedestal of life," it is important this Life Value is handled with long, silk gloves. Business partners may also be intended for and addressed here. No matter what kind of relationship you have, a range of issues are involved. You might make decisions together, pay bills, coexist in the same space, plus deal with the small things like trying to fix the constantly running toilet. Apply the following Feng Shui treatments to the Love Union/Marriage Life Value. Both the wedding cake and the business deal will be sweeter.

DO:

Know the Love Union/Marriage Life Value Does Not Symbolically Represent Any Element.

Remember this is not an indication of importance for this Life Value or in any Life Values that don't have an Element representation. Plus you have greater flexibility with what you can use for Feng Shui cures.

Know Love Union/Marriage Affects Self-Knowledge/Wisdom.

This is not difficult to grasp. Self-Knowledge/Wisdom gives you insight into why your mate squeezes the toothpaste from the top end of the tube instead of the bottom or at least gives you the patience to deal. Good judgment resides here to see it for what it is, a silly, irritating habit, not a huge, "let's go to therapy," situation.

Use Red, Pink, and White for Color Enhancement.

Please know a roomful of red balloons, pink confetti, and white streamers will not bring the love of your life any faster. Business partners will not magically knock on your front door because you serve red, pink, and white sponge cake dessert in your red, pink, and white Love Union/Marriage den. Remember, less is more.

Solve Love Relationships as well as Work Partnerships in the Love Union/Marriage Sacred Space.

This is the perfect place to set intention for that special someone to materialize in your world—to fix communication snafus and increase passion with a current mate or to call in the business partner of your dreams. This area can also encouragingly change a current working relationship. Self-Knowledge/Wisdom intentions go on the Love Union/Marriage Sacred Space. There is no Element representation or cycle to include. But the Love Union/Marriage area responds to Fire. It symbolically denotes passion and excitement. This is a hot tip, not a requirement. The traditional cure to bring back spark to a passionless marriage is to hang nine firecrackers on a Love Union/Marriage wall. If this is not the chic style which complements your Frank Lloyd Wright house design, consider two candles (or the image of fire) on your Sacred Space. Use them as power objects or images with the intention to reignite a flame of desire between you and your beloved.

SAMPLE STATEMENTS FOR THE LOVE UNION/MARRIAGE SACRED SPACE:

- The Highest Good love now is here. (Place name of the person here) feels passionate and in love with me. This or something better for the Highest Good now occurs.

- Marriage is now the relationship (person of choice) and I desire. This or something better for the Highest Good now occurs.

- There is sexual attraction and passion back in my relationship with (name). This or something better for the Highest Good now occurs.

- The Highest Good partner for my (blank) business is now here. (Place name of choice) desires a working partnership with me. This or something better for the Highest Good now occurs.

- I have the wisdom to understand my mate's habit of (insert here). I am patient and at peace with it. This or something better for the Highest Good now occurs.

- I have the high self-esteem and self-worth needed to attract a mate who is my equal on all levels. This or something better for the Highest Good now occurs.

DON'T:

Do Not Use Your Desires, Fantasies, or Hopes to Manipulate Highest Good Outcomes.

Feng Shui is many things. It is the force which creates massive shifts in your life, manifest visions, and offers solutions to seemingly hopeless problems—a power tool which doesn't need electricity. Regardless, it is not an instrument to use in a scheming way. This is true for every Life Value in the Bagua, but because the Love Union/Marriage Life Value embraces relationship love, it is particularly compelling to forget about the Highest Good results in this area. Sexual energy is extremely gripping. Whether you are a man or a woman, the flow of sex-related chemicals which run through the body activates the reptilian brain. Therefore, what you might think is for the Highest Good may be far from the big picture vision reflected by the true Highest Good. Feng Shui attracts the Highest Good. If something or someone did not respond the way you imagined, it doesn't mean the Highest Good didn't occur, only that your idea and the "big picture" revelation were different. Ask for what you want, whether this request comes from a balanced, elevated place or not. But always remember to add, "This or something better for the Highest Good now occurs." This barometer phrase will keep you out of trouble. It always brings the most evolved Truth for the situation. Trust this fact and work with the results. Life changes in beautiful ways when a victim mentality evolves into the knowledge that the Highest Good always takes place.

Do Not Have Too Many Water Features in the Love Union/ Marriage Life Value.

True, there is no Element representation in this area. There is, however, another Element influence to acknowledge. Be aware of the Element Water in this Life Value. Water, in the right places and in the right amounts, stands for abundance. Yet Water can also have a negative symbology. Regard these examples: water stains on a ceiling from a leaky roof, plumbing problem, or a sink which drips. In Feng Shui, these types of Water presences are indicative of too much emotion. Therefore keep your water features out of the Love Union/Marriage Life Value. Who needs to create more emotional turmoil, even symbolically, with a mate? Move the water, repair the leak, or dam it.

Do Not Forget to Practice Proper Feng Shui Love Values Always.

Whether you are in a relationship or not, and even if you do not want to attract a mate, apply the Feng Shui Love Cures, specifically in the master bedroom, the Love Union/Marriage Life Value, and the Self-Knowledge/Wisdom Life Value areas. Have at least a full-sized bed placed in the Empowerment Position, a mattress which is not used and preferably a new one, a free and clear floor beneath the bed, two nightstands with two lamps, and pictures or sculptures of more than single images. Whenever a client is concerned that the simple arrangement of her or his space with proper love values will manifest a new main squeeze, please know these things:

1. Reactive fixation on any situation means there is work to be done in that precise area. The layout of furniture, the application of powerful love cures, as well as intentions placed on the Love Union/Marriage Sacred Space will never override the Highest Good in each situation. You will not find yourself involved in another relationship unless the big picture vision places it there. The recommended treatments do, however, activate the necessary healing to occur for true emotional balance and self-love.

2. The proper love setup is practiced for the creation of new love and improvement with any current relationship, but they also symbolically hold the space for grief, anger, betrayal, and low self-esteem to heal.

3. Love cures produce equilibrium in your life. Period. They don't exist for any other reason. Become balanced and stable. This gives you the ability to approach anything in your world.

The Love Union/Marriage Life Value is about dignity. Direct such insight to all parts of your life. Love has a way of being the greatest of teachers. How lucky we are to have such a blessed instructor in the upper-right-hand area of our home and office.

CHILD/CREATIVITY

Color: white
Element: Metal

CHILD/CREATIVITY

This Life Value area calls all the children and pets in your life. Don't forget the illustrious inner child who demands sweets on a regular basis. In addition, pregnancy yearnings are placed here. This is also the area where creativity has center stage. The Child/Creativity area is where you situate your intentions to be inspired. Inventiveness with marketing anything, business or art, takes place here as well. Imagination in every facet of life, in every manner, is focused here. In fact, complete the Feng Shui directives in this section first so the vision and ingenuity exist to Feng Shui treat the rest of the home or office. Perform the room function cures learned in Part I and then complete the following Child/Creativity Life Value cures. They provide help for the hormone-changing manic teenager and the potty-train-challenged puppy, as well as making ideas for your drawing class as simple as one, two, buckle my shoe.

DO:

Know the Child/Creativity Life Value Symbolically Represents the Metal Element.

What do you cherish the most in your life? Your children, your pets, and your treasures. They make you rich beyond measure. If you don't have children or pets, where does your fortune lie? What is your "pet" project or your brain "child?" This treasure, like gold coins, is represented by Metal.

Know the Child/Creativity Life Value Affects the Family/Health Life Value.

The piercing sound of a child's voice as she throws a tantrum sets the entire household on edge. The child's well-being plainly affects the Family/Health Life Value. For that reason, remember the Opposite-Attract Law.

Use White for Color Enhancement.

White is, of course, the best color for a painting canvas, or for the creations your young one does while hc eats, or wears, his lunch.

Use Metal and Metal Imagery.

An iron planter, a copper fruit bowl, and silverware are all examples of Metal. A picture of a train or of a knight in shining armor is Metal imagery. Apply these Metal objects and images to the Child/Creativity area. Encourage, with intention, the very things this Life Value brings you.

Use Earth and Earth Imagery.

Earth creates Metal. Any miner knows this truth. Rock, crystals, gems, and pottery are great examples of Earth. Pictures of the desert, scenes from a Native American village, and so forth are illustrations of Earth imagery. Whatever reminds you of the Earth Element is valid. With intention, bring in the Element Earth to boost symbolic growth of the Child/Creativity area.

Use Water to Douse Symbolically the Fire When the Fire Element is Unavoidable in the Child/Creativity Area.

Fire is the Destructive Element to Metal. Turn a hard Metal vase into liquid silver by holding a steady flame to it (Girl and Boy Scout lesson 3). Fireplaces notoriously exist in the Child/Creativity Life Value. Keep in mind, it makes no difference whether you ever use the fireplace or not. The language of symbols still sees Fire when its hearth-like structure lives anywhere. To move the fireplace to a more appropriate Bagua Element position is unreasonable. Perform this cure instead:

Above the hearth, attach a nice-sized mirror (or some other Water object or image). Give it the intention to symbolize Water. Then say, "Water douses Fire so my Metal stays strong. This or something better for the Highest Good now occurs." Although you have been cautioned regarding the over use of the Make My Day, Everything's Okay Cure, it is actually with fireplaces that I most often intuit the correct use of this cure. If you likewise have such a feeling, make use of this treatment in your situation.

Solve All Children, Inner Child, Pet, Conception, and Creativity Issues with the Child/Creativity Sacred Space.

Take into account all Sacred Space qualities. If you are still unsure, you know where to review. The Child/Creativity Sacred Space respects the Element Metal. So raise-your-energy Metal items or images are perfect power objects here. Earth and Earth Images are also effective for your Child/Creativity requests. Avoid Fire. Family/Health intentions can be concentrated on, but when you place Family/Health intentions on the Child/Creativity Sacred Space, you assign those intentions to Earth or Metal.

STATEMENTS FOR THE CHILD/CREATIVITY SACRED SPACE:

- The Highest Good now occurs for (insert name of child).

- The Highest Good now occurs for (insert name of pet).

- The Highest Good creativity now flows through me.

- (Insert name of child) is happy, healthy, and honest with me. This or something better for the Highest Good now occurs.

- (Insert name of pet) is housebroken. This or something better for the Highest Good now occurs.

- My inner child is completely healed and whole. This or something better for the Highest Good now occurs.

- I am creative in all aspects of my life. This or something better for the Highest Good now occurs.

- I am creative with (marketing of the new business, the solutions regarding the "X" project, my art work, my relationship). This or something better for the Highest Good now occurs.

- I become pregnant easily and the baby growing inside of me is healthy and feels loved. This or something better for the Highest Good now occurs.

- I creatively manifest all the money I need. This or something better for the Highest Good now occurs.

- Because I am healed with my (name of ancestor here), my inner child and my flow of creativity is healthy. This or something better for the Highest Good now occurs.

- I am healthy on all levels. This or something better for the Highest Good now occurs.

DON'T:

Do Not Melt the Metal Element with the Fire Element.

Admittedly, to change the chemical states of a material is a very hip, electrifying experiment. It's exhilarating to watch a solid metal transform into a bubbling viscous liquid. However, the Child/Creativity area is no place for a Bunsen burner. Do your research in another Life Value, one which supports flame.

Do Not Forget to Individualize Your Statements for the Sacred Spaces.

The sample statements given for each Sacred Space are just that, examples to get you started. They familiarize you with the ease of focused problem-solving and are a guide for possible intentions you might give a power object for that particular Sacred Space. By no means is every situation covered, so don't limit yourself to what you read in the sample statement list. Use them, instead, to educate. As the old adage promises, give a person a fish, and she will eat one meal. Teach a person how to fish, and she will eat for a lifetime. May you become a seasoned survivalist.

HELPFUL PEOPLE/TRAVEL

Color: black, white, grey
Element: None

HELPFUL PEOPLE/TRAVEL

Amazing feats, once considered impossible, happen when this zone is Feng Shui treated. Perhaps it is so definite because it is the

Opposite-Attract Law Value across from Wealth/Power, a section so important, it is given force by its very name. Another plausible explanation for the effectiveness of the Helpful People/Travel area is the special bonding agent which exists here. Both the three-dimensional Helpful People, like friends who listen to your heart and fix your leaking faucet, as well as those who help on the spiritual level (either embodied or not) such as guides, angels, gurus, and other such evolved beings, work their magic and give assistance in this area. Community is community, whether visible or invisible. Also, when you become a co-creator in your life and intentionally contribute proactive visions into the mix, you obtain a new look and, literally or figuratively, adopt success. True friends, 3-D or not, admire and support this type of attitude.

More Helpful People/Travel characters: bosses, clients, and customers. Superiors or employees can be helpful or hellish. You decide and create it. Helpful People/Travel also focuses on all forms of real estate concerns, whether you buy, sell, or rent. Houses, apartments, condos, and such are manifested here. Moreover, all legal issues are dealt with in this Life Value: helpful judges, attorneys, and juries. In addition, Helpful People/ Travel operates the balance of travel in your life. Perhaps you might travel all the time with your job or may just want to craft a vacation to Jamaica. In this area, you attain that symmetry. Complete the functional cures for the Helpful People/Travel rooms (see Part I). Next, carry out these cures for its Life Value. Then hold on for the ride of your life.

DO:

Know Helpful People/Travel Does Not Represent Any Symbolic Element.

The absence of an Element representation in no way slows down the potential for an outrageous passage. Both hands should clasp the railing. You are in the right area to pray. Requests are heard here. Do it now.

Know Helpful People/Travel Affects Wealth/Power.

Plainly you are of above-average intelligence. Just be sure you understand this Opposite-Attract Law. It ensures victory.

Use Black, White, and Gray as Color Enhancements.

Travel Advisory: Do not save the black-and-white layered dessert, now covered with grey mold, from the fabulous trip you took to Morocco last year because you want to manifest another one. True, these colors enhance your Helpful People/Travel section, but think again. A more useful and subtle application of these colors is a black throw pillow on a couch, a nice tone of grey paint on your walls, or even the intention to enhance the Helpful People/Travel area with existing white tiles on your floor.

Enjoy the Benefits of a Helpful People Box.

So you don't really believe in the science of Feng Shui? You just read this book because your mate promises to bake your favorite meal if you do. I love it when cynics progress to this particular segment as the Helpful People Box is more than just a container. It packs a powerful blow to the skeptic's belief systems because it works so elegantly and successfully! Eventually, the naysayer's lips quiver and tears fall at the mere sight of the Helpful People Box.

It is best for the Helpful People Box to be a nice-sized container. Do not choose a box which is small and compact in size. Symbolically it insists, *I need no help from the Highest Good Visible and Invisible Helpful Beings.* Conversely, don't make it as large as a trunk, which suggests little capability to complete or hope for anything without outside assistance. Have a container at least the size of a cigar box. You seek a balance here of inside help merged with outside aid. One nice-sized, any color, raise-your-energy wooden, metal, or glass (avoid plastic) box will do. With intention and choice this becomes the sacred first aid known in Feng Shui circles as the Helpful People Box.

You decide who gets put into the box. Be sure to write the barometer add-on to every slip of "dream" papers: "This or something better for the Highest Good now occurs." Suggestions to place in it are:

1. Names of people you have an advantageous and trustworthy alliance with and a desire for business and/or personal connections to continue with. (Bill is now a Helpful Person to me. This or something better for the Highest Good now occurs.)

2. Names of problem people you're not at peace with, whether it's their actions or their energy which warrants your suspicion. They will either become helpful or disappear from your life. Always remember to place them in the box in the Highest Good. Manipulation solves nothing. (Josephine is now a Helpful Person to me. This or something better for the Highest Good now occurs.)

3. Written statements about any needs which must be fulfilled by various skilled people. (The Highest Good painter, contractor, counselor, paying client… is now here).

4. Affirmations about new relationships—both business and personal—with whom you want to maintain and encourage a positive association. (Joan, my new friend; Bob, my carpenter; Sarah, a paying client… remain helpful to me. This or something better for the Highest Good now occurs.)

5. Notate real estate desires as if they have already manifested. (The Highest Good tenant for my Elm Street house; the Highest Good buyer; the Highest Good house or apartment rental… is now here.)

6. Any legal matter for which you want favorable results (The Highest Good Judge decides for my side; the Highest Good attorney, who is brilliant; the Highest Good Jury who understand my case... is here now.)

7. All mates, children, and pets (Johnny is a helpful person and takes out the trash without fuss. This or something better for the Highest Good now occurs.)

8. The desires for travel plans to go smoothly and the wish for certain destination spots to manifest easily. (Our trip to mother's is smooth, safe, and uneventful. This or something better for the Highest Good now occurs... I now create a trip to Europe without difficulty. This is something better for the Highest Good now occurs.)

9. Any situation which seems out of your personal control and you need outside spiritual assistance. (The Highest Good Invisible and Visible Helpful People are now here to assist me in easily and effortlessly resolving my issue of... financial stress, emotional instability, and so on.)

Because the Helpful People Box is so effectual, it is advised to periodically clutter-clear the slips of paper which fill it. After desires manifest, for instance, the Highest Good plumber has fixed your dripping sink, remove the small piece of paper and either burn it or throw it away. You will be surprised how often and how many dreams come true with the supreme aid of the box. Because of this potency, clients often make the box their Helpful People/Travel Sacred Space. It is easy to write down desires and intentions for actions you want to manifest. Results are always impressive when you take the time to write or type out desired outcomes.

Solve Issues Regarding All Real Estate, Legal Situations, Bosses, Patrons, Clientele, Invisible and Visible Aid, As Well

As the Balance of Travel with the Helpful People/Travel Sacred Space.

Since there is no Element representation in Helpful People/ Travel, the Sacred Space has few rules, besides affirmation laws, the barometer proclamation, and the Opposite-Attract Law. Regardless of what you have been told, Feng Shui is meant to serve you, not the other way around. If you want, it is absolutely fine to select another vertical or horizontal Sacred Space other than the box for Helpful People/Travel. But consolidation breeds simplicity, a great offspring.

SAMPLE STATEMENTS FOR THE HELPFUL PEOPLE/TRAVEL SACRED SPACE (BOX):

- The Highest Good (painter, friend, lover, carpenter, patron, lawyer, house, tenants, dentist, doctor, and so on) is here. This or something better for the Highest Good now occurs.

- (Name of person or company) is now a helpful person (entity) to me. This or something better for the Highest Good now occurs.

- (Name of problem person or company) is now helpful to me. This or something better for the Highest Good now occurs.

- My attorney, judge, and jury are helpful to me. This or something better for the Highest Good now occurs.

- (The Health Department, building inspector, electrical inspector, permit department, plumbing inspector, and so on) easily and effortlessly pass my house, office, or business investigations. This or something better for the Highest Good now occurs.

- My boss is now a helpful person to me. This or something better for the Highest Good now occurs.

- I have all the Highest Good paying customers (clientele) I could possibly want. This or something better for the Highest Good now occurs.

- I now easily manifest the trip to (name of place here). This or something better for the Highest Good now occurs.

- I travel less with my job. I am stable and important in the home office. This or something better for the Highest Good now occurs.

- The Highest Good Invisible and Visible Helpful People are now here to assist me in easily and effortlessly resolving the issue of (place an issue which seems impossible to solve here—bigger than you.)

- Abundance of all things is here. This or something better for the Highest Good now occurs.

- With the help of the Highest Good Invisible and Visible Helpful People, I now have the proper authority position with (child, pet, employee, tenant, and so forth). This or something better for the Highest Good now occurs.

After you become accustomed to the Helpful People Box, you will find yourself more relaxed around the formality of it and may start to put in the names of obscure and brief connections to authority figures (like college admission specialist, insurance agents, and so forth). Creativity is only limited by the name and statement you choose to put on the paper, in the Highest Good. You will soon discover the grace rendered by High Beings when they are certain of your requests.

RITUAL FOR EACH HELPFUL PEOPLE BOX REQUEST

1. Placement of Object

Write or type your desire on a slip of paper. Always end the statement with, "this or something better for the Highest Good now occurs."

2. Visualize/Imagine Action Already Occurring

See the manifestation of your desired outcome.

3. Speak Intention Out Loud

Say what you have written on the slip of paper. Then place it in the Helpful People Box.

Prepare for the miracle.

DON'T:

Do Not Forget to Breathe.

When females in every culture give birth, deep breaths are encouraged. Delivery is hard work; it is called labor. Feng Shui likewise supports the deliverance of change, joy, and proactive thoughts on a regular basis. Whether the end product is a screaming, wiggling, gorgeous little being whose nursery shall never be placed in the Wealth/Power Life Value of your home, or a new way to exist in the world—thank you Feng Shui treated home—to give birth is a brutal exertion but worth every drop of sweat and toil.

CENTER OF THE UNIVERSE

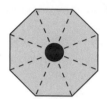

Color: yellow, earth tones
Element: Earth

CENTER OF THE UNIVERSE

The Center of the Universe sounds like it is vast and far away, but Feng Shui is not a sequel to an outer space movie. In Feng Shui, Center of the Universe exists in the very nucleus of the Bagua. Because it rests there, it naturally touches every other Life Value and by default, focuses on any of the challenges which fall into other Life Values. This is why the Center of the Universe is the simplification and centralization sphere.

Using Family/Health as an example, suppose you have issues with your mother, you were told by the doctor you need knee surgery, and there is not enough money to pay the bills this month. Of course, there are functional cures that you can make. Even still, in this case, your Family/Health Sacred Space is jam-packed. Here is a possible remedy. Move the health issues to the Center of the Universe Sacred Space. Intend your health solutions there. You can leave the ancestral and money issues with the Family/Health Sacred Space. You can simplify an area which has many issues when you move one of the Life Value problems to the Center Sacred Space. In this way, you can focus completely on each matter with full awareness. Subsequently, problems bundled into an overwhelming trauma can be sorted out and handled with consciousness. Solutions occur in a straight-forward manner when ease is the main ingredient in problem-solving.

In addition, the Center of the Universe can be used to centralize your intentions, whether for the day or for a lifetime. Suppose you want more clients in your consulting business. Such a desire is a Helpful People/Travel concern. First complete the numerous cures already mentioned in previous sections of this book, then write your intention on a slip of paper: *I now have all the Highest Good paying clients for my consulting business that I could possibly want.* This desire gets put into the Helpful People Box. Next go to the Center Sacred Space and focus the same intention on a power object honoring the Earth Element, a candle perhaps. You visualize or imagine your outcome and say: *I now have all the Highest Good paying clients for my consulting business I could possibly want.*

The Center of the Universe Sacred Space can have many different Life Value intentions on it. It is not unusual to solve Helpful People, Wealth, Health, and Career issues all at the same time. Think of Center of the Universe Sacred Space as an all-you-can-eat buffet. It is a symbolic smorgasbord with potential to put you into a peaceful, harmonious existence. To actualize this, perform the cures in this section, along with any functional treatments discussed in Part I.

DO:

Know the Center of the Universe has the Symbolic Representation of the Earth Element.

The Center of the Universe touches every Life Value. It is located in the nucleus of the Bagua and has a centering effect on each of its eight parts. No Element has such a solid and practical foundation as Earth and no Life Value provides such groundwork to resolve issues as the Earthy Center of the Universe.

Know the Center of the Universe Touches and Affects Every Life Value.

The Center of the Universe symbolically and physically has contact with each Life Value and, therefore, with every situation in your Universe. Imagine a neighbor who knows all of your business, only this one has a direct relationship to the Higher Power, or your Spiritual Source, and wants to help you.

Use Yellow and Other Such Earth Tones as Color Enhancements.

If you are unclear what colors this area responds to, think desert. There you have it.

Use Earth and Earth Imagery.

Stones, crystals, bushy plants, terracotta tiles, and Native American vases are examples of what works here. Also, consider pictures of the desert and other such earthy landscapes. Remember to ask yourself what Element an object reminds you of. If the answer is Earth, it can be used.

Use Fire and Fire Imagery.

Fire creates Earth, the ash after the bonfire. Use the Fire Element to increase the effectiveness of Center of the Universe Earth intentions. Revisit the samples of Fire and Fire Imagery in the Fame/Reputation Life Value section.

Use Fire to Burn the Wood if the Element Wood is Unavoidable in the Center of the Universe.

Wood pierces Earth. Have one candle, or a picture of a volcano, and with intention state, "Now the (candle, the energy of the volcano, or so on) has enough influence to burn Wood, so my Earth is stable. This or something better for the Highest Good now occurs." This routine is probably feeling familiar by now.

Use the Center of the Universe Sacred Space as a Simplification and Centralization Problem-Solving Tool to Decipher Many Different Life Value Issues at the Same Time.

The Center of the Universe Sacred Space is the star of the self-improvement show. Respect the Earth Element and bow deeply to the Fire Element. Choose representations of these Elements for your power objects and images. Cut down or burn the Wood Element so it doesn't stop the dream intentions of the various Life Value concerns placed here. Remember, it doesn't matter if another Life Value honors a different Element on its Sacred Space, when it is moved to the Center of the Universe Sacred Space, the Earth Element and its Element relationships are the ones acknowledged.

Many clients have expressed concern because their literal Center of the Universe is a hallway or the place where two walls corner together. They have no room for a Sacred Space. This is where the vertical Sacred Space works. One raise-your-energy picture which demonstrates Earth and/or Fire is perfect. Also choose an image which avoids the Wood Element. Don't have a picture, for instance, with a forest in the background. Select different images within the illustration to place your intentions on for specific requests. When you don't have a huge amount of space, one chi catcher for the Center and its corresponding Sacred Space is all you need.

Another solution is to place the Center of the Universe Sacred Space in some other area, your bedroom or living room for instance. Follow all Sacred Space protocols and make sure to hold in the chi for the Center of the Universe in the actual place it is located. It can share intention with another Life Value chi catcher or have its own bead hanging from the ceiling in a hallway, for instance.

Realize the following statements assume such issues are addressed in their particular Life Value and then are also given attention on the Center Sacred Space. Here are some ideas to help you understand the role of the Center Sacred Space. Take the suggestions, then alter them to fit your needs.

SAMPLE STATEMENTS FOR THE CENTER OF THE UNIVERSE SACRED SPACE:

- The Highest Good (Career, Life Path, Self-Knowledge, Wisdom, Health) is now here.

- I have perfect health with my (insert health challenge here). This or something better for the Highest Good now occurs.

- I have fantastic (creativity, love, fame, helpful people and so on). This or something better for the Highest Good now occurs.

- The Highest Good Invisible and Visible Helpful People are now here to assist me in easily and effortlessly resolving the issue of (insert challenge here). This or something better for the Highest Good now occurs.

- (Insert name of beloved here) wants to marry me. This or something better for the Highest Good now occurs.

- (Insert name of your child) develops into a great person on all levels. This or something better for the Highest Good now occurs.

- I have abundance in all areas of my life. This or something better for the Highest Good now occurs.

DON'T:

Do Not Place Wood in the Center of the Universe.

Wood is the Destructive Element to Earth. If you must have Wood, especially if it is a part of your Center Sacred Space, burn it with Fire or cut it with Metal.

Do Not Make the Center of the Universe More Important than the Other Life Values.

It's true with a name like the Center of the Universe, it becomes easy to make this Life Value just that. It is also likely you, your teenager, your mate, or even your pet, think they are the Center of the Universe. But the Center of the Universe is a symbolic gesture only. It touches and affects all the Life Values in the Bagua, so please don't ignore it. Give it credence. However, do not make it the end all of civilization as you know it.

Do Not Believe the Existence of Sacred Spaces in Your Home Will Make All Your Problems Disappear.

Of course, there is no trouble if this book becomes an overnight bestseller. The front page of the *New York Times* newspaper announces: Feng Shui Sweeps the Nation: The Latest Self-Help Panacea! But with such idealism, here's a truth to consider always: Part of the challenge and glory of playing the Life Game is to master it. The only way you become proficient at anything is to engage in it, to get your hands dirty in the mud. Life improvement takes work and dedication. Feng Shui Sacred Spaces are devices which help you to become a specialist in this spirited match of existence. Learn to determine which Life Value can best be used to address a particular problem. Go to its Sacred Space and do your magic. The problems nonetheless come—one of the clues you are still alive and kicking. However, the proactive use of Sacred Spaces takes the empowerment of Self to new levels.

STILL MORE FENG SHUI BOOTY: RELAX, THERE'S A CURE FOR ANYTHING!

The following cures can be applied to any relevant section of your home and office. Enjoy them as much as you make deep, cleansing breath a part of your every moment experience.

DO:

Feng Shui the Whole Building First, Then if Desired, Feng Shui Each Room Individually.

Many clients desire to Feng Shui every last cell of their space. To look at the microcosm inside the macrocosm of Feng Shui is perfectly reasonable and of use. First, however, Feng Shui treat the entire building of your home or office before you start to focus on the possibility to direct all nine Life Values to one particular room!

Exceptions to this rule are:

1. An office space you rent or occupy in an office complex. It is not an option to Feng Shui treat the entire building, although figure out what Life Value your office resides in within the building and whether or not the building shape is holistic. A complete square, rectangle, or circle is preferred.

2. You rent a room or live with parents who have little or no interest in the art of Feng Shui.

3. You share a multilevel family house and your upstairs and downstairs neighbors do not care about Feng Shui bathroom protocols, Empowerment Positions of beds, desks, stoves, and so forth.

4. You rent an apartment or condo in a large complex. Concentrate just on your living area. Again, figure out which Life Value of the building you reside in and whether the building shape is holistic as noted above.

With the examples given, draw a plot of the part of the building where your home or office is situated and then apply the Bagua Life Values. A Feng Shui treated space is a Feng Shui treated space, no matter how big it is. If your particular universe is not as large as the universe of the family down the street, know that their Feng Shui treated home is not more powerful. Interestingly, a large room does not require a larger chi catcher to be effective. The secret is intention. For instance, if in your four-room apartment, you intentionally honor the functional room cures for all nine Life Values and have nine Sacred Spaces to represent each of them, your breathing space is just as potent as the mansion which practices Feng Shui across town. It is a relief to know with some things in life, size just doesn't matter.

For the rest of you, apply the Bagua Life Values to a plot drawn of your entire home and/or separate office. Use the front door as the architect intended to figure out the positions of the Life Values in your space. When the Feng Shui treatments to the overall dwelling are completed, focus on individual room Feng Shui if you desire. Often clients concentrate on a particular room without a complete Feng Shui perspective first. This is not recommended, but curious nonetheless. Determine what Life Value the room in question stands for in the Bagua. Usually there are major issues in this area of life. To discover the Life Value placements in an individual room is easy. Superimpose the Bagua over the plot of just the room, using the door which opens into the room as the main door, or Mouth of Chi. See diagram L-1 for visual clarity.

LIFE VALUE PLACEMENT IN A ROOM (L-1)

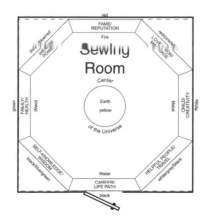

Then as you look into the room from the door, as you would the front door of the house, the door can fall in one of three Life Values—Self-Knowledge/Wisdom, Career/Life Path, or Helpful People/Travel.

After you have properly Feng Shui treated your whole house and want to work even deeper on an issue, it is effective to try this trick of the Feng Shui trade. Let's say you are concerned with a love relationship issue. The first thing you do is check your handiwork on the room function and Life Value cures in the master bedroom, the Self-Knowledge/Wisdom room, and the Love Union/Marriage room of the house. Be sure you have also created a Love Union/Marriage Sacred Space. Only then would you determine where the Love Union/Marriage area resides in each of the rooms, specifically, and most important, the master bedroom. Additionally, locate the Love Union/Marriage area in the Love Union/Marriage and Self-Knowledge/Wisdom Life Value rooms of the home or office. After they have been found, place an object or image in that area and, with the Three Secrets Reinforcement Ritual, acknowledge positive awareness has been positioned in all the areas which represent Love Union/Marriage in all ways. This is called "The Bases Are Loaded Technique." See diagram L-2 for visual clarity.

BASES ARE LOADED TECHNIQUE (L-2)

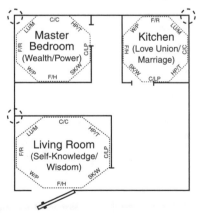

Use it for any Life Value issue (and its Opposite-Attract Law Life Value) you want to spotlight. This does not take the place of a Life Value Sacred Space, nor is it necessary to create a Sacred Space in the relevant area of each room to authenticate this procedure properly. Remember to respect the Element relationships always and that *less is more*. May you score a home run with this technique!

Place Mystical Alarm Systems on All Doors Which Lead to the Outside.

"If someone wants to get in your house, no state of the art security system can keep them out," declared a workshop participant.

"Actually, there is one thing which will keep all intruders out," I said.

"Oh, really… what?" Her eyes danced in pure delight. She was certain she would hear about the latest foolproof, underground, sonic, interstellar, satellite home security system. Her excitement was evident.

"It is called the mystical alarm system."

Her gleeful eyes changed to disdain. Yet here is the fact. There is a phenomenon in China where if a shop or house has a mystical alarm system, break-ins do not occur. It is strongly recommended you put this alarm on every door (including sliding glass doors) which leads to the outside, be it a passageway to the yard, the garage, the deck, the screen room, or any such area considered to be exterior to your home or office. Thankfully, this effective mystical alarm system is easy on the pocketbook. Obtain some red cord. The color red is important in this particular cure because red is aggressive and protective. If you have an unchangeable aversion to red, however, choose a cord of another color which represents safety and protection for you. Next, find a small bell, even a jingle bell, the red cord can easily slip through. One bell is enough, although some clients hang a multitude of bells in odd increments up to the power number of nine on the cord. See diagram L-3 for examples.

MYSTICAL ALARM SYSTEM
SAMPLES (L-3)

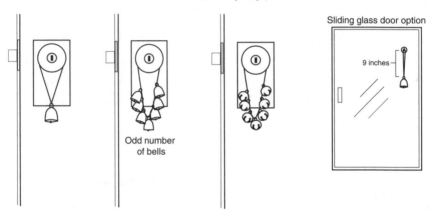

Odd number of bells

Sliding glass door option

9 inches

Then hang it on the inside doorknob, or some creative adaptation if a doorknob doesn't exist. You can even make the loop exactly nine inches around. See diagram L-4 for clarity.

(L-4)

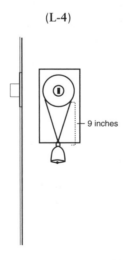

9 inches

It is not necessary for the bell(s) to ring when the door is opened, but many like this added security. And, what is the mysterious feature which makes the mystical alarm system so powerful? The workshop partaker raises her head expectantly. Intention.

SAVED BY THE BELL CURE

1. *Placement of Object*

   Position a red cord loop with at least one bell that hangs from it around the inside door knob for any door leading to the outside.

2. *Visualize/Imagine the Action Already Occurring*

   See all intruders staying out of your private space, home, or office, be it a thief or someone who poses as a friend.

3. *Speak Your Intention Out Loud*

   "I now am safe. This or something better for the Highest Good now occurs."

Fascinatingly, if you have a door leading to the outside in the Love Union/Marriage area of your space, a mystical alarm system declares new love is safe love. You can make such symbolic gestures with any Life Value rooms which have a door leading to the outside. "It is now safe for the doors of opportunity of Love Union/Marriage, Career/Life Path, Helpful People/Travel, and so on, to open easily and effortlessly for me. This or something better for the Highest Good now occurs." With mystical alarm systems and proper intention, all doors of opportunity in each Life Value have the potential to be secure. If you are violated in any area, even after the installation of the mystical alarm systems (a very rare, but possible occurrence), it is then that an understanding of the Highest Good reason behind this negative encounter must be explored. Let go of any inclination to fall back into a victim stance in these instances. When you stay empowered, you discover the beneficial parts to whatever episode that might transpire in your life.

Use Chimes to Stimulate the Chi in Any Life Value Area.

Wind chimes can be hung inside the house with the intention to stimulate chi in a certain Life Value. A particularly good placement is near the Sacred Space of a Life Value or, if possible, hang from the ceiling in a corner where the specific Life Value exists. See diagram L-5.

CHIME IN TIME CURE (L-5)

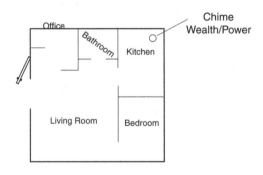

For instance, the desire to increase Highest Good paying clients for your massage business can be activated by hanging a wind chime, or even a mobile, suspended from the ceiling somewhere in the Helpful People/Travel area of your home. With intention, this stimulates the chi to support the realization of your desire for more patrons. Chimes symbolize movement, even when the wind is not blowing.

It's important to understand the difference between a chi catcher and a wind chime. The chi catcher holds the life force of the qualities of a Life Value inside your room, space, and world.

This action is necessary to manifest any expectations you have regarding this Life Value. A chime takes the life force now being held inside the space and motivates it to action. However, this specific treatment should be used with discretion, much like the Make My Day, Everything's Okay Cure. To have a wind chime in every room and for each Life Value is unrealistic about the things you want to create in your life. In fact, experience no more than one or two chimes which hang at a time, with intention, in different areas of your home and office. For example, when you write a book, suspend a wind chime in the Child/Creativity area; when you desire the Highest Good mate, hang an intentioned wind chime over the Love Union/Marriage section; when you seek to improve your health, dangle it over the Family/Health sector. Do not overuse the chimes to encourage too much movement at one time in your life. Symbolic acts can be vigorous and fierce. Treat chimes like strong medicine, a little goes a long way.

A CHIME IN TIME CURE

1. *Placement of Object*

   Decide which Life Value contains the quality you want to stimulate. Suspend a wind chime from the ceiling either near that Life Value Sacred Space or in the actual area in the home or office where the Life Value exists.

2. *Visualize/Imagine the Action Already Occurring*

   Picture the desire you have in this area of life becoming activated and encouraged and see it as already manifested.

3. *Speak Your Intention Out Loud*

   "The wind chime now stimulates and activates the chi to manifest my desire for (blank). This or something better for the Highest Good now occurs."

Though rich, first-rate chocolate is satisfying and compelling, it is addicting as well. So is the Chime in Time Cure. Treat with care.

Avoid the "Chinese Death Bed."

Whenever I want to boost my "good Feng Shui teacher" ego, I merely have to say the sentence, "Your sex life can be negatively affected by having the Chinese Death Bed placement." Immediately, dreamy stares looking off in space become concentrated gapes directed toward me. Pencils which doodle shapes and spirals that in no way correlate to symbols of the English language stop completely.

In China, when people go to a funeral home to pay respects to someone recently departed, they enter into a room with the coffin directly in front of the door. The corpse rests in peace with feet facing the entrance. See diagram L-6.

CHINESE DEATH BED POSITION (L-6)

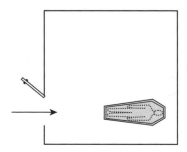

In Feng Shui, this same idea applies to the bed position in the master bedroom. This particular recommendation pertains only to adults. The child's bed position, beside the empowered arrangement, needs not be addressed. If a bed is in the Empowerment Position, which allows the occupants of the bed to see the door when their heads are on their pillows, it follows that the feet face the door at some angle. The Chinese Death Bed position occurs only when the feet are directly across from the entrance to the room. When a bed is in such a position, the sex life activity between partners can drop to a low or never frequency. See diagram C-1, page 63.

Like every Feng Shui belief, to have the bed in a Chinese Death Bed position doesn't automatically assume your nights with your beloved are passionless. It does, however, mean the "hot and heavies" are that way because you push against currents instead of letting the natural flow of the Universe take effect. Having the bed in the Empowerment Position still takes precedence, even if it's only possible when the bed is directly across from the door. In such case, the following cure for Chinese Death Bed should be employed.

LOVE BUNNY CURE

1. *Placement of Object*

   The same chi catcher used to hold Life Value chi inside the space now has two assignments. Be sure to suspend the chi catcher between the bedroom door and the empowered bed. First place intentions for it to hold in chi. Then add the intention for this cure so the chi catcher now also acts as the protector.

2. *Visualize/Imagine the Action Already Occurring.*

   See the chi catcher create a force field which extends from the ceiling to the floor of the room. It stops all direct energy from reaching the bed. Imagine this energy in the form of darts which come at the occupants of the bed.

3. *Speak Your Intention Out Loud*

   "Our intimate time is healing, regenerative, and passionate. This or something better for the Highest Good now occurs."

Cure Sha Corners.

Chi is a magical, amorphous substance which reflects back exactly what it discovers on its journey. For instance, if you don't have an obvious entrance, chi shall pass you by. If your environment is blocked with furniture or clutter, chi too refuses to move. If your atmosphere is free, clear, and flowing, so is chi. Chi is like instant soup. To get the full effect and enjoyment of the tasty powder, you must add water to make it a broth. Similarly, combine empowered arrangements with life force chi and witness the exaltation of your space.

Because of chi's reflective nature, it is valuable to rid the surrounds of all dangerous sha corners so the quality of the chi in your environment is safe, nurturing, and healthy. A sha is created when two flat surfaces come together at a point, whether this translates into a sharp edge or a corner which juts out from a wall. See diagram L-7.

A sha corner is important to locate and correct in Feng Shui because chi becomes sharply shaped when coming off these corners. In fact, another term for chi which bounces off of these sha corners is poison arrows. Pay attention to the imagery of the name, poison arrows. A poison arrow which heads into a wall is of little concern. A poison arrow which is aimed at an inside entrance to the home, office, or a room, is of great concern as it affects the feeling of safety in one's space. Also of interest is the poison arrow which points towards desks, beds, dining rooms, stoves, and so on. If there is an area where you spend a large amount of time and poison arrows are directed toward its general vicinity, this constant energy barrage could affect your sense of inner peace and focus. See diagram L-8.

EXAMPES OF SHA CORNERS (L-7)

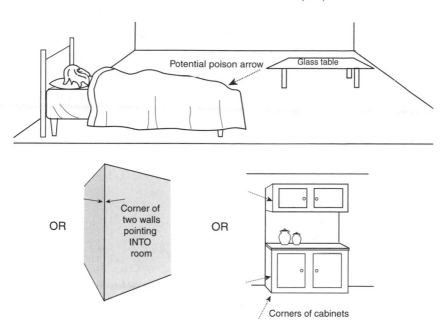

Potential poison arrow

Glass table

OR

Corner of two walls pointing INTO room

OR

Corners of cabinets

EXAMPLES OF POISON ARROWS THAT
NEED TO BE CURED (L-8)

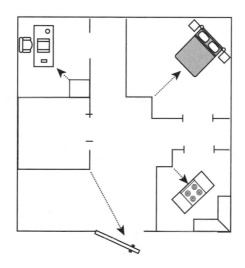

Thankfully, this less than ideal chi state is easy to fix. The most beneficial thing is to go around your home and office and look with Feng Shui detective vision for sha corners. If the poison arrows are directed toward a wall or any other unimportant place, disregard. However, if a poison arrow is aimed at potent places or its presence affects your sense of calm, perform this cure. See diagram L-9 for clarity of less important sha corners.

DO NOT WORRY ABOUT THESE TYPES
OF SHA CORNERS (POISON ARROWS) (L-9)

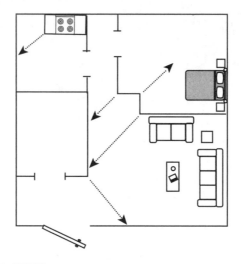

SHARP SHOOTER CURE

1. Placement of Object

From the ceiling directly in front of the sha corner, suspend a crystal (or chi catcher) hung by nine inch fishing line or thread. Options are to suspend a plant or place a ribbon which hangs down about nine inches to cover the corner.

2. Visualize/Imagine the Action Already Occurring

See the object suspended from the ceiling as having enough authority to act as a force field buffer which extends from the top of the corner, from the ceiling, all the way down to the floor. It completely softens the sharp edge and the quality of the chi responds to it.

3. Speak Your Intention Out Loud

"Now there are no poison arrows in my space. The quality of all chi in my space is safe, nurturing, and healing. This or something better for the Highest Good now occurs."

When a poison arrow is aimed toward a door which happens to stand for the Love Union/Marriage area, it is certain the client feels unsafe in love. This same assumption can be made for any poison arrow, directed at any door or object of import, which shows its way into a Life Value room. You can affect your willingness to take risks when you transform these symbolic dangerous situations into safe ones.

Hang Faceted Crystals in Any Western Facing Windows.

In China, western facing windows in office buildings are boarded up with wood. The reason behind this is the afternoon, western sun is very harsh. Therefore the timber covering the windows keep workers at the office for longer hours. How this translates into Feng Shui is that you can experience severe lessons in any Life Value which has a room with western facing windows or receives rays from the afternoon setting sun. For example, suppose you have an emotional health issue and, by coincidence, your Family/Health kitchen has a wall of western facing windows. A cure could positively affect the starkness of your depression. Or perhaps you receive the afternoon sun through a window in your Wealth/Power study. Your path toward abundance can be made much easier when the view of the western sun is Feng Shui treated. It is not necessary to cure every western facing window if more than one exists in a room. In other words, if you have three sets of western facing windows in your Fame/Reputation den, you only need to cure one. The treatment is simple and transforms road blocks into pathways, beautiful trails which lead to blessed life assistance. It is imperative for the effectiveness of this cure to use an actual faceted crystal which will convert the sunshine into colors of rainbows when it is touched by its light. See diagram L-10 for visual clarity with How the West Was Won Cure.

HOW THE WEST WAS WON CURE (L-10)

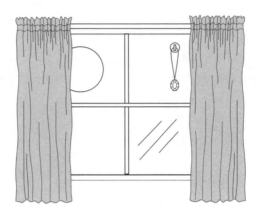

HOW THE WEST WAS WON CURE

1. *Placement of Object*

On a west facing window pane, attach a suction cup with a hook. Hang a faceted crystal suspended from a fishing line or thread (at odd increments of 1-inch to 9-inch).

2. *Visualize/Imagine the Action Already Occurring*

See the sunlight reach the faceted crystal and see the facets transform the light into the entire spectrum of colors. Watch the sparkles dance on the walls of the room. Then symbolically imagine how harsh lessons in any particular Life Value transform into positive experiences.

3. Speak Your Intention Out Loud

"My harsh lessons with (insert Life Value quality here) now turn into rainbows. This or something better for the Highest Good now occurs."

Perform the Second Recommended Cure for Stoves Residing in the Family/Health and Child/Creativity Life Values.

The Fire Element is harmful to both the Wood of Family/ Health and the Metal of Child/Creativity. Still, many have kitchens in these Life Value areas. A stove, which is the symbolic representation of prosperity, has also the Fire Element. This Destructive Element Cycle must be remedied. Give the empowerment mirror for the stove a second task. First, perform the Cure for Empowerment for the range discussed in Part I. Then carry out the following cure with the same mirror. Your next duty is to intend the mirror to represent Water symbolically and douse the Fire of the stove. A mirror, either the flat, large kind or the small, convex kind will only take on the qualities of Water if you so intend it. So, Life Values which benefit from an empowered stove, but not a Water effect, are out of harm's way. If you used a shiny teapot on your stove rather than a mirror to reflect the burners, fill it with Water and give it the added mission of dousing the Fire.

COOL THE BURN II CURE

1. Placement of Object

Focus attention on the mirror (or water-filled teapot) which is already used for the stove empowerment cure.

2. Visualize/Imagine the Action Already Occurring

See the mirror (or teapot) transform into Water and douse the Destructive Element of Fire.

3. Speak Your Intention Out Loud

"Water now douses the Fire so my Family/Health Wood grows into prosperity (my Child/Creativity Metal is stable for holding prosperity). This or something better for the Highest Good now occurs."

Without a doubt, there exists a need for detail in the science of Feng Shui. It is not a rapid endeavor. It takes time to carry out all of the cures or even to notice when a treatment could be beneficial for a certain area in your space. Feng Shui is an art which transforms your home or office over a period of time. It has the ability to convert sour grapes into a fine wine with patience and proper curing. Just don't give yourself decades to complete the Feng Shui treatments. This is your life, not a Cabernet Sauvignon.

If a Bed, Desk, Couch, and Such Must Reside in Front of a Window to Be in the Empowerment Position, Hang a Protection Crystal in the Window.

The science of Feng Shui demonstrates proper chi management. It is intelligent to position your bed, desk, and other furniture in the Empowerment Position so you can see the main door to the room. Then your energy is used for the intended activity in that room. It is not wasted on the subconscious inquiry into who or what is behind you. Sometimes the building layout is such, however, that ideal placements cannot be met. For example, you may be able to position a piece of furniture so it is empowered, yet this means your back is to a window. Although the Empowerment Position is your top priority, this arrangement can create feelings of insecurity. The best scenario would portray the piece of furniture which has a solid wall behind its empowered stance. See diagram L-11 for clarity.

EMPOWERED FURNITURE POSITIONS (L-11)

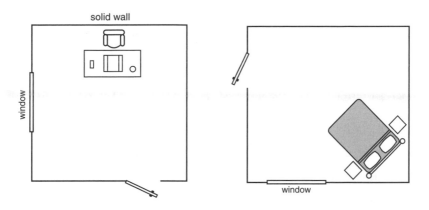

There are many cases where complete empowerment is not possible, at least in the furniture arrangement. Still, practice the Empowerment Position with recommended items. This is the first step. Then if a window is situated behind you while in such commanding placement, perform the Window as Fortress Cure even when coverings such as blinds or curtains obscure vision into or out of the building. If the window also happens to be facing the western direction, it is fine to give the faceted crystal two assignments, one to change the harsh light into rainbows, the other to protect your back. See diagram L-11a.

WINDOW AS FORTRESS CURE (L-11A)

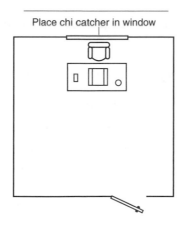

WINDOW AS FORTRESS CURE

1. *Placement of Object*

    Suspend a crystal from the window hung from a fishing line or thread (at odd increments starting at 1-inch to 9-inch). If the window sill is large enough, protection plants can be used instead. See description of Botany Cure for Protection on page 97, Part I.

2. *Visualize/Imagine the Action Already Occurring*

    See the crystal (or plants) create an invisible barrier, a translucent force field as impenetrable as steel, over the window.

3. *Speak Your Intention Out Loud*

    "No negative energy or experience, on any level, can infiltrate through the invisible safeguard covering the window. This or something better for the Highest Good now occurs."

Cure Overhead Beams.

Western architecture adores inside beams which show from the ceiling. In fact, if they are not already present in the basic structure of the house, oftentimes they are cosmetically added for aesthetic value. True, such an addition can be artistically pleasing to the eye and increase the rustic nature and warmth to a house. Yet Feng Shui maintains a rather heavy belief about overhead beams. Because chi is persuaded by its surroundings, beams have an oppressive, weighty effect on it as well as on the occupants of any building which contain these overhead rafters. Depression, claustrophobia, and other such emotional or mental maladies have been improved by the performance of the following cure. This remedy can, with intention, be applied to just one beam per room and have enough influence to treat all the other beams in that room. If your space has beams in every Life Value area, please perform this cure on one beam in every room where they are present. See diagram L-12 for visual clarity about the Beam Me Up, A Loti Cure.

BEAM ME UP, A LOTI CURE
OVERHEAD BEAM EXAMPLES (L-12)

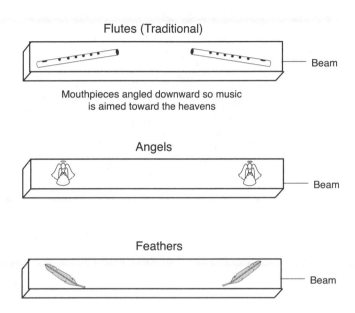

Flutes (Traditional)

Beam

Mouthpieces angled downward so music
is aimed toward the heavens

Angels

Beam

Feathers

Beam

BEAM ME UP, A LOTI CURE

1. *Placement of Object*

   On one side of the chosen beam attach two angels (or two crystals, two feathers, two bamboo flutes, or whatever two objects are in your style to lighten or lift up the beam symbolically). Have the two objects separated by a few feet.

2. *Visualize/Imagine the Action Already Occurring*

   See the chosen objects lift the mass of the beam up towards the heavens. They are transformed into beams of light. See the one beam's conversion affect all other beams in the same room. Each beam turns into a beam of light.

3. Speak Your Intention Out Loud

"The beams in this room are now shafts of light, bringing joy, spaciousness, and healing into this building. This or something better for the Highest Good now occurs."

Cure Washing Machine.

A washing machine contains a sizable drain that pumps water out after every load. In the language of symbols, that is an enormous withdrawal from your abundance bank account of life. Depending on which Life Value the washing machine resides in, you can bet the qualities of that Life Value are affected. Because the washing machine has the same challenging quality as a toilet and abundance drains away, the cure is similar but adjusted for the distinctiveness of the washing machine. Just as it is not recommended to combine whites with colors, so too should you keep the recommended cure separate from items on the laundry room shelf, such as laundry soap and fabric softener. For this reason, you are encouraged to use a bag which is hung on a nail behind the washing machine. See diagram L-13 for visual clarity on the Wash That Drain Right Out Of My Lair Cure.

WASH THAT DRAIN RIGHT OUT OF MY LAIR CURE (L-13)

WASH THAT DRAIN RIGHT OUT OF MY LAIR CURE

1. Placement of Object

Fill a medium-sized fabric bag of your choice with uncooked popcorn, rice, or salt and hang it on a nail on the wall behind the washing machine.

2. Visualize/Imagine the Action Already Occurring

See the abundance of all things overflow in your life. Realize this vision: You stand outside, arms out, head up toward the heavens, to receive the shower of chi glitter which gently falls down to you.

3. Speak Your Intention Out Loud

"Even though my abundance drains out, I still have plenty in all areas of my life. This or something better for the Highest Good now occurs."

Plug Drains in Bathrooms and Kitchen Sinks.

You are aware of the symbolic implications of water flowing down drains, whether it is a trickle or a gush. It is wise to keep your water, your abundance, intact. The conservative way is to pull up the pop up handle behind the bathroom sink to close the drain when not in use. Use an inexpensive round plastic plug or disk for the kitchen sink, as well as the bath/shower drain. For you with an artistic flair, and if the Element relationship cycles allow it, use seashells, for example, in your Career/Life Path Water bathroom to cover the drains. Use rocks in your Fame/Reputation Fire kitchen sink to add more Earth Element to further dam the Water so your Fame Fire can burn. Many creative objects can be used to cover the drains. See diagram L-14.

EXAMPLES OF DRAIN PLUGS (L-14)

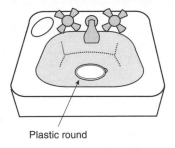

Plastic round

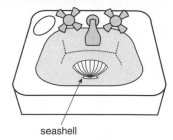

seashell

Plug when you can, breathe when you can't. In the meantime, perform this cure every time you finish with a sink or a shower. You'll be glad you did.

EVERYTHING AND THE KITCHEN SINK CURE

1. *Placement of Object*

   Cover, close, and/or leave the drain cover near the drain in question.

2. *Visualize/Imagine the Action Already Occurring*

   See all forms of abundance, especially the qualities of the Life Value which are affected by the drain stay in the room and in your life.

3. *Speak Your Intention Out Loud*

   "No abundance is lost here. This or something better for the Highest Good now occurs."

If You Live or Work on an Upper Level Floor, Ground Your Space to the Earth Plane.

When you live or work far above the first floor, it becomes vital to your well-being, and to the manifestation of your life dreams, to ground symbolically to the earth. Clearly this becomes necessary if you work on the 30th floor of a high rise building. Sometimes, when a client lives or works on the upper story of a multilevel house or if their building structure is on stilts and not touching the actual earth, this cure is also recommended. This treatment is advised for anybody with two-story houses who is having difficulty actualizing their dreams. As an illustration, suppose you have trouble finding an equal, healthy love partner. Your master bedroom is upstairs. Because the Bagua Life Values are applied to the upstairs rooms as well as the downstairs, it is important to acknowledge the Love Union/Marriage and Self-Knowledge/Wisdom areas on the upper level as well. The house's upper level is also called the top position. Adults, especially parents, should have their master bedroom upstairs in the top position Wealth/Power room. There can be discipline problems if a child sleeps over the parents, even if the adults are in the first floor Wealth/Power position. Although the upstairs can bring you the greatest status, it also separates you from the nurturing force of the earth. The following cure will help reconnect you. See diagram L-15 for visual clarity with the Grounded for Life Cure.

GROUNDED FOR LIFE CURE (L-15)

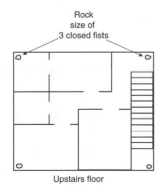

Rock size of 3 closed fists

Upstairs floor

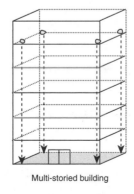

Multi-storied building

Rock hidden in soil of plant

Conservative Option

GROUNDED FOR LIFE CURE

1. *Placement of Object*

   Situate a rock, about the size of three closed fists, in each of the four inside corners of the upper floor of the building, or on your floor if you are in a high-rise structure, or on the main floor if the building construction is raised off the ground.

2. *Visualize/Imagine the Action Already Occurring*

   See the four rocks push and weight the elevated floor downward until it touches the earth.

3. *Speak Your Intention Out Loud*

   "My space, as well as my life, is grounded. I manifest easily, fully connected to the nurturing, vigorous qualities of the earth. This or something better for the Highest Good now occurs."

This cure is also the opportunity to stabilize the four different Life Value qualities which exist in those four corners even if you have an irregular shaped structure. They are the Self-Knowledge/Wisdom, Wealth/Power, Love Union/Marriage, and Helpful People/Travel areas. When you perform the Three Secrets Intention Ritual, you can also add these phrases to the intention statement: "I now ground (Love Union/Marriage, Wealth/Power, and so on) in my life and in my manifestations. This or something better for the Highest Good now occurs."

Know Feng Shui is a Language of Symbols. Learn to Read the Symbols You Are Giving Yourself—Consciously and Unconsciously.

To have Feng Shui detective vision, the ability to translate objects into physical, emotional, or mental patterns, is valuable. If you can take the mystery out of why you have a certain issue in a particular Life Value area by simply locating and removing the offending article, you are steps ahead in the who-dun-it or, in this case, the what-dun-it game.

DON'T:

Do Not Place a Sink Across from the Stove.

This is a simple Element issue. Water douses Fire and the stove (Fire element) represents prosperity in your universe. The Water sink extinguishes it and symbolically makes increasing affluence like a barefoot climb up a steep, rocky mountain (the perfect martyr role). The Feng Shui treatment to cure this is uncomplicated. Suspend a new chi catcher, or use one already holding chi in the room for the specific Life Value represented there. If the latter is your choice, know this chi catcher now has two assignments. Also make sure the designated chi catcher is suspended from the ceiling between the sink and the stove. Perform the intention ritual to hold in the chi, then do the following cure. Afterward get ready for the riches. Remember, it might show itself in your bank account or your life account. Both kinds of wealth bring peace of mind. See diagram L-16 for clarity.

I SINK, THEREFORE I AM

CURE FOR SINK ACROSS FROM STOVE (L-16)

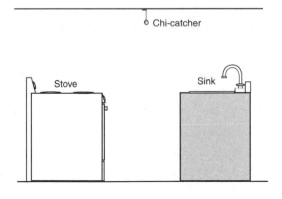

I SINK, THEREFORE I AM CURE

1. *Placement of Object*

Suspend a chi catcher from the ceiling at increments of 1-inch, 3-inch, 5-inch, and so on. Be sure the chi catcher hangs between the sink and the stove.

2. *Visualize/Imagine the Action Already Occurring*

See the smothering qualities of the Water unable to reach the Fire of the stove because the chi catcher acts as a force field barricade.

3. *Speak Your Intention Out Loud*

"The Water of the sink no longer extinguishes the Fire of my stove. I am prosperous in all areas of my life. This or something better for the Highest Good now occurs."

Here is a scenario which might baffle you. Suppose you have a stove in the Child/Creative or Family/Health Life Value section. You also have a sink across from that stove. What do you do? Everything! Empower the stove, then douse the Fire of the stove with the Water of the mirror using the Cool The Burn II Cure. Get your Element relationships in good form. Then stop the Water as it extinguishes the Fire prosperity of the stove, a different symbolic issue altogether. Perform the I Sink, Therefore I Am Cure. Now you're set.

Do Not Block a Door, Even if it is Never Used or Always Locked.

A door represents passage, access, or doors of opportunity involving whatever Life Value(s) the door enters. If the door is always locked or is rarely used, it makes no difference. A door not being used because it is broken is important to fix regardless of whether or not it is needed. Dreams, once shattered, find new vigor when the doorway leading into a related Life Values can open and close smoothly.

The habit of disabling a door by putting a trashcan, kitty litter, or table in front of it is likewise common. Take a stab at any symbolic implications you conclude from the specific objects which blockade a particular Life Value door. What symbolically prevents entry into the possible rewards of the Life Value? Clients often claim the door has an obstacle in front of it not because they want things that way, but because there simply isn't enough room for all of their things. Here is that interesting Feng Shui philosophy on clutter again: Your home and office is never too small for all of your things. If you are space deficient, there is a clutter-clear in your near future.

Do Not Stay Within Your Comfort Zones with Feng Shui Cures.

You might think the hardest part about Feng Shui is moving your antique desk into the Empowerment Position or the challenge of hanging chi catchers from your high ceilings. Or even the huge clutter-clearing project of the Family/Health extra room.

Feng Shui is incredibly tangible. It takes time, physical energy or outside help, and patience. But the toughest part of Feng Shui is invisible to the eye. It is called change. Change occurs when you move outside the box of your comfort zone. Regard the true definition of comfort zone: What you are accustomed to, or what you feel safe with, despite whether it is positive or negative. For instance, your comfort zone might be never having enough cash on you, always being late, or having low self-esteem no matter what you accomplish. It is a pattern you repeat over and over. You feel at ease with it. It fits like a glove, even if the glove is tattered, worn, and doesn't keep your hands warm anymore. It's remarkable how easy it is to attract the same mess again, regardless of whether you believe you want it or not. You possess a mighty will.

Enter Feng Shui. You alter the symbols in your environment to fit the wanna-be appearance. For instance, move the desk into the Empowerment Position. This affects your psyche. You shift from a victim to a power state. There might be a healing crisis as you sit in this authoritative stance. Your comfort zone is threatened, yet you are given the opportunity to transform, to create new comfort zones which serve you better. Clutter-clear to invite in a stream of chi. This fresh force affects the Life Value area which is now free. It can be profound, but scary. Likewise, when you replace single images with pictures of more than one, you alter the subconscious belief system which says, *I deserve to be alone*. Healing crises usually take place as new comfort zones are formed. Know this and go easy on yourself, but don't give up.

Stay conscious of the process and do not freak. For instance, you might be compelled to return your desk to its former place against the wall because you hate this new position. Your recently cleared extra room might mysteriously fill with up-to-the-minute junk boxes. You might unintentionally replace single images with more single images. Comfort zones are subtle and dangerous. It is not easy to adjust to new ones.

Thus, try to keep your Feng Shui applications good for at least six months, even if you strongly dislike a particular treatment, because it affects an area in your life you need to amend. Keep the remedy around long enough to modify the pattern permanently. Finally, have a friend check your Feng Shui handiwork. Their detective vision can be sharper than yours and their objective perspective will provide a fresh viewpoint.

Do Not Forget to Prepare "As If" It's Already Happened.

Forget the future tense of every word. You are advised to omit these compromised declarations from your Feng Shui vocabulary: Someday, might, am not, could, perhaps, and other such surrendering words. If a word doesn't pack the punch of materializing exactly what you want right now, then change the way it is said or written, even if you don't believe it. Consider this: The barometer phrase, "This or something better for the Highest Good now occurs" brings in the bigger picture vision regardless of whether you can see it. So ask for anything and dream big.

Prepare your bedroom for the Highest Good mate. Don't wait until you are ready to move in together. Make your stove empowered, even if you live alone and only cook for yourself. Do bathroom cures in your Family/Health washroom, especially if you are sick and various treatments haven't made a difference so far. Be patient and courageous. The Highest Good transformation is assured. Imagine there is a pint-sized coach who stands on your shoulders all day, whispering in your ear, "You are a winner!" or "You create this now!" and other such rah-rah cheers. Do whatever it takes. Make the Feng Shui alterations in your life arrangements and invite your dreams into your world. The more you ground wishes and dreams into the present, the more awe will become an everyday occurrence. Intend it now.

FENG SHUI BOOTY WITH A TANG

Overwhelming feelings can be soothed by rounds of deep breathing. If this seems impossible to fulfill, keep in mind: Feng Shui is a process, not an overnight perfection program. Don't try to absorb, and consequently complete, every step and cure you've just read in a matter of days. If you do, call me. I want to hire you to Feng Shui consult my place.

There is no time limit on the transformation of your life. Let it occur naturally as you apply the Feng Shui treatments to your home and office. A few clients have come to me, shivering in terror, under this false premise of required timelines.

"I was told by a knowledgeable Feng Shui person to complete three cures in three days or else."

"Or else what? You lose your parking place at the office? The dry cleaning shop cancels your order? Prime time television quits showing bad sitcoms?"

Your life can be better than you ever imagined. How exciting life is when you shift your microcosm world to shape your macrocosm world optimistically! Lose the dogma, the stringent rules, the rigid belief systems, and the feeling of dread associated with the principles of Feng Shui. Remember the power of intention, and just begin.

PART III

CHILL OUT, IT'S PERFORMANCE TIME

THE BEST IS YET TO COME

If you've reached this point in the book, you hopefully feel encouraged by what you've read so far. This next part will take you deeper into the Feng Shui practice and expand it with ritual. Always remember, however, you're in the driver's seat and the one with the ignition keys. You decide how fast to accelerate, when to slow down, and when to brake. Get to know the thrill of being empowered.

Even still, lots of information coming into your brain can be terrifying. If something occurs too fast or is too different from your reality, shut the book. The information will still be there when, and if, you become ready. Also, don't forget to enjoy. You are being given tools to convert your surroundings and life into a well-oiled machine. Listen to the hum and the purr, but know great force without control is useless. This book is an instruction manual in life maintenance but also in how to control the new changes you create. You can relax and take pleasure in the buzz. Know it will not engulf you.

THE BOO CHRONICLES: RITUAL

Regardless of your politics, religious convictions, gender, and socio-economic status, there are parameters within which your belief systems, values, and comfort zones reside. It makes little difference if your boundaries extend to the right or left. Feng Shui constantly asks you to "think outside the box." Another way to say it is: Have a Bagua State of Mind. Wherever your beliefs lie, they should easily fit inside the Bagua shape. However, the Bagua, an eight-sided figure with numerous angles, by its natural outline, holds ideas and beliefs uncommon to western thinking. See diagram M-1.

BAGUA STATE OF MIND (M-1)

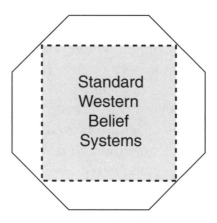

The possibilities inherent in Feng Shui principles may not be apparent to those who haven't experienced them. New concepts might threaten ideas of reality as you know it, much like how the general populace scoffed at Christopher Columbus's insistence that the earth was round, not flat. Yet regardless of how matter-of-fact you are, they are still familiar unseen realities. Examples are a certainty in the existence of a Higher Power, love between two people, or the sensation of any deep emotion. These occurrences are accepted as valid, although the force is invisible.

Some people might be left behind in this next part of the book. This portion deals with the invisible. If pessimism in regards to this information resonates with you, join the club. You are hardly alone. History tends to repeat. People often disbelieve concepts and values out of the ordinary. For instance, airplanes, trips to the moon, and studying the human cell were at one time fantasies. Now they are everyday happenings. It is this kind of thinking which wins the "Bagua State of Mind Award." In exploring these unmarked territories, wonder converts to certainty. With a similar line of thought, know a mental microscope develops when Feng Shui detective vision is activated for over 50 hours. Use it to perceive and feel what can't be seen and to make the unseen visible. It is a very handy tool. May you aquire the latest model of the mental microscope (the B-9999 series) to benefit from in your own environment.

Some of the following rituals are strongly recommended, even semi-compulsory. Do them whether or not you believe in them. Others are presented for your use when and if needed. None of them will alter your merits or religious principles. They improve the caliber on every level of your home, office, and life. Don't fret. If you *must* freak out about something, get a medical microscope. Stick a small part of your little finger under the lens and focus. Now, count the hundreds of microorganisms living on your skin right now. No, soap will not help! The invisible is alive and well. Be responsible for its quality.

DRAGON'S BLOOD SPACE CLEARING

It is not essential to find a mystical creature, the dragon, to perform this rite. You can breathe easy again. Dragon's Blood is a red resin derived from various plants. The resin historically used in this type of ritual was from the Dragon Tree (*Agavaceae* family; Genus/Species *Dracena draco*). When Dragon's Blood melts, it looks like blood boiling. I know, not very pleasant. Here is my version of how it got its name. Obviously, Dragon's Blood's creepy title came from a bored worker whose task it was to package the resin. He was jealous of the CEO, who was out having a wine luncheon with his beautiful mistress. The CEO wanted the resin named Heart Vibe. Envy is a green monster indeed.

Dragon's Blood resin, with its antiseptic smell, is respected because of the smoke's ability to scour the energy of a dwelling. If you are familiar with the Native American ritual of burning dried sage for purification of a space, appreciate that smoldering Dragon's Blood resin is 100 times stronger, not in aroma, but in effectiveness. Dragon's Blood resin reaches deeply into the many energy layers of a building and purifies them indiscriminately.

This is important because history in a space, whether rented or owned, also tends to repeat itself. It is wise to "energy clean" the area you move into. This attention to atmosphere quality removes patterns, thought forms, belief systems, and entities as well as the irk of the former occupants. Even a very sensible person would admit a building where a murder took place feels different than a day spa facility.

What is an example of a pattern in a building? You are probably aware of such cases as a restaurant which doesn't make it financially and closes its doors. A new restaurant moves into the same building. It has a better menu, tastier food, friendlier service. For sure it will be a success. However, six months after opening, it too closes its doors. Another restaurant moves into the same structure. A few months later, it fails.

Here's an example of a belief system and thought form in a building. The former woman occupant, whose husband died 15 years before, lived the rest of her life lonely, grieving, and bitter about her fate. Charlotte, a single woman hungry for relationship love, moves into the house as a renter. Although she thinks she takes all the right steps to find true love, it still evades her. The invisible airwaves can be merciless and, among other things, she is subconsciously affected by the grief and bitterness floating in the atmosphere. Another example would be the couple who got a divorce and sold the house. The next occupants are honeymooners who get along famously until they move into this new dwelling. Then, mysteriously, they fight all the time. After a few months of this, the woman leaves. Thought form and belief system examples go on. Old and new sickness, death, separation, bankruptcy, and more can float in the character of a space. Interestingly, people are attracted to a space which accommodates the very issues which fit into their comfort zones. For instance, the man with money problems feels great in the apartment where the former occupant declared bankruptcy. A woman with health issues feels at home in the dwelling where a previous resident had a chronic disease, even if that occupant has been gone for over 10 years. A family who lost a child to a tragedy and moved to ease the memory are magnetized to a new home where a similar death thought form resides.

You won't necessarily take on a certain value or belief system just because it exists in a place. Plus it's not just difficult things that float in the air waves. Because Feng Shui practices preventative maintenance, every action and cure is recommended to ensure you move with, not against, the life currents. These ideologies raise your awareness to possible contributing factors in any situation, thus you take responsibility for your environment, even if you can't see all the aspects of it. Rest assured, you can become a millionaire, even if your home had a former occupant who met with financial ruin. Likewise, you can meet the perfect Highest Good mate, regardless if an isolated spinster lived in your house before. Anything is possible, yet whenever these thought forms and belief systems exist persuasively in your environment, you work against the tide to manifest dreams.

What are some examples of entities? Perceptions are largely shaped by the media—from Casper the Friendly Ghost to *The Amityville Horror*—where the apparitions are so powerful, angry, and aggressive, the lives of the occupants are devastated. However, real life is rarely like that. Spirits are energy patterns left over from departed beings. The hovering energy is usually harmless and simply has some unfinished issue. Many of these energy patterns act out a comfort zone behavior (yes, even ghosts have them). Somehow, your presence, and perhaps your family's, are a threat to what they perceive as their space. Their "announcement" behavior might be subtle or brazen. It is also vital to note not every building has a ghost or ghosts. Nor is it necessary to accept the idea of apparitions if this is not your truth.

Without a doubt, however, historic buildings, which now are private homes and offices, have layers of energy from generations past to remove. Not to be ignored, new construction contains the possible vex, patterns, and belief systems of the architect, the contractor, and the construction workers. If you are aware of an intense past in a dwelling, consider the Dragon's Blood Ritual. It could optimistically change the results for you, the new occupant. Everyone should space clear their environments, regardless of circumstances and details surrounding the abode. Start with a clean slate. Even if you don't believe in all of this mumbo jumbo, the aftereffects of an energy wash are undeniable.

THE RITUAL[5]

Materials Needed:

1. Dragon's Blood resin, frankincense resin, and myrrh resin (two packets of each is recommended)

2. Two packets of specialty charcoal used for resin incense burning

3. Aluminum pie pans (one for each "station")

4. Ceramic dinner plates and oven mitts

5. Disposable lighter

Incense resins are colored chunks the size of small pebbles which come in little packets. They can be purchased or ordered from various shops which carry incense. Get help from a spouse or friend(s) when doing this deep cleansing. Not only is it less overwhelming, but feedback from clients has proven the purification is more effective when done with at least one other person. Get as much help as you need to make this a fun workable ceremony. Hold space clearing parties. Hard work mixed with good friends and strong heart forces make everything easier. Note: The Dragon's Blood Space Clearing Ritual is for stand-alone structures which do not share walls with other buildings or construction. A separate procedure for apartments and offices is dealt with next.

Instructions:

1. Create multiple stations for incense burners. Fashion a station with an aluminum pie pan filled to the top with sand or dirt. Put one of the charcoal circles on top of the dirt in the center of the pan. Position this pan in the middle of a ceramic dinner plate. Place this makeshift, inexpensive incense burner over an oven mitt then set this station on the floor in any room or on top of a table. Be Very Careful! The

5. The prototype for the Dragon's Blood Ritual is taken from the book, *Spiritual Cleansing* by Draja Mickaharic. It is an obscure text, and the ritual in this book is quite different from the one I designated for Feng Shui space clearing, but I am indebted to the author for his knowledge and insight.

Charcoal Burns Very Hot! See diagram M-2 for visual of station.

INEXPENSIVELY MADE STATIONS TO
BURN RESIN INCENSE (M-2)

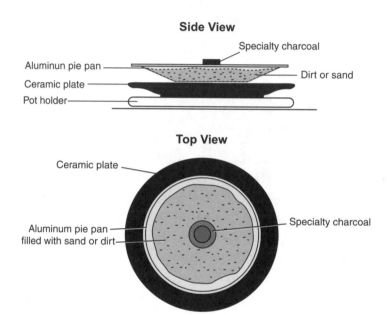

2. Make sure you have enough stations so every square inch of your space receives the influence of the Dragon's Blood resin smoke. It isn't necessary to place a separate station in every room, but more stations are better with this cleansing, as opposed to being conservative with the number of stations formed. Use your intuition.

3. Put stations on every floor of your structure. The ritual clears out negative influences on all floors simultaneously. If the Dragon's Blood smoke is not introduced on every level, this leaves a vulnerable area for the negative influences to relocate in the dwelling. These forces can easily re-enter a

space when the ritual is over. The Orange Peel Toddy (see page 256) exists for office spaces, apartments, multifamily dwellings, and other shared-wall locations, when situations and/or neighbors make doing this ritual impossible. One station is usually enough in basements. Similarly, open the access door to an attic and place a station on the floor under the cavity. Smoke travels upward into the attic. Some clients place a station in all out buildings for thoroughness.

4. Before you light anything, open all windows and doors which lead to the outside. Next, open up doors in each room of your space including closet doors, bathroom doors, toilet lids, and the oven door. Also open kitchen cabinets, drawers in chests, and so on. This allows all energies out when intimidated by the Dragon's Blood smoke. Because the front door, back door(s), and windows are open, it gives negative influences an exodus. If you cannot vacate your house with the front door open because of fear of intrusion, still open doors between rooms, cabinet drawers, and such and be sure to have at least one window or outside door open in every room if at all possible. Thus an exit for the smoke and the energies is created.

5. Gather the resins together and visualize their effectiveness when burned. Visualize or imagine the smoke escorting the negative influences out the windows and doors and then up to the skies to be neutralized. No negativity invades any neighborhood structure. Then visualize or imagine your Higher Power (or light) entering into the Dragon's Blood, frankincense, and myrrh resins.

6. To burn the resin, you must first ignite the charcoal on each station. Hold the flame of a lighter under a charcoal you clasp with a pair of metal tongs. It's simple to ignite this charcoal as it is made with a flammable substance. When it catches, it

starts to shoot off small sparks. This is your signal to place the ignited charcoal back on the station's soil. See diagram M-3.

SAFE HANDLING OF SPECIALTY CHARCOAL (M-3)

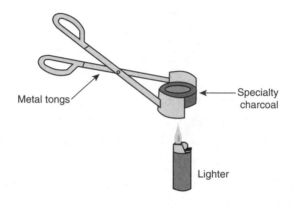

7. When each station's charcoal stays lit, communicate this fact to your fellow helpers. When every person has lit stations, add about a thumbnail size of Dragon's Blood to each station. Too large a piece of resin can put the charcoal out when it melts. Avoid this! Before starting the ritual, prepare the Dragon's Blood by using a hammer to break it into smaller pieces, even into a powdery substance. In addition, be sure to place only the Dragon's Blood resin on the charcoal at this time since you want to encourage the departure of everything. The frankincense and myrrh resins have a different action which will come in later.

8. When each station smolders with the Dragon's Blood resin, leave the building! Take your children, pets, and, of course, the helpers with you. Stay away for 20 minutes. This assures safety for you and your loved ones as these energies clear out. Don't just walk across the street or down past a few neighborhood houses to watch the process. Energies latch

onto anything which will keep them there. Do not forget the power of a comfort zone. If you maintain visual contact with your building, these patterns have connection with you. Easily they will come into your personal breathing space and return to the structure when you do. Instead, take a walk, bring your dog to a nearby park, or place your cat carrier in the backseat of your car and go on a short drive. Because you have asked at least one person to assist you, multiple cars are parked outside your house. If everybody loads up in one or two vehicles, the rest of the cars can stay to give the illusion people are still in the house. Be sure to roll down one window a small amount in each remaining car so the smoke of Dragon's Blood, as it leaves the structure, can clear out the vehicle as well.

9. Pets which accompany you include any that live inside the dwelling such as dogs, cats, hamsters, birds, and so on. Do not trouble yourself with fish in aquariums. They are protected by the water which surrounds them. Program this protection. Imagine a circle of light surrounds the tank and permeates the cells of the water with goodness. House pets are not left outside in the backyard because, like you, they can become a target for detrimental influences to attach to and return when you let the pets back inside. Feral cats, horses in corrals, chickens, as well as other farm animals in general, do not have to be moved because they spend their existence outside. They would, however, benefit from an intentional protection placed around each of them in your mind's eye when doing step 5. Imagine or visualize a circle of light surrounding each one and see negative influences unable to penetrate their being.

10. After approximately 20 minutes has passed, return to your space and sense whether or not the Dragon's Blood resin smoke was effective in ridding your dwelling of unfavorable

patterns. Nearly 95% of my clientele have experienced complete clearing from just one burn of the Dragon's Blood resin. However, you may return and intuit the structure is not entirely cleansed. For instance, you might feel a twist in your tummy or intuit something isn't quite right. If such is the case, add more Dragon's Blood resin to each station (step 7). Leave again for 20 minutes. Two rounds are usually successful in energy cleansing any building thoroughly. A completely optimal purification makes the structure feel very empty, devoid of anything.

11. After 20 minutes has passed (the first or second time), return to your space. The Dragon's Blood resin should have burned out completely. You and your helpers can go back to each respective station. Use the same ignited charcoal, which is getting a light grey in color, to place frankincense and myrrh resin together in the center of it. If it is necessary to cleanse the building for two rounds, start new charcoals on each station.

Frankincense and myrrh's aromatic smoke brings back the affirmative energies and Higher thoughts. At this time, everyone should imagine the positive notions, grace, and good energies being invited back in. Visualize or imagine glitter coming through the windows and doors to fill the room. You and your loved ones may stay during this part of the process. Frankincense and myrrh attract protective, grounded, and nurturing powers to infuse your dwelling. Dragon's Blood resin pushes everything, positive and negative, out of your space. The smoke from frankincense and myrrh resin calls whatever is in the Highest Good back into your abode. A few clients, aware of a sweet presence living in their house, have been reluctant to remove it. If the presence is indeed in the Highest Good for your life, such gifts will return on the smoke of frankincense and myrrh.

12. Apply the Three Secrets Reinforcement Ritual. Stand in the center of your home and visualize or imagine that the ritual was effective. Positive things and desires come to you easily and effortlessly.

THE BOO RITUAL CURE

1. *Placement of Object*

Stand in the center of your dwelling.

2. *Visualize/Imagine the Action Already Occurring*

See the smoke of the Dragon's Blood escort dark, weak, and sickly energy out of the building through the open doors and windows. See the smoke of the frankincense and myrrh invite positive, empowered, Higher thought energy into your space.

3. *Speak Your Intention Out Loud*

"My dwelling is purified completely by the Dragon's Blood Ritual. It is protected and full of light, joy, and healing energy. All my dreams manifest easily. This or something better for the Highest Good now occurs."

If properly done, never again does a deep cleansing need to occur in this particular space. However, if you rent out the dwelling, and then in the future inhabit it again, this deep cleansing is recommended to remove patterns of others. Furthermore, if you really want your space's energy polished, repeat the Dragon's Blood ritual monthly. Because the stations described above are difficult to pick up and easily move, choose your own fire-safe burner to use for future treatments. Then, using this one receptacle, walk from room to room letting the smoke of the Dragon's Blood resin saturate the space. Doors and windows are opened to let the negative energies out. Like before, open doors of closets, bathrooms, and such. Perform all preparatory actions, repeating instructions of steps 5 through 9. Nobody needs to leave during these times as this sanitizes you and your loved ones' own personal patterns. Pets are best left indoors during this touch-up cleansing. Remember to always conclude the ceremony by a burn of the frankincense/myrrh resins. Finally, do the Three Secrets Reinforcement Ritual at the end each time to assure effectiveness.

THE "ORANGE PEEL TODDY" FOR SHARED-WALL SPACE CLEARINGS

If you live in an apartment or a multifamily dwelling where the other families aren't open to a Dragon's Blood cleansing, or if you share an office space or cubicle in a building, then the "Orange Peel Toddy" ritual is for you. The Dragon's Blood ritual is not useful in a building where the patterns can hide. Afterwards all damaging energies return to their original posts and, believe me, they will. This next ritual is based on a traditional Feng Shui purification ceremony. However, the rite received a boost. The original orange peel cleansing now shares a similar potency and effectiveness as the Dragon's Blood ritual.

PREPARATION OF ORANGE PEEL TODDY ELIXIR

Materials Needed:
1. Organic orange
2. Purified water
3. Cypress essential oil
4. A small tigereye stone
5. Glass jar with screen for lid
6. Container for completed elixir

Most items are found at health food and metaphysical stores. The traditional Feng Shui ceremony calls for just an orange and water. The ritual is most precious and potent when all components are prepared from the highest, purest materials. Thousands of years ago, water was uncontaminated and oranges were untreated. Today, these details need to be mentioned.

Actions for Creating the Purification Elixir:

1. Peel the orange and divide the peel into nine sections. Place the nine pieces into the jar and add purified water to the rim. This closely mimics the traditional cleansing liquid Feng Shui doctrine has used for centuries. The orange can be eaten or thrown away. It is only the orange peel that you need in this particular ceremony.

2. Insert the tigereye stone into the concoction. Tigereye is commonly a brown and yellow gem known for its protective qualities. Add a small tigereye stone, about the size of an American quarter, to the orange peel water. The tigereye qualities are then infused into the water. Studies are available about the malleable characteristics of water. In essence, water is influenced by the thoughts which surround it, words spoken to it, and the energies of what is placed in it. When viewed under a microscope, an otherwise stunning water crystal becomes distorted and fractured when the ideas in the energy field are fearful and limiting. However, when positivism is in the water's proximity, its crystal reflects a similar beauty in form. Thus it is easy to program the water to be the protector of your aquarium fish during the Dragon's Blood ritual. These same principles pertain when you make gem remedies. The gem's attributes are absorbed into the water. Such is the function of tigereye gem in this elixir. Its protecting traits become a natural configuration in the formula.

3. Place the screen over the mouth of the jar to avoid insects and other contaminants getting into the mixture. Put the jar outside where it receives the moon rays and the sun rays for three days and nights. This is effective even on cloudy days and new moon nights. Another option is to cover the mouth of the jar with cheesecloth. You can use any natural material which allows the liquid to breathe. Avoid, however, using the jar's actual lid, as this inhibits the natural air flow benefit. Also stay away from plastic.

4. Traditional Feng Shui ideals promote keeping the filled jar under the rays of the moon for three nights. I maintain the jar should be left outside for five nights. To receive the benefits of the sun rays, leave the jar outside during the day as well. This encourages the power of yin (moon) as well as the strength of yang (the sun) to infuse the blend. Do not keep the jar inside your house thinking a window that receives these rays from the sun and moon is sufficient. Find a safe spot for it outside, a balcony, backyard, or even a tolerant neighbor's enclosure. In this way, the liquid mixture may sun and moon bathe properly, absorbing the needed traits from those celestial bodies.

5. After this concoction has been outside for the proper amount of time, retrieve the jar. Remove the orange peel and tigereye stone with a strainer, saving the liquid in a separate container. This fluid becomes the special elixir for space clearing. You may throw away the orange peel. Some clients bury them. The tigereye can be kept for future doses. Just be sure to place the stone in a sacred spot, not, for instance, in a crowded kitchen drawer hidden under take-out menus.

6. Add nine drops of cypress essential oil to the elixir. This oil purifies sick rooms. Its woodsy scent overcomes any unpleasant odors as well as cleans out all impressions of

illness. Aromatherapy is extremely powerful, and the use of essential oils becomes more common all the time.

You now have the specialty elixir to energy wash your shared-walled dwelling. Left-over formula can be kept in the refrigerator, appropriately labeled, to be used again. Don't drink it, however. It might look like lemonade, but it doesn't taste like it. Add nine drops of cypress essential oil whenever the elixir is dormant for a few weeks. For all deep initial cleansings, however, use freshly prepared elixir.

THE RITUAL

The following ritual is based on the traditional rite, but it has been strengthened and modernized.

1. Open up doors and windows leading to the outside.

2. Open up doors in each room, including closet doors, bathroom doors, toilet lids, oven doors, kitchen cabinets, and so on. These two actions give negative influences an opportunity, regardless of where they originate, to evacuate. If you have safety issues, do not open all outside doors and windows, but have at least one window or outside door open in every room if possible.

3. The most powerful time to perform this ritual is either around noon or midnight. This is because the sun or the moon, depending on which phase you pick, is highest in the sky. Solar or lunar forces have the strongest influence on the earth's atmosphere at these times. If performing the ritual at such times is not possible, have ease, it will work at other times as well.

4. Place your container of elixir on the table. Set your intention. Visualize the removal of all negative patterns, thought forms, belief systems, and entities from your dwelling. See them exit

out the windows and doors. Sometimes in an office none of the windows open, so instead see the trail of negative energy pass through the window panes. Envision the clearing of negative influences as harmless to all neighboring homes, offices, and spaces. All exiting energies rise to the heavens to be neutralized. Concurrently, see that you are surrounded by a circle of protective light. You are sheltered from all harmful, predecessor energies as you are the most recent inhabitant of the space. Also picture your Higher Power (or light) infusing the elixir.

5. Flick this mixture around your space with the fingers of your hand, letting the drops of the mixture reach everywhere, including walls and fixtures. Keep up your focus of intention. Some clients use a spray bottle to distribute the elixir. To mist is fine, convenient, and just as potent if done with intention.

6. Repeat step 5 for three days. Stir or shake the mixture each time you begin the cleansing. The first day encourages weak configurations to leave. The second day coerces the stronger patterns to vacate. The third day—the one that clients seem to miss somehow—is the most vital to the purifying process. The constant barrage of clearing elixir encourages the exodus of the negative stimulus in the area. The strongest, most influential negative forces finally surrender and withdraw on this last application. Be sure to include it.

7. At the end of the three-day treatment, promote the return of Higher thoughts and grace by either burning frankincense and myrrh (see the Dragon's Blood ritual) or, if incense is not appropriate, some other form of invitation. Visualize or imagine streams of glitter come into the space, filling it with joy, luck, and your Higher Power. Any type of welcoming rite is appropriate here. Use your intuition.

8. Sometime after the ritual and the call for the return of the Higher thoughts and grace, stand in the center of the

room and perform the Three Secrets Reinforcement Ritual. Visualize or imagine the ceremony's effectiveness as well as the ease with which all dreams manifest now.

THE BOO TWO RITUAL CURE

1. *Placement of Object*

   Stand in the center of your dwelling, office, or cubicle.

2. *Visualize/Imagine the Action Already Occurring*

   See the spray (or flicks) of the elixir enter the room and encourage the dark, weak, and sickly energy to exit out of the building through the open doors and windows or through the window pane glass. See the smoke of the frankincense and myrrh, or the rite of your choice, invite positive, empowered, Highest Good energy into your space.

3. *Speak Your Intention Out Loud*

   "My dwelling purifies completely with the Orange Peel Toddy Ritual. It is protected and full of light, joy, and healing energy. All of my dreams manifest easily. This or something better for the Highest Good now occurs."

For extra protection and complete thoroughness after all steps are taken, a purification of self is advisable. This is done with some Dragon's Blood resin, a sheet, and a burning station. See step 1 of the Dragon's Blood ritual for instructions and a visual on how to make a burning station. Do this personal clearing outside! Take a chair to some exterior, private location. Drop a small amount of Dragon's Blood resin, about the size of your little fingernail, on a station's lit charcoal. Remember, it burns very hot, so use caution! Sit in the chair and cover yourself completely with the sheet so Dragon's Blood smoke completely fumigates you. Do this for at least 10 minutes. Clients rave about this particular personal purification. If you don't have an outside patio, deck, or backyard to complete this step properly, get a friend to let you use her backyard. It is not unusual for me to come home and smell the distinctive aroma of Dragon's Blood floating on the breeze from my backyard. A quick investigation discloses a huddled, Halloween ghost-like figure purifying over rising smoke.

The CMA Clause: These two rituals are given to you for informational purposes. When you purify your own environment, it empowers. If you feel, however, you need the services of a professional to bless your space in whatever spiritual practice, please do so. The Dragon's Blood ritual and the Orange Peel Toddy are the perfect adjunct to any intentional purification ritual. They do not interfere or obstruct alternative clearings. Even if they are not something which resonates with your personal style, please cleanse your environment in a fashion which fits your beliefs. Remember the power of intention to bring in effectiveness to whatever ritual you choose. Intention + purification = satisfied customers!

Try not to be discouraged if these last few pages have befuddled you. This information is about energy—an invisible phenomenon which is as bona fide as the easy chair you sit on, but hard to see with your physical eyeballs. Many steps to each space clearing ritual can likewise cause apprehension. These ceremonies are given as guides but do not take the place of your intuition. Consider these suggestions like training wheels. At first, you faithfully ride your bike with them on, but eventually they come off and you steer the bike as if carried on the wind. After your awareness upgrades about the quality of energy in your surroundings, you will never again be satisfied with a feeling less than pleasing. Of course, the neighbors might think you're eccentric. Let them. You have The Bagua State of Mind Award hanging on your wall and a microscope for detecting negative energy in your back pocket. Finally, please recognize this viewpoint: If you don't possess your dwelling, something else will.

LAND CLEARING CEREMONY

This particular rite has to do with the land surrounding your home or office. This ritual is based on a similar one in traditional Feng Shui but is updated and westernized. The terrain under your dwelling (whether you rent or own) may be a small lot large enough only for your building, a vast tract of land spanning acres, or something in between. Before the modern-day neighborhood complete with tract housing, your property could have been the host to many things. A temporary campsite for a band of gypsy nomads, a site where an act of violence occurred, like a tribal war, or possibly even a Native American burial ground are examples. It is difficult to look out your window and imagine buffalo roaming through tall grass, a village of teepees, or a canon waiting for the next round in a historical battle. We live in a very "Me-Now" world. Even when there is an obsession with the historical past, it often is motivated by special interests. The Bagua State of Mind asks you to respect the distant history and the far-off future of any plot of land, whether or not you personally benefit from such care. Our society comfort zone is to take from this planet. Our food, our shelters, our clothes, even the air we breathe come from the abundant generosity of the earth. Even if we minimize our consumption and try to focus on simply "taking in the beauty," we still have an impact.

This next ritual gives you an opportunity to give back. Positive force, directed at the earth, goes a long way in healing the past and supporting a future. Optimistic energy brings about the creative, transformative powers the planet needs to progress to the next step in harmony with humankind. Carry out this ritual regularly, as it properly honors the land where your house or office resides. As you transform your surroundings into a healing haven, and if many others assume this level of accountability with their part of the planet, magnificent things can happen. It is when your hands are open to give that the greatest, abundant gifts appear. It is when your hands are open to give that you not only live, but thrive.

THE LAND CLEARING RITUAL[6]

Materials needed:

1. A large glass bowl

2. 3 or 4 pounds of birdseed

3. Saffron (a spice used sparingly in cooking)

4. A healthy understanding of the Three Secrets Reinforcement Ritual

The Steps:

1. Fill a bowl, one which makes you pop, with birdseed. Traditional Feng Shui methods call for dried rice to be used in this ceremony. I suggest birdseed as it has a similar grain symbolism as rice and is beneficial for all wild animals. Note: neither the dried rice nor the birdseed is recommended if you have a hunting cat. Seed on the ground will clearly put birds and small animals in a vulnerable position. Instead:

   a) Refer to the section of the elixir preparation for the Orange Peel Toddy and substitute this powerful potion instead. Add saffron to the mixture after the designated time in the sun and moon.

   b) Use flick motions to distribute the elixir with your fingers, up, out, and down, similar to that indicated for the birdseed formula.

---

6. David Daniel Kennedy is exceptional with his easy-to-understand language on how the Land Clearing Ritual, the Tree Of Life Ritual, and the Red Cloth Ritual are explained. They can be found in his book, Feng Shui For Dummies. I used his descriptions of these rituals as a prototype. I am also indebted to Rachel Long for her herb consultation which led to the use of saffron (the non-toxic, but equally powerful alternative to cinnabar) and the use of turquoise powder as a strong protection additive in some of the rituals.

2. Add five pinches of saffron to the birdseed. For centuries, the Chinese used cinnabar in all sacred rituals. The long-established use of cinnabar in Feng Shui is based on the same practice. Here is a concern. Cinnabar is an ore (mercury sulfide) and although it's unlikely anyone would have a life-threatening response to the powder, even if a small amount were swallowed, exposure over time can result in mercury accumulation in the body with serious health consequences. Although it is used in some Chinese medicines, I would advise against contributing to increasing toxicity levels on the earth. Therefore, the customary use of cinnabar in this ritual seems counter to what the offering is accomplishing. This ceremony is about benevolence and therefore must harm no one and nothing.

    Enter saffron. It is a non-toxic alternative to cinnabar used by Tibetans in their ceremonies because it adds sacredness, preciousness, and potency to any ritual. There are very expensive versions of the spice at specialty kitchen and cooking shops. Less costly varieties are available at most grocery stores. Use your intuition on which quality is best for you, both financially and spiritually. With proper intention, any kind of saffron is effective.

3. Mix the birdseed and the saffron together with your middle finger. Women use the left hand and men use the right. At the same time, visualize or imagine the Higher Power (or light) as it enters the birdseed, blessing and infusing it with the power to purify your property. Stir the concoction in a counter-clockwise manner at least nine times (or multiples of nine—18, 27, and so on) while you visualize this penetration.

4. Begin at the Mouth of the Chi. On land, this is where the driveway meets the road of your property. It doesn't matter whether actual earth or pavement is there. Throw three handfuls of birdseed as high as you can into the air. Visualize or imagine your life and the property uplifted and empowered.

5. Pitch three handfuls of birdseed outward, parallel to the ground. This action feeds the hungry ghosts of the land and shows all energies present you are compassionate. Visualize or imagine the resolve of challenging issues as all negativity leaves your lot.

6. Throw three handfuls of birdseed straight down to the ground. This action symbolizes the planting of seeds for new growth. Visualize or imagine your dreams coming to you easily and effortlessly.

7. Continue to throw the seed in these three different ways. Walk clockwise around the perimeter of your property and stop where your instinct tells you. Perform steps 4, 5 and 6 each time you intuitively halt in another spot. Visualize or imagine the action symbolized with each toss of the birdseed. Upward throws are positive and uplifting, parallel throws assist you to clear issues and negative influences, and downward throws plant seeds of new energies and growth. If you have a small lot, use your intuition to determine how you ceremoniously nurture the earth patterns. If you have a large property, specifically multiple acres, do this ritual on the 200 feet which surround your home. Again, use your insight.

8. When you are in close proximity to your dwelling, stop your clockwise journey and throw three handfuls of birdseed against your front door. This action sanctifies your home, office, and its occupants. Visualize or imagine sacredness in your space now.

9. Resume your clockwise journey back to the Mouth of Chi on your property and conclude this ceremony by pitching three handfuls of birdseed high into the air. As you do this, silently request good fortune from the Higher Power (or light).

10. Perform the Three Secrets Reinforcement Ritual. Visualize or imagine the ceremony was effective, and see all of your dreams manifest easily and effortlessly.

HOLY GROUND CURE

1. *Placement of Object*

   Stand at the Mouth of Chi of your land. If you live or work in an apartment or building complex, the Mouth of Chi is where the driveway to your particular building meets the road.

2. *Visualize/Imagine the Action Already Occurring*

   See the three separate procedures of distributing seed on your land as a healing for it and you. The weak and sickly energy on the terrain transforms to frequencies of hope, health, and joy. See positive forces feed strong nurturing energy to the earth.

3. *Speak Your Intention Out Loud*

   "My property is purified completely by the Land Clearing Ritual. My land is cherished. It now emits a protection, full of light, joy, and healing energy for my home (office) and all who enter it. Every one of my dreams manifests easily. This or something better for the Highest Good now occurs."

This rite does many things. It attracts birds and small animals to luxuriate on the abundance of food on the property. This increases the chi of the land, which benefits you, the earth, and all other beings. It is also a tool which shows the Higher Power, or whatever is your spiritual source, you are prosperous. It is a wonderful exercise to do when you feel patterns of poverty consciousness. Remember abundance is not just with money, but love, health, time, creativity, and so on. Poverty-consciousness is the feeling of lack in any area and this ritual heals such misleading viewpoints. Finally, it demonstrates to the earth spirits, invisible patterns, and energies of the land you care for, either through ownership or rental, that you are a good force. Expect the flow of the Highest Good to emanate from your entire space when all is in harmony. This sets you up to receive help from outside sources, Visible and Invisible.

It's recommended that you do this ceremony at least once a year or as often as you intuitively want. Watch the birds and animals gather what you spread. Enjoy the reward of establishing abundance awareness as well. Do this ceremony in conjunction with the Dragon's Blood or Orange Peel Toddy Rituals. Carry out the space clearing of the building first. The land clearing does not have to occur on the same day, but it is remarkable how a purified earth under any dwelling affects the overall ambiance of the home and office.

THE TREE OF LIFE PROCEDURE

Execute this ritual when you have a dead tree, a dying tree, or simply must remove a tree for some purpose. A dead or dying tree negatively affects the energy of household or office occupants who are in close proximity to it. Don't make this ceremony a priority for a tree on your property which isn't in visual range from your dwelling. This rite is only for sick, dying, and dead trees in the general vicinity of your building. Because the Family/Health Life Value has the symbolic Element representation of Wood, an ailing tree, the greatest symbol of Wood, can affect health, well-being, familial relations, and finances. What follows is an uncomplicated yet immensely crucial ceremony if you have a tree in this condition. Much of your hard Feng Shui work can be overshadowed by a dead tree or even a non-vibrant tree near your dwelling.

THE TREE OF LIFE RITUAL

Materials Needed:

1. Large glass bowl which makes you pop

2. One pound of birdseed

3. 1/3 teaspoon of saffron

4. Nine turquoise beads, crushed to a fine powder

5. An understanding of Three Secrets Reinforcement Ritual

The Action:

1. Put birdseed in bowl. As in the Land Clearing Ceremony, do not use birdseed if you have a hunting cat. Refer to the Land Clearing Ritual for an alternative. Adjust accordingly.

2. Add saffron and turquoise powder. Turquoise can be acquired at a bead store for an economical price. The beads don't have to be large. It is the gem's qualities, used by many cultures as a protective force, which permeate the birdseed. Note: The hammer is your friend.

3. Stir the mixture counter-clockwise nine times (or multiples of 9—18, 27, and so on). Women use the left middle finger and men use the right. Honor the process when mixing. Visualize or imagine your Higher Power (or light) infiltrating the blend.

4. Circle the trunk of the particular tree clockwise with the concoction. Be liberal with your distribution of the mixture. Visualize or imagine shielding qualities as you see a circle of impenetrable light extend from the trunk all the way to the top of the tree. Picture it nourishing the tree. It also stops the tree's energy from leaking out to structures on the land.

5. Create a trail of the mixture from the tree to your front door.

6. Perform the Three Secrets Reinforcement Ritual. Visualize or imagine health, protection, and peace for all the occupants of your home or office.

7. At this point the necessary action can be done with the tree, whether this is to remove it or leave it as is. It no longer affects the condition of your environment.

STOP THE "TREE"SON CURE

1. *Placement of Object*

   Stand between the remedied tree and your home or office.

2. *Visualize/Imagine the Action Already Occurring*

   See the mixture as a protective force which shields you from the negative influences exuded from the ailing or dead tree. This fortification is absolute to your house as well. The trail to your door generates vibrant health and peace to all occupants. Picture the mix focusing strong, caring, healing energy to the Wood being as well.

3. *Speak Your Intention Out Loud*

   "Myself, loved ones, visitors, and animals, whether in my house or on my land, are now completely sheltered by the Tree of Life Ritual. This or something better for the Highest Good now occurs."

THE RED CLOTH CUSTOM

This is a dramatic, highly effective, extremely popular ceremony to help you to strut about your space like a peacock in all his majesty. This ritual can be used to assist you with various challenges. For the rite to be the most helpful, first decide on the things you want to improve.

If you desire:

1. More passion in your relationships. Now you know why this ritual is extremely well-liked. Phone calls from satisfied customers are the norm.

2. More health and vitality in your physical bodies. Some people challenged with illness have adopted this ritual. It offers hope and positive results.

3. More enhancements for improved prosperity. The Red Cloth Custom is a detail to add to the essential treatments already covered, which can fill in the holes of whatever poverty-consciousness issues you might still accommodate.

THE RED CLOTH RITUAL

Materials Needed:

1. A red cloth big enough to cover the entire mattress of your bed. Thus, a queen-size bed needs a queen-size red flat sheet. A king-size bed needs a cloth or sheet big enough to cover the entire mattress, not two single sheets sewn together. Bright reds are more effective than maroons.

2. An understanding of the Three Secrets Reinforcement Ritual.

The Action:

1. Place the red cloth or sheet between the mattress and box springs of the bed. Alternatives to this are to situate the cloth or sheet between the futon and futon frame or even under the mattress pad of a foam mattress that is on the floor. For chi flow, however, it is better to have the bed off the ground.

2. Perform the Three Secrets Reinforcement Ritual. Remember to visualize the desired results.

THE RED CLOTH CURE

1. Placement of Object

Position a red cloth or sheet, which is large enough to completely cover the mattress, between the mattress and the box springs. Adapt for your style of bed.

2. Visualize/Imagine the Action Already Occurring

See whatever you desire manifest. Picture the red sheet constantly communicating this point, whether it is intimate relations with a partner or fantasy mate yet to materialize, magnificent health, or more riches with all things. Although it is tempting to program it all, focus on one ambition at a time. When it manifests, change intentions to express another desire.

3. Speak Your Intention Out Loud

"My dream of (insert request) manifests easily and effortlessly. This or something better for the Highest Good now occurs."

THE QUESTION MARK REGARDING RITUAL

To do or not to do, that is the question. Why should you take silly actions on things you can't see, don't feel, and hardly even think about? Besides, you don't want the dreaded "Why is Bill on his front lawn throwing birdseed in the air with his eyes closed as he mutters something?" inquiry from neighbors who scratch their heads as they peek out their window. You are afraid the homeowner's association will ban you from the meetings because funny smelling smoke oozes out your screens on a regular basis. Finally, you refuse to believe a stupid red sheet will improve your sex life, and what if the cleaning service finds it when they make the bed!

Arguments for the Inclusion of Feng Shui Ritual in Your Life.

1. Ritual is language understood by your Higher Power. Ritual is prayer in motion.

2. Ritual is performed everyday with common things. You have a practice of cleaning the house on Wednesday, reading the morning paper as you drink your first cup of coffee, or

going out for breakfast after church on Sunday. These rituals just happen to reside within your comfort zones. Consider a Bagua State of Mind and expand your possibilities.

3. "Fake it 'til you make it" also works with ritual. Even if you do not relate to this section at all, if you follow instructions, the rituals will be effective, regardless if you believe or not. Needless to say, any ritual or practice, performed with reverence and belief in its positive outcomes, will exponentially increase the results. Of course, the Three Secrets Reinforcement Ritual included at the end of every suggested ritual helps to secure this.

4. Whether the feel of your home and office is dramatically improved and you sense it, or you just go through the motions because it is strongly recommended and your partner is Feng Shui crazy, it still does not matter. Improvement occurs in your life regardless. You don't need to affirm the effectiveness of rituals to see the marked enhancement in your world. Just do it!

GREAT BIG FIREPOWER: PEP TALK OF THE DECADE

The treatment of Feng Shui to your home and office is not easy. There is a big difference between reading this book and the application of this science throughout your environment. The latter is much more difficult. So, here are some final do and don'ts to simplify and prioritize the task before you.

DO:

Realize Feng Shui Only Works if You Do It.

It makes no difference how intelligent, rich, or fabulously good looking you are. If you don't incorporate the principles of Feng Shui into your environment, absolutely nothing will happen. I guarantee it. Feng Shui is an experiential task. It does not promote the "know it all" Feng Shui academia, rather the "do it all then see the wonders soar" approach. It is advantageous to learn the theories, better yet, use them in your surroundings. It's a type of self-love you'll be glad you did. Promise yourself to direct just one Feng Shui feat a day. Clutter-clear a drawer. Get supplies to make chi catchers. Install mystical alarm systems on appropriate doors. Remember, miracles take place each step, not just at the end of all treatments. Feng Shui is a process, a multi-layered onion that makes you cry but also adds spice to your world.

Prioritize these Feng Shui Applications First.

Before overwhelming thoughts lead you off to other distractions, do these things next. The quality of your universe will immediately change for the better.

1. Cure the shape of your building with intention so the missing pieces of the Bagua are represented. For a review on this procedure, reread the text and subsequent cure starting on page 44, Part I.

2. Invite chi to your front door. Prepare your Mouth of Chi for the honored guest that it is. Expect incredible shifts in your life. For a review on this procedure, please reread the text starting on page 130, Part I.

3. Hold in the chi wherever necessary. If you live or work in a one-room studio, one chi catcher can hold the life force for all parts of the Bagua (with intention), except for the bathroom, which has a closed door. Have a separate chi catcher for that particular Life Value. If you have many rooms, you will need numerous chi catchers even when one Life Value spans multiple rooms. A separate chi catcher in each independent room is advised. For a review on this procedure, reread the text and cure starting on page 51, Part I.

4. Fix all leaks and bathroom/utility drainage. If there are numerous steps to perform in the bathroom, at least start. Shut the lid to the toilet and close the door to the room. For a review of bathroom protocol, please reread the text starting on page 50, Part I. Drainage issues with washing machines can be reread on page 232, Part II.

5. Clutter-clear the Life Value areas where your biggest challenges exist. Don't forget to clutter-clear also the Opposite-Attract Law Life Value for complete thoroughness in problem-solving. Watch the gifts on the physical, emotional, mental, and spiritual planes appear. For review on this procedure, please start rereading text on page 13, Part I.

6. Arrange a time to do the Dragon's Blood, Orange Peel Toddy, or a space clearing ritual in your own style. Whether you feel it or not, the quality of your atmosphere will improve significantly when you do this step. The space clearing rituals given in this book, proven to be effective, can be reread in the text starting on page 246, Part III.

7. Breathe deeply. Have a good time with the progression. Feng Shui has the word fun in its pronunciation. It is Fung Sway. Don't fear the Fung. Feel the Fung. Do the Fung. Enjoy the Fung. Let Fung wash over your being until you Sway with joy.

8. Don't give your power away to me, it, or anything. Let Feng Shui integrate into your being, not the other way around. You don't have to be a highly advanced mystic living in a cave in the Himalayas to get Feng Shui results.

Place Mirrors in Appropriate Places.

Mirrors are used to situate you in Empowerment Positions and to cure garages, create makeshift storage units, or teenager storage units by deflecting away negativity and more. To review such procedures, reread the mirror chapter starting on page 119, Part I.

Create a Sacred Space Representation for Every Value in the Bagua.

Every dwelling has nine Sacred Spaces, even if there are several floors or the shape of the building is irregular. After you have anchored the missing pieces, you still embody the absent Life Value with a Sacred Space in some room of the building. When you set intention to hold in chi, include the Life Value of the room and the Life Value of the Sacred Space you placed there. To review information on Sacred Spaces, please reread the text starting on page 29, Part I.

Remember if an Object (or Action) Raises Your Energy, It Is Most Likely Okay.

Normally people, when in public, are regular individuals with ordinary needs and customary likes and dislikes. However, when I enter a room or go to an event, something happens. Their intellect defers to their pounding heart.

"I know it is horrible Feng Shui to have vertical blinds. I read it somewhere!"

"I feel terrible about the swimming pool in the backyard. I heard it was, you know, bad to have..."

"Gosh, I really need to get rid of all my ceilings fans! I know it is cutting chi, but it does get over 100° in the summer!"

At these times, I feel like a Catholic priest on confessional duty astonished by all the guilt, the anguish, and supposed Feng Shui sin. Like the cleric, I absolve them with a short, but imperative, "If it raises your energy, (my child), it is fine to have the pool, the vertical blinds, and the ceiling fans. Just do the appropriate intentional cures and three Hail Marys!"

It's true there are rules and regulations in this Feng Shui philosophy. You have three sections on them at your disposal in this book. However, there is a theory you also balance with that. Consider always what raises your personal energy in your environment. This does not give permission to commit Feng Shui blasphemy (keep the bathroom door closed!), but it should calm your nervous system.

Begin Your Feng Shui Treatments in the Areas of Your Home or Office For Which You Have the Most Enthusiasm.

After you have completed the priorities in your structure, don't let the parental mind bully you to focus on a room and its Life Value until your heart is ready. You may know you need attention in the Wealth/Power office. Abundance, especially of money, would make everything so much easier. Still, every cell in your being wants to transform the Child/Creativity living room. Feng Shui is about going with the flow, even when you harness its principles into your environment. No one can tell you where, why, and when better than your own hunches. Imagine your instinct wears a magician's hat. Sometimes when you sleep, this inner being astral travels to another land. While there, your essence drinks liquid wisdom from a silver chalice. Then it reintegrates back into your physical being, waiting for you to make a decision. Next time you need to make a choice, let the gut have a word or two.

Know Any Building is a Self-Healing Unit.

When you accidentally cut your arm, there is a step-by-step process of healing which occurs in spite of you. Without conscious thought, the cut scabs, then peels, then scars. It heals without input from the peanut gallery. You can worry. You can mess with it, but except for some more serious physical condition, your arm shall return to a state of wellness. This is called homeostasis, a state of equilibrium between different but interdependent elements, a return to health.

A dwelling has the same ability to achieve homeostasis once the curative qualities of Feng Shui are applied. When you rearrange furniture, hold in the chi, change the symbols in your environment, and employ other such Feng Shui ideals, it is virtually impossible for healing in the building—which is your life—not to take place. When the vibrant chi is free to flow in a structure, it will work its magic in every room and Life Value. Superficial problems mend right away. But just as with a deeper cut, it takes more time to repair multilayered issues associated with a particular part of the dwelling. You can worry. You can mess with it by picking at the treatments you've already done. In spite of this, a building with Feng Shui applications always works towards a state of balance. Let go and allow the recovery to happen on its own regardless of the input from the peanut gallery.

Treat Intention Like an Active Verb.

Too many times, intention is used as an excuse. For example:

"I intended to go to the store. Oh well, we will just have jelly beans for dinner again."

"I intended to help you. Just got busy when I put together the erector set for Jimmy."

"Someday, I intend to go to Jamaica. For now, I just want a bus ticket to Arkansas."

Intention is magic superglue. It sticks dreams and manifestation together. In the art of Feng Shui, it is crucial. Please do not just intend to perform the many Three Secrets Reinforcement Rituals to solidify your Feng Shui changes. True intention is an act; there are no brownie points given for being well-meaning.

DON'T:

Do Not Give Up! Get Support with Issues Which Immobilize You.

You might have a burning desire to apply Feng Shui to your environment. Great! Passion helps with all things. But it still won't make it trouble free. Some actions go smoothly. Others seem impossible. Through the tears, read the phone number of an open-minded friend in your address book. Choose one who is good with foreign languages, the lingo of symbols. Call and ask for help. Have pals verify your Feng Shui achievements. This gives oomph to the daunting task.

Whenever there is blockage with any multidimensional endeavor, you can bet the saboteur, fear, is present. It crept in when you weren't looking. Not to fret, that's when a friend can add warm fuzzies to counter the razor-sharp edges of change. Anything is possible when you have a support system. Get out a pen and a piece of paper. Write to the Highest Good Invisible and Visible Helpful People to assist you. Put this request in your Helpful People Box. Then anticipate acts of genius.

Do Not Have Memory Loss About These Things:

1. Change is a hard thing to do. Modifications can be as intense as walking outside in the middle of a winter blizzard in your bathing suit.

2. Comfort Zones are subtle until you break out of their limiting container. Then they become giants, awakened from a contented slumber and none too happy that a bitty gnat (you) has rustled them awake. Realize their growl is worse than their bite. Endure the yip-yip for a short time. Medicate with copious amounts of breath, trust, and Helpful People, both Visible and Invisible. Soon the new, more advanced comfort zones will bully your old ones into submission. Call it survival of the hippest.

3. Walk on the path where self-love grows. When you are on the same side with all your parts, subconscious included, self-sabotage has no place to breed. Confidence expands. Intend your home and office to be easily Feng Shui treated, without struggle, and with plenty of time to smell the roses.

4. Expect chaos as a means to order. Whenever you make adjustments in your surroundings, like moving an item into the Empowerment Position, you disrupt a comfort zone. In your excitement about transformation, you might shift many patterns in your world consecutively, for example, an entire house in one weekend, the ever popular Feng Shui marathon. Expect a visitor then—a tourist, who delights in turmoil. The name of this day-tripper is chaos.

   The washing machine broke since you put a chi catcher up in the Self-Knowledge/Wisdom laundry room. All forms of creativity have been lost when you moved the desk into Empowerment Position. You did the proper bathroom protocols but now the faucet drips. You clutter-clear your

Helpful People/Travel guestroom, but instead of feeling great about things you just experience anxious nervousness. Flow Schmo! The only flow you have is the current of money out the door since you put a mirror behind the stove! Two of the burners quit operating and it's going to cost all your newfound abundance to fix it.

This may never happen to you. But know as you change a pattern, regardless if the new configurations are for the better, there is a short period when the feathers thrown up in the air, so to speak, fall slowly to the ground to land again in their new alignment. While you wait for this fresh arrangement, a void remains to be filled. That's when chaos gets a passport to your world. Take heart; this havoc only gets a tourist visa. Such a vacationer doesn't stay around once the Feng Shui principals integrate. Chaos is bored and restless in such a graceful atmosphere and buys a one way ticket to Clutterville.

5. To evolve is not painful. The resistance to evolution is. As a culture, we are taught to hide our empowerment as individuals; to not think, to not have opinions, and to not dream outside of the norm. Such a stance is perilous. To exist as a species on earth, we must progress to a place of true empowerment, power *with* rather than power *over*. We then become a community with the good of the whole in mind and pass on this legacy to our grandchildren. The art of Feng Shui achieves this same end.

For The Feng Shui Maniac: Super Sonic Powered Sacred Spaces.

Avoid this next step in your Feng Shui practice until nothing else seems to work. Give your new life at least one month to test the results of your Feng Shui devotion. Great things might happen.

Horrible things might happen (can you say, "healing crisis?"), or even more confusing, nothing at all seems to happen. If you have conscientiously performed all treatments related to your issue and find your concern still exists, consider the following actions. In this sample, let's use the low self-esteem matter.

The importance of healing subconscious as well as conscious emotional patterns is based on a principle called the Emotional Release Technique. It is easy, quick, and successful. Please see the support pages at the end of the book for more information. The following steps are applied to any issue which is a multilayered pattern.

1. Locate the relevant Sacred Space which addresses your concern.

   In the example we're using, self-esteem is dealt with on the Self-Knowledge/Wisdom Sacred Space. Other examples would be: health—Family/Health; struggles with a teenager —Child/Creativity; job—Career/Life Path; relationship— Love Union/Marriage; money—Family/Health; lack of time— Wealth/Power.

2. Choose a power object or image to handle your concern. Choose power objects (images) which respect any Element Cycle relationships pertaining to a particular Sacred Space. There is no Element with the Self-Knowledge/Wisdom Life Value.

3. Create an affirmation which establishes the result you seek in the present tense. For instance, "My self-esteem is fantastic. I love myself completely. This or something better for the Highest Good now occurs."

4. Remove the barometer statement from the phrase and repeat it out loud. "My self-esteem is fantastic. I love myself completely."

5. Sense the area around your heart and gut. Get an impression between the two regions where there is tightness. If both are constricted, choose either the heart or the gut to work with first. Then imagine a hollow cylinder sticking out from the center of this area. Disengage your intellect. Bow your head, with your neck extended as your chin tucks towards the chest area. See diagram N-1 for clarity.

EMOTIONAL RELEASE TECHNIQUE
FOR SUPERSONIC SACRED SPACES (N-1)

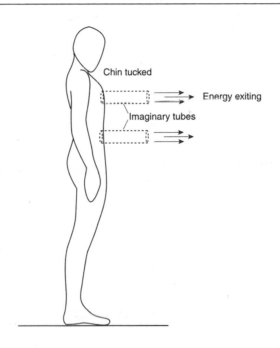

6. Like a gushing oil well, allow the constricted energy to rise up the cylinder, flow out, and become neutral as soon as it leaves the tube. It's not important to comprehend what the energy is, just allow it to leave your body.

7. Intuit whether the feelings of the force exist because: a) you are trying to be accepted; b) trying to control the situation; or c) trying to feel safe. These three impulses are motivators behind all behaviors. Choose one of them. Realize this is a false belief which leads to constricted energy and not a remedy to anything. Let this awareness be until you feel the root of this belief system rise up the tube, flow out, and become neutralized.

8. Do a similar process described in steps 1-7 on the Opposite-Attract Law Sacred Space. Go to the Love Union/Marriage Sacred Space. Choose a power object (image) and say out loud, "I have healthy self-esteem which ensures the choice of my Highest Good equal in all of my relationships."

9. Repeat this entire procedure (steps 1-8) for nine consecutive days (or multiples of 9—18, 27, and so forth). After a nine-day cycle is completed, state the original affirmation out loud. Keep the same power object (image), and allow Feng Shui and the Sacred Space to work their astonishing enchantment. "My self-esteem is fantastic. I love myself completely. This or something better for the Highest Good now occurs."

The results can be profound. Feng Shui converts flourish.

THE END OF THE BEGINNING: CONFESSIONS OF A FENG SHUI CONSULTANT

Make no mistake, Feng Shui is fantastic. It changes existence. But be prepared for the realities of life as well. The following certainties are composed from my own experiences:

1. From time to time, you forget to close the drains in your bathtub or kitchen sink.

2. Occasionally, your work desk gets disgustingly messy. A big pile of papers, which resemble Mount Everest, keeps you from finding bills.

3. Frequently, a problem comes up, and although you know which Life Value Sacred Space to place a positive affirmation on, you choose TV therapy instead.

4. There are periods when you amass a mound of clutter for weeks on end.

5. From time to time, you benefit from the objective eye of a child, yours or a friend's, who offers Feng Shui advice.

What does this all mean? That you are gloriously human—life ebbs and flows—and sometimes you flow and at other times you ebb. Walk your talk. However, also breathe and enjoy the passage of living. Perfectionism all the time is tedious. Don't be boring.

Hang chi catchers. Your life positively alters. Find the empowerment placement of the bed, desk, and stove. In fact, choose the Empowerment Position with all of your life situations. The shift will be subtle but profound. Follow the bathroom cures, then examine how abundance in your life magically appears. Honor yourself. Cover the television. Observe how nurturing communication, towards self and others, becomes the healthy norm. Clutter-clear your home and office. Note when you are surrounded by things which raise your energy, you function at maximum excellence. Realize you only proceed as quickly as you are emotionally and spiritually prepared to change. Feng Shui, performed with intention, guarantees this transformation in your life. So be gentle and support yourself.

This artful science is powerful medicine. Not only is it an extraordinary problem-solving tool, it is also a mystical journey towards self-improvement and growth. It is unbelievable until you are actually on its path, acknowledging the awesome modifications in your world. If you choose to direct Feng Shui to your life, prepare to be blown away. The beliefs and ideals you hold to be true shall be revolutionalized. Miracles are commonplace. Limitations to what's possible get smaller and smaller until they disappear altogether.

Feng Shui will teach you—there is indeed a manual to life. Read the symbols. Not just in your home and office but in your day-to-day world. Everything you need to know is constantly revealed. Perhaps you are undecided about something in your day and see a rainbow in the sky. Go for it. An ambulance speeds by when you are thinking about whether you should invite an acquaintance into your world as a friend. Reconsider. Feng Shui makes life interesting. It gives you a huge advantage over being a victim to circumstance. This science comes close to revealing the secrets to life mastery. Yes, problems still exist. Existence continues to have snags. What you want and what you get might be sadly different. But Feng Shui teaches you to use your microcosm universe, your home and office, like a map to perceive and enhance your life radically. May you, your mate, and your children never walk on Feng Shui eggshells in your home and office. It is not worth it. Neither is this the true meaning behind the gift of Feng Shui. My personal Feng Shui discipline is constant but not flawless. I have a life; so do you and your loved ones. A sanctuary is hardly a place you return to and fear you may have something out of place. Your Feng Shui remedied home and office can be a safe haven where you are served, restored, protected, and assisted with solutions to your problems. But only your relaxed, intuitive High Self can co-create such an environment with you.

Please remember a Feng Shui treated building naturally heals itself and your life because of homeostasis. Breathe your sigh of relief. Slowly and steadily employ the Feng Shui principles in this book. Your life, your world, and your universe take on completely different features, ones which only appear when regular therapeutic, affirmative forces, and hopefulness are released consistently from every cell in your environment. You become a walking endorphin as your life begins to pamper you. Enjoy it. Feng Shui provides such charm. It is that magnificent.

1

SPREADING THE WORD:

REFERENCES

BLACK HAT TIBETAN **REFERENCES**

Interior Design with Feng Shui, Sarah Rossbach. Penguin/ Arkana 1987.

Feng Shui: Harmony By Design, Nancy SantoPietro. The Berkeley Publishing Group 1996.

Clear Your Clutter With Feng Shui, Karen Kingston. Broadway Books 1998.

Move Your Stuff, Change Your Life—How To Use Feng Shui To Get Love, Money, Respect, And Happiness, Karen Rauch Carter. Simon & Schuster 2000.

Sacred Space: Clearing and Enhancing the Energy of your Home, Denise Linn. Ballantine Books. 1995.

Feng Shui for Dummies, David Daniel Kennedy. IDG Books Worldwide, Inc. 2001.

Feng Shui and Health: The Anatomy of A Home, Nancy SantoPietro. Three Rivers Press 2002.

BAGUA STATE OF MIND REFERENCES

These titles might not have anything to do with Feng Shui or they could. What is certain is they will stretch the mind and change your life.

Creative Visualization, Shakti Gawain. Bantam Books 1978.

The Creative Visualization Workbook, Shakti Gawain. New World Library 1982.

MAP: Medical Assistance Program, 2nd edition, Machaelle Small Wright. Perelandra, Ltd 1994.

The Four Agreements, Don Miguel Ruiz. Amber-Allen Publishing, Inc. 1997.

The Mastery Of Love, Don Miguel Ruiz. Amber-Allen Publishing, Inc. 1999.

Don't Sweat The Small Stuff In Love, Richard Carlson, PH.D. and Kristine Carlson. Hyperion 1999.

A Deadly Arrangement: Happiness, Harmony, Homicide, Denise Osborn. The Berkeley Publishing Group 2001.

The Eleven Commandments of Wildly Successful Women, Pamela Boucher Gilbert. Macmillan Spectrum 1996.

The Complete Book of Essential Oils & Aromatherapy, Valerie Ann Wormwood. New World Library 1991.

Animal Talk, Penelope Smith. Pegasus Publications 1989.

Non-Toxic And Natural: How to Avoid Dangerous Everyday Products and Buy or Make Safe Ones, Debra Lynn Dadd. Jeremy P. Archer, Inc 1984.

Celebration of Breath, Sondra Ray. CelestialArts 1986.

Commune with the Angels, Jane M. Howard. A.R.E. Press 1992.

Stone People Medicine, Manny Twofeathers. Wo-Pila Publishing 1996.

Healing Mudras: Yoga for Your Hands, Sabrina Mesko. Ballantine Publishing Group 2000.

When Elephants Weep: The Emotional Lives of Animals, Jeffrey Moussaieff Masson and Susan McCarthy. Delacorte Press 1995.

30 Simple Energy Things You Can Do to Save The Earth, The Earth Works Group. Javnarama 1990.

The Recycler's Handbook: Simple Things You Can Do. The Earth Works Group. Earth Works Press 1990.

BAGUA STATE OF MIND ACTIVITIES

Gabrielle Alizay
   P.O. Box 2673
   Santa Cruz, California 95063
   email: galizay@homepeace.com
   www.homepeace.com
   www.fengshuigeek.com
   www.fengshuicarkits.com

For a free gift, go to www.homepeace.com/freedownloads.htm

Spring Forest Qigong for Health
Presented by the Learning Strategies Corporation, 2000 Plymouth Road, Minnetonka, Minnesota 55305-2335 USA
Phone: 800-735-8273, 952-476-9200
Fax: 952-475-2373
Email: Mail@LearningStrategies.com
www.LearningStrategies.com

The Abundance Course
Presented by: Lawrence Crane Enterprises, 15101 Rayneta Drive, Sherman Oaks, CA 91403
Phone: 888-333-7703, 818-385-0611
Fax: 818-385-0563
www.ReleaseTechnique.com

The End: Personal Growth Through Technology
Presented by: Centerpointe Research Institute, 4720 S.W. Washington St. Suite 104, Beaverton, OR 97005
Phone: 800-945-2741, 503-672-7117
Fax: 503-643-3114
Email: info@centerpointe.com
www.centerpointe.com

Network Chiropractic
National Network Chiropractic
Phone number: 303-678-8101
www.associationfornetworkcare.com

The Feldenkrais Method
www.feldenkrais.com/

The Cloning of Success
www.smartstreetkid.com

Emotional Freedom Technique
www.emofree.com

INDEX